Voices of
Civil War America

Recent Titles in
Voices of an Era

Voices of Civil War America

Contemporary Accounts of Daily Life

Lawrence A. Kreiser, Jr.,
and Ray B. Browne, Editors

VOICES OF AN ERA

GREENWOOD

AN IMPRINT OF ABC-CLIO, LLC
Santa Barbara, California • Denver, Colorado • Oxford, England

Library of Congress Cataloging-in-Publication Data

Voices of Civil War America : contemporary accounts of daily life / Lawrence A. Kreiser, Jr. and Ray B. Browne, editors.
      p. cm. — (Voices of an era)
  Includes bibliographical references and index.
  ISBN 978-0-313-37740-2 (hardcopy : alk. paper) — ISBN 978-0-313-37741-9 (ebook)
  1. United States—History—Civil War, 1861–1865—Sources.   2. United States—History—Civil War, 1861–1865—Personal narratives.   I. Kreiser, Lawrence A.   II. Browne, Ray B. (Ray Broadus), 1922–2009.
  E464.V65   2011
  973.7'8—dc22   2011015584

ISBN: 978-0-313-37740-2
EISBN: 978-0-313-37741-9

15 14 13 12 11   1 2 3 4 5

This book is also available on the World Wide Web as an eBook.
Visit www.abc-clio.com for details.

Greenwood
An Imprint of ABC-CLIO, LLC

ABC-CLIO, LLC
130 Cremona Drive, P.O. Box 1911
Santa Barbara, California 93116-1911

This book is printed on acid-free paper (∞)

Manufactured in the United States of America

Contents

DOCUMENTS OF CIVIL WAR AMERICA

Contents

PREFACE

This volume in the *Voices of an Era* series presents a range of primary documents that illuminate the character and social history of the United States during the tumultuous period encompassing the Civil War and the Reconstruction era. It intends to help students evaluate the meaning and importance of contemporary accounts and to incorporate those documents into school and research projects. It is also designed to support the current academic movement toward document-based teaching, with educators and students engaging firsthand source materials as the building blocks of the past.

Each of the documents highlighted in this volume follows a similar format. That is:

- An **Introduction** providing relevant historical background for the selection
- A **Keep in Mind While You Read** section providing context points to help evaluate the document
- An **Aftermath** section describing the results and consequences that flowed from the document
- An **Ask Yourself** section listing questions about the document as well as ways that the document might illuminate both life at the time and life today
- A **Topics and Activities to Consider** section suggesting several themes or ideas to explore in a paper, essay, online project, or class presentation
- A **Further Reading** section listing important print and electronic resources for additional research

Many of the documents also are accompanied by **Sidebars** and **Definition Fact Boxes**. The Sidebars provide information about a topic related to the document under consideration. An explanation of any terms in the documents that are either colloquial or relatively obscure is found in the Definition Fact Boxes.

A **Biographical Appendix**, listing any names used in the Introduction and Aftermath sections, is found at the end of the volume, as is a **Glossary** that lists any terms in the same two sections that are perhaps unfamiliar to many readers. A **Bibliography** listing selected print sources and nonprint sources—such as Web sites, DVDs, and films, among other materials—concludes the volume.

Acquisitions Editor Mariah Gumpert oversaw the publication process for *Voices of Civil War America* from start to finish. Mariah provided incisive comments and questions that kept the project focused and on track. She also displayed a large amount of patience in answering questions and addressing concerns, often delivered when right up against a deadline.

My family—Alicia, my wife of now 15 years, and Julia and Anna, my grade-school-aged daughters—provided more encouragement in seeing this project to completion than I have words to describe. Their good humor in allowing me time to work on the manuscript, plus their welcome distractions in all sorts of games and activities—including frequent drawing and painting and tossing the softball—made everything even more worthwhile. I am blessed that we share our lives together.

Ray Browne, the listed coeditor of this volume, died during the fall of 2009. Ray was the catalyst for this project. He did all of the initial work with Greenwood to establish the scope of the volume and to determine the project deadlines. With his love of life and learning, Ray inspired many and is missed by all who knew him. To Ray, and his wife Pat, this book is dedicated.

INTRODUCTION: CIVIL WAR AMERICA AND RECONSTRUCTION

Perhaps no other event has dominated everyday life in the United States as the Civil War and Reconstruction did during the mid- and late19th century. Between 1861 and 1865, Americans fought the largest and costliest war yet waged in North America. About 3 million men served in the Union and Confederate armies, or about 10 percent of the nation's population in 1860 (31 million people). The percentage of manpower mobilized during the Civil War is higher than the nation has achieved at any time since, including World War II. Nearly every Civil War era family had a father, husband, son, or brother in the military, making the maneuvers and battles of armies very closely watched affairs. A great deal of worry went along with the watching. By the end of the fighting, the Union and the Confederacy had lost a combined 620,000 men dead to battle and disease. Another 500,000 Union and Confederate soldiers had suffered wounds. All told, two percent of the American population had become casualties. A similar level of destruction in the United States today would result in 6 million people killed, wounded, and missing—a nearly unthinkable cost.

The Reconstruction era (1865–77) that followed Union triumph in the Civil War marked a significant transformation in American life. Most immediately, four million African Americans made the transition from slavery to freedom. For the first time, black people enjoyed citizenship and, for men, suffrage. A surge in white violence and intimidation soon made these rights and liberties in name only. While African Americans began a long struggle to gain equality, the United States became ever more urban and industrial. The majority of Americans still lived in the countryside. But the pace quickened toward the United States becoming the strongest industrial nation in the world by the early 20th century. Much of the growth in manufacturing output was fueled by the labor of immigrants. Irish, Germans, and, beginning in the mid- and late 1860s, Chinese all arrived in large numbers. Americans also were on the move during the postwar era. Individuals and families continued to move westward, as they had done since the Colonial era. By the late 1800s, the population of the West was the fastest growing in the nation.

Many of the trends begun during the 12 years of Reconstruction continue through the modern day. Readers in the early 21st century only have to glance at headlines in the newspaper or on the Internet to see discussion of whether all civil liberties should be extended to all Americans, whether immigration should be more tightly regulated, and whether the economy is on the upswing or downslide. Little wonder that Allen Nevins, a distinguished historian working in the 1920s, noted that the postwar era marked the "emergence of modern America."

This book, a volume in the *Voices of an Era* series, explores daily life during the tumult and upheaval of the Civil War and Reconstruction era. Emphasis is on the ordinary rather than the momentous. Documents were selected to illustrate, among other topics, the foods Americans ate, the lessons they studied at school, the jobs and professions they worked, and the games they played. The opening chapter on politics is the exception, by exploring the national scene. These documents attempt to give a general overview of some of the most important decisions made during the time period under consideration. Topics explored in the chapter run chronologically from the Kansas-Nebraska Act in 1854, which ultimately brought the nation to civil war, through the inauguration of Rutherford Hayes and the end of Reconstruction in 1877.

The observations drawn about daily life in the mid-19th century are, by necessity, general. Differences based on gender, race, economics, and a range of other factors existed, as they do today. While highlighting some of these identifiers, this book focuses on *middle-class* Americans. The term is rather nebulous, since no single definition exists. For these purposes, middle-class Americans were those who participated in the prosperity that marked much of the mid- and late19th century. A severe economic downturn swept across the nation between 1873 and 1877. Otherwise, for most Americans, the standard of living was increasing. Wages varied widely. But, by way of illustration, in 1870, a "common" farm laborer earned $16.57 per month, with board. A town laborer earned $1.55 per day, without board. By comparison, a Union private earned $13 per month throughout most of the Civil War. Also improving the standard of living, prices, after soaring during the war, dropped. Savings on food and housing allowed for more spending on nonnecessities. Consumers had much to choose from, with expanding manufacturing output and transportation networks bringing material goods and luxury items across much of the nation. Shoppers in the late 1860s and early 1870s enjoyed a range of selection largely unknown by their grandparents and great-grandparents.

Living in the modern day, it is easy for readers to slip into stark generalizations about the past. Some readers might view a previous era as a time of strong values and simple pleasures. Other individuals might condemn the past as backward and primitive. The Civil War and Reconstruction era, as with any other, was a mixture of both. Many Americans distrusted, if not outright disliked, anyone who was not white, native born, and Protestant; or outside the majority of the population. Other Americans lived quite happily without cars, computers, and cell phones—technologies they knew nothing about but that we consider indispensable. Whatever else we think about the past, the bar is set too high if we view people outside the standards of their time. Like any other time period, the Civil War and Reconstruction era had bad times and good times, villains and heroes—much like our own will to students and scholars looking back decades from now.

How to Evaluate Primary Documents

A text to a coworker about an upcoming business presentation; a postcard to a family member while on vacation—all of these are correspondences that many of us do almost routinely. These conversations might also help scholars working years and decades down the road to better understand us and, by extension, our society. The thought is both unnerving and exhilarating. Few of us write with an eye toward posterity. What if, in texting the coworker, we are in a hurry and use no punctuation or capitalization? What if we use shorthand, such as *2* for *to*? Might historians working in the next century believe we were poor spellers or, worse, poor writers? What if societal values change, and our words make us look poorly by the standards of later centuries? At the same time, many of us might find exciting that we are creating historical documents through our written and oral communications. The vacation postcard might give insight to a scholar not yet born about how and where Americans living during the early 21st century liked to travel. Did we go by plane or car? Did we vacation with friends or family? Did we travel to a historic site or an amusement park? These seemingly innocuous decisions all contribute to the historical record and to our portrayal by future generations.

Scholars term any document that gives first-hand insight into a particular person, place, or event a *primary source*. In addition to the business text and vacation postcard previously mentioned, newspaper editorials, diary entries, letters, photographs, and a range of other materials might serve as primary sources. Any material that that does not give a first-hand account is a secondary source. The distinction sometimes depends on the circumstances. A term paper that you write on Pearl Harbor is a primary source if analyzing how college students today perceive American entry into World War II. But the same term paper is a secondary source if analyzing the surprise attack itself. A YouTube video showing a math professor working though a classroom problem might serve as a primary source for teaching styles at colleges and universities. The same clip, however, is not a primary source if discussing the lecture style utilized by English professors.

Scholars working with primary-source material must be sensitive to the author's attitudes and audience. Attitudes represent a person's outlook and beliefs. These might change over time, or by circumstance. Alternately, attitudes might encompass a long-standing worldview. The key to making the distinction is to attempt to place the primary source in historical context. Might a soldier criticizing the generalship of George Washington during the Revolutionary War be genuine in his conviction? Does he discuss poorly executed maneuvers or battlefield defeats? Or might his attitudes be influenced by other factors mentioned in the same letter or diary entry—such as sore feet and an empty stomach? There are few absolutes in dealing with primary sources because, unless we are dealing with a current topic, we cannot go back in time and talk to the authors. Still, once the attitude of an individual is generally determined, his or her sentiments are compared to those expressed by other people in similar circumstances. Did other soldiers criticize or praise George Washington? Once a weight of evidence is accumulated, scholars draw their conclusions. The findings often establish more scholarly debates, as other researchers agree or disagree with the original arguments.

In using primary sources, scholars must also take into account the author's audience. An audience is the intended recipient of the letter, email, or other form of communication. The Revolutionary War soldier mentioned previously might phrase a letter differently if writing to a friend, a family member, or, perhaps, directly to George Washington. He might use more earthy expressions if writing to his friend rather than to Washington, because of the nature of the relationship. He might avoid any criticism altogether in writing to the parents, so as not to cause any needless worry. Scholars must bear these concerns in mind and not take every expression (or lack of expression, as the case may be) at face value.

Working with primary sources is richly rewarding. First-hand accounts allow readers to experience history as it happens, rather than after the fact. The element of contingency— that the flow of American history might have gone in many different directions—is exhilarating. Some of the primary sources selected for this volume were written before anyone knew that the Union would win the Civil War, or that the fighting would end in 1865. Other documents were penned while the federal government still was debating Reconstruction policies, and while the West was still considered the frontier. The documents impart an immediacy that makes the past seem to come alive. Real people were leading real lives, a fact that their words bring home to us.

CHRONOLOGY OF EVENTS

1860

	The population of the United States reaches 31 million people. New York City, with 813,000 people, is the most populous city.
November	Abraham Lincoln and the Republican Party capture the White House, with a plurality of the popular vote.
December	South Carolina secedes from the Union.
	More than 1,000 steamboats ply the Mississippi River.

1861

March	Abraham Lincoln is inaugurated as the 16th president of the United States.
April	The Confederate States bombard Fort Sumter in Charleston harbor, beginning the Civil War.
July	The Confederacy defeats a Union offensive aimed at capturing Richmond in a battle at Manassas, Virginia, the first large-scale fighting of the war.
	Gilbert Van Camp is awarded a contract to supply the Union army with canned foods.
	America's first commercial pretzel bakery opens in Lititz, Pennsylvania.

1862

April	Congress abolishes slavery in the District of Columbia.
April	Union forces throw back a Confederate offensive after two days of bloody fighting around Shiloh, Tennessee.
June	Robert E. Lee assumes command of the Confederate forces defending Richmond, soon thereafter renamed the Army of Northern Virginia.
September	The Union Army of the Potomac wins a battlefield victory at Antietam in western Maryland in the bloodiest single-day of fighting in the nation's history.
	Congress passes the Homestead Act.

1863	January	The Emancipation Proclamation takes effect.
	July	The Union achieves twin military successes by defeating a Confederate invasion of the North at Gettysburg, Pennsylvania, and by capturing the Confederate defensive stronghold at Vicksburg, Mississippi.
	October	Abraham Lincoln declares the last Thursday in November a day of national thanksgiving.
	December	The Capitol Dome in Washington, DC, is capped after years of construction.
1864	March	Ulysses S. Grant is made General-in-Chief of the Union army, a position that he holds until the end of the war the next year.
	June	The Union army puts Petersburg, Virginia, under siege, after suffering heavy casualties that spring during the Overland Campaign.
	September	The Union army captures Atlanta, a major Confederate supply and transportation center.
	November	Abraham Lincoln handily wins reelection.
1865	April	The Confederate Army of Northern Virginia surrenders at Appomattox, Virginia, effectively ending the Civil War.
	April	Abraham Lincoln is assassinated.
		The Union Pacific Railroad begins to build track running westward, to meet the Central Pacific Railroad working eastward and complete a transcontinental railroad.
		The 13th Amendment abolishes slavery in the United States.
		The typewriter is patented and becomes widely produced several years later.
1866		New York, Philadelphia, Baltimore, and New Orleans experience bouts of cholera, smallpox, and yellow fever, killing many residents.
		Race riots occur in Memphis and New Orleans.
		The first cattle drive moves 2,000 longhorns north from Texas.
1867		The United States purchases Alaska from Russia for $7.2 million.
		Little Women, by Louisa May Alcott, is published.
	December	R. H. Macy's in New York becomes the first department store to stay open late into the evening, setting a sales record.
1868		The 14th Amendment grants the rights of citizenship to African Americans.

	May	Memorial Day (initially known as Decoration Day) is first observed.
	November	Ulysses S. Grant and the Republican Party easily defeat Horatio Seymour and the Democratic Party during the presidential election.
1869		The transcontinental railroad is completed, to great national fanfare.
		The Cincinnati Red Stockings become the first baseball team to hire professional players.
		Boston receives its first shipment of fresh meat from Chicago by way of the newly invented refrigerated rail car.
1870	January	Construction begins on the Brooklyn Bridge that, when completed 13 years later, is the longest suspension bridge in the world.
		Hiram Revels is the first black man to win election to the Senate, as a Republican from Mississippi.
		The 15th Amendment extends suffrage to African American men.
1871		Ulysses S. Grant signs the Civil Rights Act, attempting to protect southern black people from violence visited by the Ku Klux Klan.
		Ezra Sutton, an infielder for the Cleveland Forest Citys, is reportedly the first player in professional baseball to hit a home run.
1872	January	Yellowstone National Park is established.
		The Freedmen's Bureau, a government-run organization designed to help black people make the transition from slavery to freedom, is abolished.
		Montgomery Ward & Co. is founded in Chicago.
	November	Ulysses S. Grant wins reelection.
1873	March	The Comstock Law makes it illegal to send by mail any "obscene, lewd, or lascivious" books.
		Levi Strauss and Jacob Davis receive a patent to use copper rivets to strengthen their denim work pants, and production of Levi's jeans begins soon after.
		Cable cars begin service in San Francisco.
1874		The Philadelphia Zoo opens, the first public zoo in the United States.
	November	The Gamma Phi Beta sorority is established at Syracuse University and is the first to use the term *sorority* to describe a women's Greek letter organization.

1875	May	The first Kentucky Derby is run.
	June	Arguably the first game of college football is played, pitting Tufts University against Harvard University.
		Congress passes the Civil Rights Act, prohibiting discrimination by race in public accommodations and jury duty.
1876		Alexander Graham Bell patents the telephone and, shortly after, makes the first successful telephone call.
		The Centennial Exposition begins in Philadelphia.
	June	Several hundred men of the U.S. 7th Cavalry Regiment, including Lieutenant Colonel George Armstrong Custer, the commanding officer, are killed at the Battle of the Little Bighorn.
	December	*The Adventures of Tom Sawyer* by Mark Twain is published in the United States, after earlier going into print in England.
1877	March	Rutherford Hayes, a Union veteran and a Republican, follows Ulysses S. Grant into the White House.
	August	Brigham Young, the Mormon leader who helps to establish a thriving church and community in Utah, dies.
		Reconstruction is ended, with civil rights for black people in the South left on paper but not in practice.
		The first college lacrosse game is played between New York University and Manhattan College.

POLITICS

1. Senator Stephen Douglas's Support of the Kansas-Nebraska Bill (1854)

INTRODUCTION

What caused the Civil War is one of the more frequently asked and debated questions in American history. Did the presence of slavery since the beginning of the nation make civil war unavoidable? If not, did politicians blunder into the war? The problem with these interpretations is that they raise as many questions as they answer. If the very existence of slavery made an armed showdown between the North and South inevitable, why did the Civil War occur in 1861, rather than decades earlier? If bumbling national leaders descended the United States into an otherwise avoidable conflict, why does Abraham Lincoln consistently rank among one of the most skilled presidents in the nation's history?

Many modern-day historians date the coming of the Civil War to the debate over the WESTWARD EXPANSION of slavery in the mid-1850s. Senator Stephen DOUGLAS, a Democrat from Illinois, sparked much of the controversy. Ambitious and combative, Douglas hoped to establish a transcontinental railroad running west from Chicago. The route would be the first of its type and would bring almost immeasurable economic gain to Illinois and the rest of the Midwest. The Nebraska Territory was the stumbling block. A vast stretch of land running west from Missouri and Iowa, the Nebraska Territory needed to gain admission into the Union before work on INTERNAL IMPROVEMENTS might begin. The MISSOURI COMPROMISE OF 1820, however, stipulated that any territory running west from the southernmost boundary of Missouri, meaning the Nebraska Territory and the neighboring Kansas Territory, come into the Union as a free state. Southern politicians adamantly opposed the idea, correctly recognizing that the free states would increasingly outnumber and, in all likelihood, outvote the slave states in the Senate. One southern politician vowed to see the Nebraska Territory "sink in hell" before entering the nation as possibly several free states. Douglas found a solution in the idea of *popular sovereignty.* In "An Act to Organize the Territories of Nebraska and Kansas," known more widely across the United States as the Kansas-Nebraska Bill, Douglas called for settlers in the western territories to vote whether they wanted to gain statehood as free or slave. A popular vote by local residents, Douglas reasoned, was American democracy at its best. Opposition was swift across much of the North. Many of Douglas's fellow northerners argued that southerners were determined to spread slavery across the West. The ultimate goal of this SLAVE POWER CONSPIRACY was to spread slavery into the East and make the United States an entirely slave-owning nation.

KEEP IN MIND AS YOU READ

1. The Democrats and the Whigs were the two major political parties in 1854. In general, the agrarian-oriented Democratic Party favored states rights and limited government. In opposition, the industrial-oriented Whig Party favored a stronger federal government and internal improvements.

2. The free states held the balance of power in Congress by 1854. Sixteen free states to 15 slave states gave the North more votes in the Senate (with two senators per state). A much larger population, thanks largely to immigration from Ireland and Germany, gave the North the edge in the House of Representatives (with representation based upon population). By 1860, the North numbered 22 million people and the South 9 million people. Broadly stated, the role of Congress is to make laws. Southerners worried that legislation to abolish slavery might initiate in a Congress dominated by the free states.

3. Congress earlier had accepted the idea of popular sovereignty in the Compromise of 1850. Under the legislation, territorial governments of the New Mexico and Utah Territories were allowed to vote whether to enter the Union as slave states or free states.

4. Sectional tension was running high by 1854. Northerners resented the fugitive slave law stipulated in the Compromise of 1850. The federal government might force private citizens to help capture runaway slaves, if needed. Southerners bitterly resented the harsh portrayal of slavery and slave owners in *Uncle Tom's Cabin,* written by Harriet Beecher Stowe and published in 1852.

Document: Douglas's Support for the Kansas-Nebraska Bill

Mr. President, I have not brought this question forward as a Northern man or as a Southern man. I am unwilling to recognize such divisions and distinctions. I have brought it forward as an American Senator, representing a state which is true to this principle, and which has approved of my action in respect to the Nebraska bill. I have brought it forward not as an act of justice to the South more than the North. I have presented it especially as an act of justice to the people of the territories, and of the states to be formed therefrom, now and in all time to come.

I have nothing to say about Northern rights or Southern rights. I know of no such divisions or distinctions under the Constitution. The bill does equal and exact justice to the whole Union, and every part of it; it violates the rights of no state or territory, but places each on a perfect equality, and leaves the people thereof to the free enjoyment of all their rights under the Constitution. . . .

I say frankly that, in my opinion, this measure will be as popular at the North as at the South, when its provisions and principles shall have been fully developed and become well understood.

Source: *Congressional Globe,* 33rd Congress, 1st Session, Appendix, p. 338. The *Congressional Globe* also is posted online. A searchable archive provided through the Library of Congress in Washington, DC, is found at: http://memory.loc.gov/ammem/amlaw/lwcg.html.

AFTERMATH

The Kansas-Nebraska Act passed later that year, declaring that any state might come into the Union "with or without slavery, as its constitution may provide." The wording might have made the Civil War all but inevitable, by shattering the national political parties. The Democratic Party split into a northern wing and a southern wing. The Whig Party collapsed. The Republican Party emerged in the furor over Kansas-Nebraska, vowing to halt the further expansion of slavery into the territories. By the election of 1860, American political parties were largely regional. The Republican Party drew its strength from the free states, while the Democratic Party drew its strength from the slave states. Political leaders catered toward their home region, often eschewing compromise and stoking regional passions.

ASK YOURSELF

1. Debate over the Kansas-Nebraska Bill aligned many members of Congress along regional lines, rather than party affiliation. Is there any issue that might have the same result today—such as gay marriage, gun control, or abortion?
2. Douglas attempted to soothe regional tensions by arguing that he was neither for the North nor for the South. Do politicians today seem to seek bipartisan support over controversial issues? If not, are politicians and the nation better served by appealing to only one side of any controversial issue? Is there a right and a wrong in most political debates, and no room for middle ground?

TOPICS AND ACTIVITIES TO CONSIDER

- Families often moved west prior to the Civil War by covered wagon, a long and expensive journey. Consider how families are more mobile today. Is moving any easier because we have access to airplanes and moving trucks? Or is any long-distance move difficult to undertake, regardless of the time period? Read a first-hand description of traveling westward in 1865 at "The Old West: Crossing the Plains, 1865," Eyewitness to History: http://www.eyewitnesstohistory.com.

BLEEDING KANSAS

Kansas exploded into violence with the passage of the Kansas-Nebraska Act. Free-soil and pro-slavery settlers hastened into the region, understanding that a popular vote would determine Kansas's admission into the Union. In the volatile atmosphere, mob rule often held forth. A band of pro-slavery men attacked and destroyed much of an abolitionist settlement at Lawrence on May 21, 1856. Two days later, John Brown, a fanatical abolitionist, and his sons murdered five slavery men at Pottawatomie Creek. The deepening bloodshed drew in federal troops, who managed to suppress the worst of the violence. After several proposed constitutions were rejected by voters, Kansas joined the Union as a free state in 1861. By this time, the border warfare in "Bleeding" Kansas had claimed the lives of more than 50 people. The killing in the state would continue with the start of the Civil War that same year.

↝ How has easier mobility in families and individuals moving from one region of the country to another changed American culture? Do people moving across the country cause their adopted regions to lose their distinctiveness over time, and is this good or bad?

Further Reading

Ayers, Edward L. *What Caused the Civil War? Reflections on the South and Southern History.* New York: Norton, 2005.

Johannsen, Robert W. *The Frontier, the Union, and Stephen A. Douglas.* Urbana: University of Illinois Press, 1989.

Johannsen, Robert W. *Stephen A. Douglas.* New York: Oxford University Press, 1973.

Rawley, James A. *Race and Politics: "Bleeding Kansas" and the Coming of the Civil War.* Philadelphia: Lippincott, 1969.

Varon, Elizabeth R. *Disunion! The Coming of the American Civil War, 1789–1859.* Chapel Hill: University of North Carolina Press, 2008.

Wunder, John R. and Joann M. Ross. *The Nebraska-Kansas Act of 1854.* Lincoln: University of Nebraska Press, 2008.

Web Sites

For an analysis on the events that led to the start of the Civil War, see James Oliver Horton, "Slavery and the Coming of the Civil War: A Matter for Interpretation." The essay is from *Rally on the High Ground: The National Park Service Symposium on the Civil War,* posted at: http://www.cr.nps.gov/history/online_books/rthg/chap5.htm. Contemporary newspaper editorials on the Kansas-Nebraska Act are found at "Secession Era Editorials Project," Department of History, Furman University, http://history.furman.edu/editorials/see.py. The text to the Kansas-Nebraska Act, as well as a photograph of the document, is posted at: http://www.ourdocuments.gov. The site is labeled as a *cooperative effort* among National History Day, The National Archives and Records Administration, and USA Freedom Corps.

2. REACTION TO LINCOLN'S FIRST INAUGURAL ADDRESS IN THE *STAUNTON* (VIRGINIA) *SPECTATOR* (1861)

INTRODUCTION

The Republican Party won the presidential election of 1860, making Abraham Lincoln the nation's 16th president. Born in Kentucky in 1809, but spending most of his life in Illinois, Lincoln was a moderate on slavery. Lincoln called not for the ABOLITION OF SLAVERY in the South, but for the halt of its spread into the West. Closing the territories to slavery would benefit free laborers by keeping wages competitive and allowing for upward mobility. Lincoln refused to make any concession on the issue, arguing that other political demands from the slave states surely would follow. "If we surrender," Lincoln predicted, "it is the end of us." Lincoln faced an unprecedented challenge when he stood to deliver his inaugural address on MARCH 4, 1861. The DEEP SOUTH had viewed the election of Lincoln as a direct threat to the legality of slavery. Certain that the closing of the West to slavery would inexorably lead to the abolition of the institution in the South, white southerners believed their standing within the American nation was on the wane. Secession offered the only recourse to maintain their way of life. Under the idea, southerners argued that the American Union was a compact of states. Should a state believe its rights threatened by the national government, it had the right to withdraw from the Union and reassert its fundamental sovereignty. Led by South Carolina in December 1860, the other six states of the Deep South quickly left the Union. Lincoln, like many other political leaders across the United States, never recognized the legality of secession. Drawing on already well-established arguments, Lincoln declared that the Union was eternal. Otherwise, minority parties and views would hold the government hostage by threatening to secede. Political debate and the ballot box were the way to amend grievances, rather than breaking apart the nation.

On a gray and blustery day that seemed to match the mood of the nation, Lincoln addressed the so-called Confederate States in his inauguration speech. Lincoln reiterated his stance that the Union was perpetual. He also promised his "dissatisfied fellow countrymen" that the federal government would not initiate the use of military force to keep the nation together. "You can have no conflict, without being yourselves the aggressors." Lincoln closed by reminding his listeners that "We are not enemies, but friends. We must not be enemies. Though passion may have strained, it must not break our bonds of affection. The mystic chords of memory, stretching from every battle-field and patriot grave, to every living heart and hearthstone, all over this broad land, will yet swell the chorus of the Union, when again touched, as surely they will be, by the better angels of our nature."

An editorial written in the *Staunton Spectator* eight days after the inauguration stated that Lincoln had missed an opportunity to resolve the sectional crisis. As president, Lincoln was duty bound to enforce the laws of the land. But if Lincoln had called for a National Convention, the seven seceded states might have gained national approval for their action. While relatively even in tone, the Democratic newspaper fundamentally misunderstood that Lincoln was not going to allow the Union to dissolve.

KEEP IN MIND AS YOU READ

1. Abraham Lincoln had little national political experience before assuming the presidency. Lincoln had served multiple terms in the Illinois State Legislature, as a Whig. In 1847, he won election to the House of Representatives for a two-year term. Here Lincoln became known primarily for his opposition to the Mexican-American War (1846–48). Despite only a brief stay in Washington, Lincoln had gained national prominence by 1860. Lincoln had engaged Stephen Douglas, the author of the Kansas-Nebraska Bill, in a series of spirited debates for the Senate in 1856. Lincoln lost the election, but his eloquence and sharp mind drew much admiration. Four years later, Lincoln forcefully argued the right of the federal government to limit slavery in the territories at Cooper Union in New York City.

2. Many white southerners sincerely believed that slavery formed the foundation for American democracy. Every Western society produced a group of people so poor and so powerless that they had little to lose in pushing for a new system, violently if necessary. Political and economic upheavals across much of Europe in 1848 only confirmed these views. Better to have potential revolutionaries easily identifiable, and, literally, under lock and key through black slavery, than loose amid the mass of free laborers in the North. Whites might share a rough political equality amid the presence of slaves, because virtually no whites had any interest in seeking dramatic change.

Document: "Lincoln's Inaugural," Staunton Spectator, *March 12, 1861*

On the first page of this paper will be found a correct copy of the Inaugural Address of the President. We know that it will be read with great interest by all of our readers. . . . The Constitution invests the Executive with no discretionary powers in regard to the enforcement of the laws, but, on the contrary, makes it his imperative and sworn duty to see that they be faithfully executed. It is for the very reason that it is the duty of the Executive to have the laws enforced, and the duty of the people to yield obedience to them, that we have several times recommended the call of a National Convention for the purpose of obtaining the consent of the three-fourths of the States to the peaceful withdrawal of the seceded States, and the release of the Executive from his obligations to enforce the laws in them. . . . We believe that this policy must be adopted, or that civil war, the direst of all calamities, will ultimately be the result. We regret that the President did not express a desire to be relieved, in the mode suggested, from his obligations to perform a duty which threatens such direful consequences. . . . To involve the country in civil war, as long as there remains any means to avoid it, would be more than folly and madness—it would be in the highest degree criminal. We cannot believe that any President would willingly involve the country in civil war.

The Inaugural Address is understood by some to indicate a purpose to enforce the laws at all hazards, and by others that the laws will be enforced only so far as it can be done peacefully.—It cannot be known certainly which is the proper construction, till the policy of the administration shall be more clearly indicated by its acts. If it shall, in reckless disregard of the peace of the country, persist in enforcing the laws where it must result in a conflict, the inevitable result will be that the whole South will be united in armed opposition to such a policy.

Source: "Lincoln's Inaugural," *Staunton* (Virginia) *Spectator*, March 12, 1861, p. 2. Listed at: Edward L. Ayers, "The Valley of the Shadow: Two Communities in the American Civil War," Virginia Center for Digital History and University of Virginia Library: http:// valley.lib.virginia.edu/news/ss1861/va.au.ss.1861.03.12.xml#02.

AFTERMATH

Confederate forces fired on the Union-controlled Fort Sumter, located in Charleston harbor, South Carolina, on April 12, 1861. After a 33-hour bombardment, the fort surrendered. Lincoln soon after called for 75,000 volunteers to put down the "insurrection." The call for troops drove the Upper South—Virginia, North Carolina, Tennessee, and Arkansas— from the Union. The *Staunton Spectator* stood prophetic, with the South now in "armed opposition" to the federal government. The Civil War had begun.

ASK YOURSELF

1. In all but the final version of his inaugural speech, Lincoln closed with the question for the South, "Shall it be peace or sword?" Compare the line to Lincoln's now famous closing words regarding the "mystic cords of memory." What ending is more effective, and why?

THE CONFEDERATE INAUGURAL ADDRESS

Jefferson Davis, a Mississippi planter and the newly installed President of the Confederate States of America, had delivered his inauguration speech on February 18, 1861, in Montgomery, Alabama. Davis argued that the "sovereign States" of the Deep South had the right to withdraw from the American Union, because the federal government had become "destructive" toward their rights. In doing so, the seceded states "merely asserted" a right that the Declaration of Independence "had defined to be inalienable; of the time and occasion for its exercise, they, as sovereigns, were the final judges, each for itself. The impartial and enlightened verdict of mankind will vindicate the rectitude of our conduct, and He who knows the hearts of men will judge the sincerity with which we labored to preserve the Government of our fathers in its spirit." Davis made no mention of slavery in his speech. Alexander Stephens, the Vice President of the Confederacy, was far less circumspect. Speaking in Savannah, Georgia, in late March, Stephens declared that "our new government" has as "its corner-stone" the "great truth that the negro is not equal to the white man."

2. The *Staunton Spectator* advocated a strategy for Lincoln to let the South secede while still fulfilling his duties as president. If Lincoln failed in this, the fault for a civil war rested with him. Does the critique seem fair? Was Lincoln exercising a policy "more than folly and madness" by attempting to maintain the American Union?

TOPICS AND ACTIVITIES TO CONSIDER

- ❧ A number of songwriters penned lyrics to support Lincoln's bid for the White House in 1860. Some of these titles are posted at: Today in History: March 4, Songs of the Campaign and Presidency, American Memory from the Library of Congress: http://memory.loc.gov/ammem/today/mar04.html. Does music play a powerful role in presidential elections today? What might the lyrics read if you had to write a song to support a presidential campaign?

- ❧ Lincoln arguably faced the most serious crisis in American history when coming into office in the winter of 1861. The following link, run by Bartleby.com—which bills itself as the "preeminent Internet publisher of literature, reference and verse . . . with unlimited access to books and information on the web, free of charge"—lists all inauguration speeches, from George Washington through Barack Obama: http://www.bartleby.com/124/. What speeches do you think are the most stirring, and why?

Further Reading

Abrahamson, James L. *The Men of Secession and Civil War, 1859–1861*. Wilmington, DE: SR Books, 2000.

Donald, David H. *Lincoln*. New York: Simon and Schuster, 1995.

Goodwin, Doris Kearns. *Team of Rivals: The Political Genius of Abraham Lincoln*. New York: Simon and Schuster, 2005.

Klein, Maury. *Days of Defiance: Sumter, Secession, and the Coming of the Civil War*. New York: Alfred A. Knopf, 1997.

Marvel, William. *Mr. Lincoln Goes to War*. Boston: Houghton Mifflin, 2006.

McPherson, James M. *Battle Cry of Freedom: The Civil War Era*. New York: Oxford University Press, 1988.

Web Sites

For a picture of Lincoln's inauguration address, as well as more historical background, visit: American Treasures of the Library of Congress: http://www.loc.gov/exhibits/treasures/trt039.html.

The Lincoln Archives Digital Project catalogues "federal records created during the Lincoln administration." The project has made available over 6,000 documents, as well as photographs, maps, political cartoons, and newspapers. The address is: http://www.lincolnarchives.us.

3. A "Disgrace to the American People": The Illinois Legislature Denounces the Emancipation Proclamation (1863)

INTRODUCTION

The Union went to war in 1861 to, in the words of Congress, "defend and maintain the supremacy of the Constitution and to preserve the Union." All of this might be accomplished without touching slavery in the Confederate States. Lincoln initially turned back any move against slavery, fearing to alienate the BORDER STATES of Kentucky, Maryland, and Missouri. Slave owners sometimes even came into Union lines, to reclaim their PROPERTY that had run away. By the next year, however, Lincoln, as well as many other Union observers, recognized the military benefit that the Confederacy was drawing from the labor of slaves. Southern men might shoulder a musket while slaves worked in the fields and constructed defensive works. Lincoln understood that expanding Union war aims to strike against slavery would correspondingly weaken the Confederacy. When to announce the new policy proved the issue. The Union needed a battlefield victory, to avoid the appearance of announcing the emancipation of the slaves as a last-ditch effort to stave off losing the war. Ferocious fighting between the Union Army of the Potomac and the Confederate Army of Northern Virginia around ANTIETAM Creek in western Maryland on September 17, 1862, provided the opportunity. The Union army scored a strategic victory when, two days after the battle had ended, the Confederate army retreated back into Virginia. Lincoln issued a preliminary emancipation proclamation on September 22, declaring slavery ended in any state still in rebellion against the government at the start of 1863. No Confederate leader heeded the warning and, on January 1, Lincoln signed the final proclamation. Lincoln believed that signing the measure was one of the most just decisions of his political career. Members of the Illinois legislature, in Lincoln's home state, took a very different view.

KEEP IN MIND AS YOU READ

1. Some modern-day scholars suggest that, in issuing the preliminary emancipation proclamation, Lincoln was merely responding to the thousands of slaves who had freed themselves by escaping into the Union lines. The slaves won their own freedom, and Lincoln merely confirmed the fact. Other scholars criticize the president for freeing the slaves only where his power failed to extend—in

the Confederate-held territory—and not where his authority did reach. Both arguments overlook the revolutionary nature of the Emancipation Proclamation. Lincoln had turned the war into a contest to reshape American society and assured that, with ultimate Union triumph, slavery was on the road to extinction.

2. The Confederate States, after long and bitter debate, authorized the recruitment of slaves into the military only a few weeks before the end of the war in the spring of 1865. There is considerable controversy as to whether blacks in any numbers would have taken advantage of the opportunity, since no guarantee was made for their freedom if the Confederacy won the war.

Document: The Illinois Legislature's Reaction to the Emancipation Proclamation

Resolved: That the emancipation proclamation of the President of the United States is as unwarrantable in military as in **civil law;** a gigantic usurpation, at once converting the war, professedly commenced by the administration for the vindication of the authority of the constitution, into the crusade for the sudden, unconditional and violent liberation of 3,000,000 Negro slaves; a result which would not only be a total subversion the Federal Union but a revolution in the social organization of the Southern States, the immediate and remote, the present and far-reaching consequences of which to both races cannot be contemplated without the most dismal foreboding of horror and dismay. The proclamation invites **servile insurrection** as an element in the emancipation crusade—a means of warfare, the inhumanity and diabolism of which are without example in civilized warfare, and which we denounce, and which the civilized world will denounce as an ineffaceable disgrace to the American people.

Source: Resolution of the Illinois State Legislature, January 7, 1863. Listed at: http://edale1.home.mindspring.com/Resolution%20of%20the%20Illinois%20Legislature%20in%20Opposition%20to%20the%20Emancipation%20Proclamation.htm.

civil law: Slaves were considered property rather than people at the start of the Civil War. The fear was that by striking against private property in freeing the slaves, President Lincoln had greatly exceeded his authority. The worry was that future presidents might use the precedent to strike against homes, land, and other property owned by individuals and groups not in favor with the administration. Taken to an extreme, such action would descend the United States from democracy into dictatorship.

servile insurrection: A slave uprising. In the Emancipation Proclamation, Lincoln asked the "people so declared to be free to abstain from all violence, unless necessary in self-defence." The wording was far too vague for opponents of the Emancipation Proclamation, as "self-defence" might be used to excuse nearly any action.

AFTERMATH

As suggested by Illinois State Legislature, initial reaction to the Emancipation Proclamation across much of the Union was cool, if not outright hostile. The Democratic Party picked up seats in the off-year Congressional elections. At the same time, many Union soldiers protested that they had volunteered for almost any reason but to free the slaves. Outrage was the reaction in the Confederacy. JEFFERSON DAVIS derided the Emancipation Proclamation as the "most execrable measure recorded in the history of guilty man." Still, over time, the Emancipation Proclamation turned into a war-winning weapon for the Union. In 1865, by the end of the fighting, 180,000 African American soldiers had served in the Union army.

The numbers represent almost 10 percent of the Union manpower mobilized. Whites in the Union army and on the home front came around to give begrudging respect to black soldiers for their bravery and courage.

ASK YOURSELF

1. Might the acceptance of blacks into the Union military have opened the door for African Americans gaining rights of citizenship and, for black men, the right to vote in the postwar era? Why?
2. Politics often is a matter of timing. Do modern-day politicians wait to announce major policy proposals when events give them momentum, as Lincoln did after the Union victory at Antietam?

TOPICS AND ACTIVITIES TO CONSIDER

- The push to end slavery influenced American popular culture. In 1862, Julia Ward Howe penned "The Battle Hymn of the Republic." The song was one of the most popular in the Union, and remains well known today. Some of the lyrics read:

   "As He died to make men holy/Let us die to make men free/His truth goes marching on."

   Does any movement or cause have the same influence on American life today?
- How emancipation came about is a question that scholars continue to debate. Was President Lincoln the driving figure, or did he merely respond to events? Try to list some of the arguments to either side of the question after listening to the lecture by Allen Guelzo, "The Emancipation Moment: Abraham Lincoln and the First of January, 1863" posted at: http://teachingamericanhistory.org/seminars/2004/guelzo.html. Allen Guelzo is the Henry R. Luce III Professor of the Civil War era at Gettysburg College. The site is maintained by TeachingAmericanHistory.org, a project of the Ashbrook Center for Public Affairs at Ashland University, Ohio.

Further Reading

Franklin, John Hope. *The Emancipation Proclamation*. Garden City, NY: Doubleday, 1963.

Guelzo, Allen C. *Lincoln's Emancipation Proclamation: The End of Slavery in America*. New York: Simon and Schuster, 2004.

Holzer, Harold and Sara Vaughn, eds. *Lincoln and Freedom: Slavery, Emancipation, and the Thirteenth Amendment*. Carbondale: Southern Illinois University Press, 2007.

McPherson, James M. *Crossroads of Freedom: Antietam*. New York: Oxford University Press, 2002.

Web Sites

For more background information on the Emancipation Proclamation, plus photographs of the hand-written document, go to: http://www.archives.gov/exhibits/featured_documents/emancipation_proclamation/. The site is maintained by the National Archives, located in Washington, DC.

Learn more about the fighting at Antietam at: http://www.nps.gov/anti/index.htm. The Antietam National Battlefield is maintained by the National Park Service.

4. A Reaction to the Gettysburg Address in *Harper's Weekly* (1863)

INTRODUCTION

The months that followed Lincoln's signing of the Emancipation Proclamation went badly for the Union. In the East, the Army of the Potomac suffered the collapse of yet another offensive to capture the Confederate capital city of Richmond during three days of vicious fighting around CHANCELLORSVILLE, Virginia. In the West, the Union siege of Confederate-held VICKSBURG, Mississippi, seemed to go on indefinitely. The situation turned even more grim during the early summer. Confederate General ROBERT E. LEE and his Army of Northern Virginia again pushed northward, crossing into northern Maryland and southern Pennsylvania by late June. Lee hoped that the capture of a major northern city—perhaps Philadelphia, New York, or Washington, DC—might gain European recognition of the Confederacy. But first Lee had to defeat the Union Army of the Potomac. The clash came at the crossroads town of Gettysburg. Union and Confederate soldiers fought ferociously during the first three days in July, inflicting and enduring horrific losses. By the time Lee admitted defeat and retreated southward, 45,500 Union and Confederate soldiers were killed, wounded, and missing. The Union had won a major battlefield triumph, soaring morale in the army and on the home front to one of its highest points.

KEEP IN MIND AS YOU READ

1. Governor Andrew Curtin of Pennsylvania authorized David Wills, a local attorney, to purchase land for a cemetery for Union dead soon after the end of the fighting at Gettysburg. Wills purchased 17 acres, and work began. That autumn, a committee planned a dedication ceremony for November 19. EDWARD EVERETT, a nationally known orator, received invitation as the primary speaker. Lincoln received invitation to "make a few remarks" almost as an afterthought, because few on the committee believed that he would accept.

2. At the dedication ceremony, Everett spoke for nearly two hours. This was not unusual for the day, since listening to speeches was a popular form of

entertainment. Lincoln, by contrast, spoke for only about two minutes. His words ran:

Four score and seven years ago our fathers brought forth on this continent, a new nation, conceived in Liberty, and dedicated to the proposition that "all men are created equal."

Now we are engaged in a great civil war, testing whether that nation, or any nation so conceived and so dedicated, can long endure. We are met on a great battle-field of that war. We have come to dedicate a portion of that field, as a final resting place for those who here gave their lives that that nation might live. It is altogether fitting and proper that we should do this.

But, in a larger sense, we can not dedicate—we can not consecrate—we can not hallow—this ground. The brave men, living and dead, who struggled here, have consecrated it, far above our poor power to add or detract. The world will little note, nor long remember what we say here, but it can never forget what they did here.

It is for us the living, rather, to be dedicated here to the unfinished work which they who fought here have thus far so nobly advanced. It is rather for us to be dedicated here to the great task remaining before us—that from these honored dead we take increased devotion to that cause for which they gave the last full measure of devotion—that we here highly resolve that these dead shall not have died in vain—that the nation, under God, shall have a new birth of freedom—and that government of the people by the people, for the people, shall not perish from the earth.

Lincoln returned from the speakers' stand to polite applause. Many in the audience may not have recognized that the President was finished speaking, given the brevity of his address. An editorial writer for *Harper's Magazine,* with nearly three weeks to think on the dedication ceremony, found much to praise.

Document: A Reaction to the Gettysburg Address in Harper's Weekly

The solemn ceremony at Gettysburg is one of the most striking events of the war. There are grave-yards enough in the land—what is Virginia, but a cemetery?—and the brave who have died for us in this fierce war consecrate the soil from the ocean to the Mississippi. But there is peculiar significance in the field of Gettysburg, for there "thus far" was thundered to the rebellion. This it is which separates it from all the other battlefields of the war. Elsewhere the men in the ranks have fought as nobly, and their officers have directed as bravely; but here their valor stayed the flood of barbarism, and like the precious shells that the highest storm-tides strew upon the beach, showing how far the waters came, so the dead heroes of Gettysburg marked the highest tide of the war. Therefore shall their graves be peculiarly honored, and their memory especially sacred; and all that living men can bring of pomp and solemnity and significance to hallow their resting-place shall not be wanting.

The President and the Cabinet were there, with famous soldiers and civilians. The oration by Mr. Everett was smooth and cold. Delivered, doubtless, with his accustomed graces, it yet wanted one stirring thought, one vivid picture, one thrilling appeal.

The few words of the President were from the heart to the heart. They can not be read, even, without kindling emotion. "The world will little note nor long remember what we say here, but it can never forget what they did here." It was as simple and felicitous and earnest a word as was ever spoken.

Source: *Harper's Weekly: A Journal of Civilization,* December 5, 1863, vol. 7, no. 362, p. 2. Listed at "The Civil War": http://www.sonofthesouth.net/.

AFTERMATH

Like the writer at *Harper's Weekly,* Edward Everett also quickly grasped the magnitude of Lincoln's speech. "I should be glad" Everett praised to Lincoln several days later, "if I could flatter myself that I came as near to the central idea of the occasion, in two hours, as you did in two minutes." Especially important, Lincoln had successfully linked the founding of the American nation to the Declaration of Independence. Many other observers dated the United States to the ratification of the Constitution in 1788. The Constitution had recognized the legality of slavery through the 3/5s Compromise (which defined a slave as both property and person, for both economic and political reasons). But, in the Declaration of Independence, is the famous line that "all men are created equal." Lincoln, like more progressive white Americans at the time, interpreted the phrase to mean that all men have the right to make their own living and by their own labor, rather than as a call for social and political equality. This was a far cry from where the nation had stood earlier, with few white Americans even bothering to include blacks in any discussion of equal rights. Lincoln's speech is today considered one of the greatest addresses in American history.

ASK YOURSELF

1. Was Lincoln's speech especially powerful because it occurred at the dedication of the Union cemetery at Gettysburg, as suggested by *Harper's Weekly?* Do you think

GETTYSBURG AND VICKSBURG

Union triumphs at Gettysburg and Vicksburg during the summer of 1863 was one of the major turning points of the Civil War. After the fighting in Pennsylvania and Mississippi, the Union enjoyed a clear superiority in manpower and material. Union triumph on the battlefield was all but inevitable. War, however, also involves maintaining the political will to fight. The question after mid-1863 increasingly centered around whether the Union might maintain the morale to see the war through to its conclusion. If the Union became discouraged over heavy casualties and lack of battlefield progress, as very nearly happened by late the next summer, the Confederacy might win its independence. A similar scenario occurred during the Vietnam War. By the early 1970s, the United States had triumphed in every major battle. Yet the American public simply wanted out from the conflict, disillusioned about the lack of clear political objectives to win the war.

that the words would have carried the same power if Lincoln had delivered the speech at the White House?

2. In general, are shorter speeches better? Does the audience remember the main points better? Or, does the audience need the speaker to fill out his or her main points, rather than offering sound bites?

TOPICS AND ACTIVITIES TO CONSIDER

- ❧ The National Cemetery at Gettysburg has received praise both at the time and today for its inclusive design. How is the design of the cemetery inclusive, and why are the grounds considered one of the first national cemeteries in American history? Explore the history of the park at: http://www.nps.gov/archive/gett/gncem.htm. The National Park Service maintains the site.

- ❧ Abraham Lincoln wrote several drafts of the Gettysburg Address. Compare the speech written here, recorded by two of Lincoln's advisors and personal secretaries, to an earlier version. What are the differences in wording, and are they significant? The earlier version of the speech is posted at Abraham Lincoln, Draft of the Gettysburg Address: Nicolay Copy. Transcribed and annotated by the Lincoln Studies Center, Knox College, Galesburg, Illinois. Available at Abraham Lincoln Papers at the Library of Congress, Manuscript Division, Washington, DC: American Memory Project, http://memory.loc.gov/ammem/alhtml/malhome.html.

Further Reading

Boritt, Gabor S. *The Gettysburg Gospel: The Lincoln Speech That Nobody Knows.* New York: Simon and Schuster, 2006.

Sears, Stephen W. *Gettysburg.* Boston: Houghton Mifflin, 2003.

Wills, Garry. *Lincoln at Gettysburg: The Words That Remade America.* New York: Simon and Schuster, 1992.

Web Site

The National Park Service maintains the Gettysburg battlefield. Explore the history of the battle and the grounds at: http://www.nps.gov/gett/.

5. "Election Day . . . the Most Momentous Since the Days of Washington": Diary Entries by Union Lieutenant Colonel Theodore Lyman (1864)

INTRODUCTION

The Union faced a stark choice in the presidential election of 1864. Running at the head of the Republican ticket, Abraham Lincoln promised to preserve the Union and abolish slavery. No end to the war but in Union victory was possible, because the Confederacy refused to let go of its slave-labor system. George McClellan and the Democratic Party offered another alternative. A former Union general turned politician, McClellan ran on a platform calling for a compromise with the Confederate States. The Union might be restored, but only as it stood in 1860. Slavery would remain intact, and possibly even protected under a new Constitutional amendment. The campaign quickly turned nasty—Republicans cried cowardice, if not outright treason; Democrats countered their opponents placed the freedom of black slaves above the lives of white soldiers. By the late summer of 1864, McClellan looked likely to carry the White House. Multiple Union offensives had suffered massive casualties before bogging down. By August, ultimate victory, as the Republicans defined it, seemed as far away as ever. Even Lincoln gloomily predicted, "I am going to be beaten, and unless some great change takes place, *badly* beaten." Great change did come, however, over the next two months. Union forces captured Atlanta, Georgia, a major Confederate industrial and transportation center, in September. The next month, a Union army smashed a Confederate force at Cedar Creek and gained control of Virginia's Shenandoah Valley. The two Federal battlefield victories soared morale, and made military victory only a matter of time. Lincoln won reelection by a majority of 212 to 21 in the electoral college, carrying all but Delaware, Kentucky, and New Jersey. Union soldiers voted for Lincoln in especially heavy numbers. The military vote tallied 78 percent for Lincoln, compared to 54 percent of the civilian vote. Lieutenant Colonel Theodore Lyman, a staff officer, described the election process and results in the Union Army of the Potomac.

KEEP IN MIND AS YOU READ

1. The United States had never held a wartime election prior to 1864. Some observers suggested that Lincoln delay, or even call off, the vote. Lincoln refused, declaring that "We cannot have free government without elections; and if the rebellion could

force us to forgo, or postpone a national election, it might fairly claim to have already conquered and ruined us." The United States would not again simultaneously face a presidential election and a war until 1944.

2. Many Confederate military and political leaders believed that the triumph of McClellan was their best chance to win the war. When that failed to happen, Jefferson Davis continued to breath defiance, insisting that no battlefield triumphs "can save the enemy from the constant and exhaustive drain of blood and treasure which must continue until he shall discover that no peace is attainable unless based on the recognition of our indefeasible rights."

Document: Diary Entries of Theodore Lyman

November 3, Thursday Flocks of election commissioners, scurvy looking fellows, are coming down here to look after the presidential vote. Voting is a **state matter;** for some states there is no permission for soldiers to vote. Those who can, vote either by proxy or by commissioners. By proxy, they publickly [sic] declare that they wish to give to a certain person at home the power to vote for them, and to him a proper document is duly forwarded. By commissioner, they appear before this officer and their vote is registered and given to him, in a sealed envelope.

November 8, Tuesday Election day, and one of the most momentous—indeed the most momentous since the days of Washington. . . . Out of some 19,000 votes which were cast in this army, Lincoln's majority was over 8,000.

November 10, Thursday Enough news has come to confirm Lincoln's election.—No rows any where, and everything very creditable. A grand spectacle of order in the midst of most terrible war!

Source: Lowe, David W., ed. *Theodore Lyman, Meade's Army: The Private Notebooks of Lt. Col. Theodore Lyman.* Kent, OH: Kent State University Press, 2007, pp. 292–94. Reprinted with permission.

---

state matter: Nineteen states allowed soldiers to vote by absentee ballot. Indiana, Illinois, and New Jersey were among the most important of the remaining states, because of their large number of electoral votes. The three states had Democratic legislatures, and advanced the argument that allowing soldiers to vote would be tantamount to supporting military rule. In reality, Democrats in these states recognized that most Union soldiers by 1864 supported the Republican platform. Still, even if no soldiers had been allowed to vote, Lincoln would have carried the popular total and won reelection.

AFTERMATH

Lincoln's reelection made ultimate Union victory in the Civil War only a matter of time. With broad popular support at home and material and manpower superiority at the front, Federal armies had only to wear down their Confederate counterparts. That happened quickly. On April 9, 1865, only one month after Lincoln's second inaugural address, the Confederate Army of Northern Virginia surrendered at Appomattox Court House, Virginia. The Army of Northern Virginia had been the Confederacy's most successful military force. The surrender of Lee's men effectively marked the end to the war, even though other Confederate field armies would surrender over the next several weeks. Lincoln would not live to see this, falling victim to an assassin's bullet on April 15.

ASK YOURSELF

1. Is holding an election during wartime a "grand spectacle of order," as Lyman declares? Should elections be postponed during wartime, to avoid the risk of a change in leadership?

2. Some modern-day historians have taken Jefferson Davis and Robert E. Lee to task for continuing the war after the reelection of Lincoln. Thousands of lives were lost, and millions of dollars were spent, between November 1864 and April 1865. If the Confederacy no longer had hope for winning the war, these were blood and treasure wasted. The criticism is stark, but is it valid? Do any people going down in defeat recognize the true reality of the situation?

TOPICS AND ACTIVITIES TO CONSIDER

- In his third inaugural address on January 20, 1941, President Franklin D. Roosevelt made reference to Abraham Lincoln. FDR faced a similar task, in that he had to rally a nation in time of war. How do the tone and the message of the two speeches compare? FDR's 1941 inaugural is posted by following the U.S. Inaugurals link at: http://www.bartelby.org. Bartelby.com maintains the site.

- Lincoln often made use of the Bible in his public speeches. Compare Lincoln to other presidents in Will Stape, "How U.S. Presidents Treat Religion in Their Inaugural Speeches": http://www.associatedcontent.com/article/1418481/how_us_presidents_treat_religion_in_pg3.html. The site is maintained by Associated Content, which claims that its "platform enables anyone to participate in the new content economy by publishing content on any topic, in any format (text, video, audio and images), and connects that content to consumers, partners and advertisers."

LINCOLN'S SECOND INAUGURAL ADDRESS

Lincoln's second inaugural address, delivered on March 4, 1865, ranks as one of the finest. The address was brief—the fewest number of words delivered by a president during an inauguration thus far—but profound. Lincoln explained the start of the war by declaring that the North and South had sought to avoid hostilities in 1861, "but one of them would make war rather than let the nation survive; and the other would accept war rather than let it perish." With ultimate Union victory looming ever closer as the war stretched across its fourth winter, Americans might hope for a speedy resolution. Lincoln closed with his now famous injunction "With malice toward none; with charity for all; with firmness in the right, as God gives us to see the right, let us strive on to finish the work we are in." With these words, Lincoln may have been looking toward the postwar reconstruction of the South. Lincoln in late 1863 had issued his Proclamation of Amnesty and Reconstruction, which offered a presidential pardon to southern whites who accepted the abolition of slavery and took an oath of allegiance to the United States. If 10 percent of the white men in any state took the oath (based against the number of voters in the 1860 presidential election), they could reestablish a state government. The plan never gained much momentum, with Lincoln's assassination only five weeks later.

Further Reading

Connelly, Thomas Lawrence. *The Marble Man: Robert E. Lee and His Image in American Society.* New York: Knopf, 1977.

Davis, William C. *Lincoln's Men: How President Lincoln Became Father to an Army and a Nation.* New York: The Free Press, 1999.

Nelson, Larry E. *Bullets, Ballots, and Rhetoric: Confederate Policy for the United States Presidential Contest of 1864.* Tuscaloosa: University of Alabama Press, 1980.

Sears, Stephen W. *George B. McClellan: The Young Napoleon.* New York: Ticknor and Fields, 1988.

Thomas, Emory M. *Robert E. Lee: A Biography.* New York: W.W. Norton, 1995.

Waugh, John C. *Reelecting Lincoln: The Battle for the 1864 Presidency.* New York: Crown Publishers, 1997.

Web Sites

For a photograph of Lincoln's second inaugural address, as well as a transcription and analysis, go to: http://www.ourdocuments.gov. Ourdocuments.gov is maintained by the National Archives and Records Administration.

For a state-by-state breakdown of presidential elections since 1840, plus a wealth of other analysis, go to "Voting America: United States Politics, 1840–2008": http://american past.richmond.edu/voting/elections.html. The site is maintained by the Digital Scholarship Lab at the University of Richmond.

6. The 14th Constitutional Amendment and the 15th Constitutional Amendment (1868, 1870)

INTRODUCTION

With the triumph of the Union in Civil War in 1865, the nation faced the difficult task of rebuilding. During the Reconstruction era, the nation, especially the former Confederate States, had to repair from the physical damages of the war. Far more important, and daunting, the social fabric of the nation had to undergo reconstruction. How to integrate the nearly four million former slaves, now known as freedpeople, into the mainstream of American life focused an enormous amount of energy. Initially, the attempt went badly. The 11 former Confederate States had largely only to RATIFY the 13th Amendment, acknowledging the abolishment of slavery, before gaining readmission into the Union. By late 1866, former Confederate military and political officials began to win election to Congress; while the freedpeople were reduced to slavery in everything but name. President ANDREW JOHNSON, who had assumed the office after the assassination of Abraham Lincoln, stood by. A native of Tennessee and a firm Unionist during the Civil War, Johnson had vowed to restructure southern society to achieve greater equality for blacks and whites. Yet Johnson was either unwilling or unable to halt the reemergence of much of the ANTEBELLUM political, economic, and social system in the postwar South. National leaders in the Republican Party now stepped in, and increasingly dictated Reconstruction policies. Chief among these efforts was the passage and eventual ratification of the 14th Amendment (on July 23, 1868), granting rights of citizenship to African Americans; and the 15th Amendment (on March 30, 1870), extending suffrage to black men.

KEEP IN MIND AS YOU READ

1. The task before the United States to expand democracy in the South was enormous. No Western nation had constructed a biracial democracy, so there existed no precedent for Americans to draw upon.
2. Women, black and white, did not have the right to vote in the 1860s. This would change with the ratification of the 19th Amendment in 1920.
3. Andrew Johnson and Republican leaders in Congress had a showdown in early 1868. Arguing that Johnson had exceeded the authority of his office in trying to

remove Secretary of War EDWIN MCMASTERS STANTON, Republicans impeached Johnson. During the subsequent trial in the Senate, Johnson narrowly survived. He was badly diminished politically, however, and did not run for reelection later that same year.

Document 1: The 14th Amendment (1868)

Section 1. All persons born or naturalized in the United States, and subject to the jurisdiction thereof, are citizens of the United Sates and of the state wherein they reside. No state shall make or enforce any law which shall abridge the privileges or immunities of citizens of the United States; nor shall any state deprive any person of life, liberty, or property, without due process of law; nor deny to any person within its jurisdiction the equal protection of the law.

Section 2. Representatives shall be apportioned among the several states according to their respective numbers, counting the whole number of persons in each state, excluding Indians not taxed. But when the right to vote at any election for the choice of electors for President and Vice President of the United States, representatives in Congress, the executive and judicial officers of a state, or the members of the legislature thereof, is denied to any of the male inhabitants of such state, being twenty-one years of age, and citizens of the United States, or in any way abridged, except for participation in rebellion, or other crime, the basis of representation therein shall be reduced in the proportion which the number of such male citizens shall bear to the whole number of male citizens twenty-one years of age in such state.

Section 3. No person shall be a Senator or Representative in Congress, or elector of President and Vice President, or hold any office, civil or military, under any state, who having previously taken an oath, as a member of Congress, or as an officer of the United States, or as a member of any state legislature, or as an executive or judicial officer of any state, to support the Constitution of the United States, shall have engaged in insurrection or rebellion against the same, or given aid or comfort to the enemies thereof. But Congress may by a vote of two thirds of each House, remove such disability.

Section 4. The validity of the public debt of the United Sates, authorized by law, including debts incurred or payment of pensions and bounties for services in suppressing insurrection or rebellion, shall not be questioned. But neither the United States nor any state shall assume or pay any debt or obligation incurred in aid of insurrection or rebellion against the United States, or any claim for the loss or emancipation of any slave; but all such debts, obligations, and claims shall be held illegal and void.

Section 5. The Congress shall have power to enforce, by appropriate legislation, the provisions of this article.

Document 2: The 15th Amendment (1870)

Section 1. The right of citizens of the United States to vote shall not be denied or abridged by the United States or by any state on account of race, color, or **previous condition of servitude.**

Section 2. The Congress shall have power to enforce this article by appropriate legislation.

AFTERMATH

Dramatic gains came quickly, as a result of the two recently ratified Constitutional amendments. Under the 14th Amendment, blacks owned property, attended public schools (widely established in the South for the first time during the Reconstruction era), and married

previous condition of servitude: No state might restrict voting rights to only residents born free; in essence attempting to avoid extending the right to vote to black men for yet another generation.

and raised families. A strong sense of community developed, aided all the more by the emergence of black churches such as the African Methodist Episcopal Church and the Zion Church. Blacks also gained political power, under the 15th Amendment. African Americans won election for the first time to public offices, including Congress and state legislatures. Many of these leaders played important roles in rebuilding the economy and infrastructure of the South from the devastation brought during the Civil War. Blacks enjoying a degree of self-sufficiency and political power were revolutionary changes. All too soon reaction set in, and many of the gains achieved during the late 1860s and early 1870s were just as quickly undone.

ASK YOURSELF

1. Why is the right to vote granted in a separate amendment from that extending the rights of citizenship? The voting age today is set at 18. Is this better than setting the voting age at 21, as mentioned in Section 2 of the 14th Amendment?
2. Is the requirement that three-quarters of states have to ratify an amendment to change the Constitution too high a bar? Should only a majority have to move for change, as in other areas of American democracy?

TOPICS AND ACTIVITIES TO CONSIDER

- Many scholars argue that American history should be studied primarily through the prism of race and ethnicity. Why might this be true? Other scholars believe that gender is a better focus for the study of the American past. Why might this also be true?
- The American Constitution drew upon other source documents for many of its ideas. What are some of these documents, and how does the Constitution compare? For the source materials that influenced the Constitution, see: "The American Constitution—A Documentary Record," The Avalon Project: Documents in Law, History, and Diplomacy, Lillian Goldman Law Library, Yale Law School, http://avalon.law.yale.edu/.

Further Reading

Benedict, Michael Les. *Preserving the Constitution: Essays on Politics and the Constitution in the Reconstruction Era.* New York: Fordham University Press, 2006.

Brown, Thomas J., ed. *Reconstructions: New Perspectives on the Postbellum United States.* New York: Oxford University Press, 2006.

Cox, LaWanda. *Freedom, Racism, and Reconstruction: Collected Writings of LaWanda Cox.* Ed. Donald G. Nieman. Athens: University of Georgia Press, 1997.

Fitzgerald, Michael W. *Splendid Failure: Postwar Reconstruction in the American South.* Chicago: Ivan R. Dee, 2007.

Foner, Eric. *Reconstruction: America's Unfinished Revolution, 1863–1877.* New York: Harper and Row, 1988. An abridgement of Foner's work is *A Short History of Reconstruction, 1863–1877.* New York: Harper and Row, 1990.

McKitrick, Eric L. *Andrew Johnson and Reconstruction.* Chicago: University of Chicago Press, 1960.

Web Sites

The Constitution is posted online at: http://www.usconstitution.net/const.html. USConstitution.net, developed and maintained by Steve Mount, also provides links to state constitutions and the Confederate Constitution.

Explore the history behind the 14th Amendment at "Citizenship, Due Process, and Equal Protection: The Creation of the 14th Amendment," Explore History: Text, Illustrations and Cartoons from the Pages of Harpers Weekly: http://14thamendment.harpweek.com/.

7. RUTHERFORD B. HAYES'S INAUGURAL ADDRESS (1877)

INTRODUCTION

Backlash against the move toward black equality began early in the Reconstruction era. Many whites simply could not accept the transition of African Americans from slaves to citizens. Amid charges of corruption and incompetence against Republican-dominated governments, southern whites campaigned to regain state and local political control. One South Carolina politician later remembered, "We reorganized the Democratic Party with one plank, and only one plank, namely, that 'this is a white man's country, and white men must govern it.'" White Democrats squared off against black Republicans and their political allies in SCALAWAGS (native-born white southerners who supported the Republican Party) and CARPETBAGGERS (white northerners who had moved to the South after the end of the Civil War). Often the clashes turned violent, and scores of people were killed in armed confrontations across much of the region. President ULYSSES S. GRANT, a Republican and former Union military hero, sent in more federal troops. The Ku Klux Klan and other paramilitary organizations found their power curbed, especially when confronted with Congressional legislation that made interfering with voting rights a federal offense. Still, the damage was done. Northern resolve to carry forward the policies of Reconstruction had begun to wane by the mid-1870s. Many northerners increasingly wanted to move beyond the sectional tensions of the past and toward a seemingly bright future as a united nation. When Rutherford B. HAYES won the disputed presidential election of 1876, he informally pledged to end "bayonet rule" in the South. A former Union army officer like Grant, Hayes believed that the influence of southern moderates would do more to protect the rights of the freedpeople than the presence of federal troops. Hayes made clear that he was readying to end Reconstruction when he delivered his inaugural address.

KEEP IN MIND AS YOU READ

1. A financial panic in 1873 set the mind of many Americans on their own economic welfare, rather than that of others. Unemployment rose to about 14 percent.
2. The Supreme Court already had scaled back the authority of the federal government to enforce civil rights in the South. The Court declared in 1876 (*United States v. Cruikshank*

and *United States v. Reese*) that legislation authorizing the federal government to enforce civil rights applied only to its interactions with individual states. Thus, the government had no authority to prosecute individuals accused of violating either voting rights or civil liberties.

3. Democrats and Republicans disputed electoral returns in Florida, South Carolina, and Louisiana. Returns across the rest of the nation were close enough that whatever party carried the returns in these three states would win the White House. In behind-the-scenes dealings, the Republicans agreed to both end Reconstruction and channel more federal money for infrastructure development into the South, in exchange for the disputed electoral votes.

Document: Hayes's Inaugural Address

The permanent pacification of the country upon such principles and by such measures as will secure the complete protection of all its citizens in the free enjoyment of their constitutional rights is now the one subject in our public affairs which all thoughtful and patriotic citizens regard as of supreme importance. . . .

The sweeping revolution of the entire labor system of a large portion of our country and the advance of 4,000,000 people from a condition of servitude to that of citizenship, upon an equal footing with their former masters, could not occur without presenting problems of the gravest moment, to be dealt with by the emancipated race, by their former masters, and by the General Government, the author of the act of emancipation. That it was a wise, just, and providential act, fraught with good for all concerned, is now generally conceded throughout the country. . . .

The evils which afflict the Southern States can only be removed or remedied by the united and harmonious efforts of both races, actuated by motives of mutual sympathy and regard; and while in duty bound and fully determined to protect the rights of all by every constitutional means at the disposal of my Administration, I am sincerely anxious to use every legitimate influence in favor of honest and efficient local *self* government as the true resource of those States for the promotion of the contentment and prosperity of their citizens.

Source: Richardson, James D. *A Compilation of the Messages and Papers of the Presidents, 1789–1907*, vol. 7. Washington, DC: Bureau of National Literature and Art, 1908, pp. 442–44.

AFTERMATH

Many modern-day historians describe the Reconstruction era as America's "unfinished revolution." The hopes for the expansion of democracy to include both blacks and whites had failed by Hayes's inauguration. Blacks quickly became citizens in name only. Public segregation received legal sanction, ushering in an era of "Jim Crow." African American voting rights and legal rights also received severe curtailment. As grim as the picture was, the Reconstruction era established a blueprint for achieving civil rights. Extending citizenship to black Americans, and granting the right to vote to black men were revolutionary changes. Holding America to the promise of equal rights proved the objective striven for by later generations.

ASK YOURSELF

1. Is describing Reconstruction as an "unfinished revolution" a fair assessment? Many contemporary observers looked to either extreme. Some critics charged that by allowing southern Democrats to regain local political power, the federal government and the North had abandoned blacks to a "fate worse than slavery." By contrast, many southern whites argued that they had redeemed their region from corrupt and imposed Republican rule. Are either of these interpretations valid?

2. Do Americans move too quickly from the past and toward the future? Do northerners bear some of the blame for the failure of Reconstruction, because they wanted to move forward by the mid-1870s?

TOPICS AND ACTIVITIES TO CONSIDER

- *Birth of a Nation* is one of the more innovative and controversial films in American history. Produced in 1915 by D. W. Griffith, *Birth of a Nation* achieved much popular success. The movie also plays upon racial and regional stereotypes. Explore how Griffith's film influenced American attitudes toward race and the Reconstruction era at: Tim Dirks, "The Birth Of A Nation," The American Movie Classic Company: http://www.filmsite.org/birt.html.

- The apartheid system, or legalized segregation, in South Africa is sometimes compared to the Jim Crow South. Explore the history of apartheid at Monal Chokshi, Cale Carter, Deepak Gupta, Tove Martin, Robert Allen, "The History of Apartheid in South Africa," Computer Science Department, Stanford University: http://www-cs-students.stanford.edu/~cale/cs201/apartheid.hist.html.

Further Reading

Perman, Michael. *The Road to Redemption: Southern Politics, 1869–1879*. Chapel Hill: University of North Carolina Press, 1984.

Rable, George C. *But There Was No Peace: The Role of Violence in the Politics of Reconstruction*. Reprint; Athens: University of Georgia Press, 2007.

Simpson, Brooks D. *The Reconstruction Presidents*. Lawrence: University of Kansas Press, 1998.

Web Sites

For a detailed description and analysis of the Reconstruction era, see Eric Foner and Olivia Mahoney, "America's Reconstruction: People and Politics After the Civil War," Digital History: Using New Technologies to Enhance Teaching and Research: http://www.digital history.uh.edu/reconstruction/index.html.

For a breakdown of the vote by state in the presidential election of 1876, as well as links to articles on the election, see James R. Whitson, "President Elect: The Unofficial Homepage of the Electoral College": http://www.presidentelect.org/index.html.

MILITARY LIFE

8. "To Assist ... in the Defense of Our Common Country": David Pierson to William H. Pierson (April 22, 1861)

INTRODUCTION

Why soldiers fought during the Civil War is a question that fascinates historians. Union and Confederate soldiers repeatedly advanced against enemy fire that dropped men by the hundreds and the thousands. Union soldiers assaulted the Confederate-held Bloody Lane at Antietam, Maryland, several times before finally breaking through, leaving their dead and wounded "in heaps." Visiting the scene of the fighting in the 1980s, General John Wickham, the then Army Chief of Staff, marveled, "You couldn't get American soldiers today to make an attack like that." Bell Wiley was the first historian to explore soldiers' motivations in detail. Writing in the 1940s and 1950s, Wiley concluded that Union and Confederate soldiers only held vague ideas about why they fought. Rather, soldiers persevered out of a sense of loyalty to their comrades in the ranks. James McPherson, James Robertson, Reid Mitchell, and other well-known Civil War scholars have since challenged Wiley's arguments. These historians assert that Union and Confederate soldiers held a very strong sense of attachment to their respective causes, which helped them to endure the otherwise overwhelming carnage of the battlefield. Loyalty to comrades and unit certainly was important, especially in the heat of battle. But soldiers demonstrated in campaign after campaign that they were willing to sacrifice their lives, if need be, to defend the liberties and freedoms granted by their form of government. The letter excerpt is from Confederate Captain David Pierson, who volunteered in the 3rd Louisiana. The 30-year-old Pierson eventually won promotion to major and was wounded several times before mustering out in 1865.

KEEP IN MIND AS YOU READ

1. Confederate soldiers talked about fighting to protect their "way of life." The right to practice slavery was a major part of this. Even though most Confederate soldiers did not own slaves, they very much believed that the institution of slavery protected their own political freedoms and liberties. No white man would attempt to radicalize the existing political and economic system, because doing so only hurt himself. Even the poorest white man had distinction in southern society, because he was better than the millions of enslaved black persons. Confederate

soldiers therefore easily reconciled talk about fighting for liberty and freedom, because they meant it for white Americans. With most of the war occurring in the South, Confederate soldiers also fought to protect their homes and families from Union invasion.

2. Union soldiers went to war in 1861 to preserve the American nation. Democracy simply would not work, if any people or region left when unhappy with the outcome of popular elections. The Union fought to protect the rights of the many from the tyranny of the few. After the Emancipation Proclamation, Union war aims broadened to include the destruction of slavery. Many Union soldiers initially protested loudly that they would not fight and die for African Americans. As the war progressed, and soldiers recognized that striking against slavery was striking against the Confederate war effort, emancipation became more widely accepted.

3. Some Civil War soldiers fought for money and adventure. An economic downturn had hit the nation's economy in the late 1850s, which resulted in high levels of unemployment. For at least some men, military service promised a way to earn monthly pay, albeit in a dangerous way.

Document: Letter from David Pierson to His Father, William H. Pierson (April 22, 1861)

Dear Father,

By the time this will reach you I will be on my way to New Orleans to join the Army . . . I hope you will not be disturbed about my leaving so suddenly. I am not acting under any excitement whatever but have resolved to go after a calm and thoughtful deliberation as to all the duties, responsibilities, and dangers which I am likely to encounter in the enterprise. Nor do I go to gratify an ambition as I believe some others do, but to assist as far as in my power lies in the defense of our Common Country and homes which is threatened with invasion and annihilation . . . A majority of the free people of the South have through the **ballot box** and their chosen representatives have resolved to throw off their allegiance to their once-cherished Government and enact another suited to their wants and desires. For me there is but two alternatives left: either to take up arms against the South or in her defense. And between them I am not slow to choose. It would be a violation of my very natural feeling and impulse for me or any other man to rise up against the Government in which we live & under whose care we are protected. I have volunteered because I thought it my duty to do so . . . I am young, able-bodied, and have a constitution that will bear me up under any hardships, and above all, there is no one left behind when I am gone to suffer for the necessities of life because of my absence. Hundreds have left their families and their infant helpless children and enlisted in their Country's service, and am I who have none of their dependents better than they? If I loose [sic] all I have and survive, I can make it again, and if I perish it will be but a sacrifice which duty impels every patriot to make upon the altar of his Country's Glory.

ballot box: Most southerners voted for John Breckinridge and the Democratic Party in the presidential election of 1860. When Abraham Lincoln carried the White House, the seven states of the Deep South formed conventions to vote on secession. All the states voted in favor, although in many cases by a narrow margin.

Source: Pierson family papers, Manuscripts Collection 768, Louisiana Research Collection, Tulane University Libraries, New Orleans. Many of David Pierson's letters are printed in Cutrer, Thomas W. and T. Michael Parrish, eds. *Brothers in Gray: The Civil War Letters of the Pierson Family*. Baton Rouge: Louisiana State University Press, 1997.

AFTERMATH

Soldiers who served in the Union and Confederate armies reflected the societies from which they came. Men on both sides of the battle lines most often worked as farmers and farm laborers before the war, as did 4 out of every 10 American males in 1860. The Union had a greater percentage of skilled and unskilled laborers in the ranks, reflecting the more sizeable urban population of the North by the mid-19th century. Union and Confederate soldiers were young, like the rest of American society. The largest age group in both armies was men between the ages of 18 and 29 years. Most men who wore the blue uniforms of the Union and the gray uniforms of the Confederacy had yet to celebrate their 25th birthdays. Literacy rates among soldiers varied by army. In the Union army, 90 percent of soldiers could read and write, compared to 80 percent of soldiers in the Confederate army. The gap in literacy rates reflects the increasingly widespread establishment of public schools in the North. Still, on the whole, Civil War soldiers were among the most literate group of people in the world to that time. The men very much tried to detail their wartime experiences to family and friends at home, and the many letters that still exist make the Civil War a fruitful area for scholarly research.

ASK YOURSELF

1. Pierson mentions that every patriot has a duty to sacrifice on the "altar" of his country. Why the use of religious imagery?
2. Did Pierson perhaps feel social pressure to volunteer to fight? If he had stayed at home, when married men and fathers were going to war, might the community have looked poorly upon him?

TOPICS AND ACTIVITIES TO CONSIDER

- How does the letter from Pierson compare to letters written by Newton Robert Scott? Scott enlisted in the 36th Iowa in 1862, and his letters to Hannah Cone, his future wife, are posted at Bill Proudfoot, "Letters from an Iowa Soldier in the Civil War," Civil War Virtual Archive: http://www.civilwarletters.com.
- Compare the Louisiana Ordinance of Secession to those of the other Confederate States, in order of secession, at The Blue and Gray Trail, http://blueandgraytrail.com/event/confederate_order_of_secession. Do the documents read as you might expect, given that delegates were declaring their independence from the United States?

Further Reading

McPherson, James M. *For Cause and Comrades: Why Men Fought in the Civil War*. New York: Oxford University Press, 1997.

Mitchell, Reid. *Civil War Soldiers: Their Expectations and Their Experiences*. New York: Viking, 1988.

Robertson, James I. *Soldiers Blue and Gray*. Columbia: University of South Carolina Press, 1988.

Wiley, Bell I. *The Life of Billy Yank: The Common Soldier of the Union*. Indianapolis, IN: Bobbs-Merrill, 1952.

Wiley, Bell I. *The Life of Johnny Reb: The Common Soldier of the Confederacy*. Indianapolis, IN: Bobbs-Merrill Co., 1943.

Web Sites

For excerpts and images from letters written by thousands of Civil War soldiers, see "'I Take Up My Pen': Letters from the Civil War," Gilder Lehrman Institute of American History, New York: http://www.gilderlehrman.org/collection/online/gettysburg/index.html.

The United States Civil War Center, housed at Louisiana State University, Baton Rouge, promotes the study of the Civil War by making available a wealth of information related to the conflict. The website is: http://www.cwc.lsu.edu.

9. Hardtack and Coffee, or the Unwritten Story of Army Life (1887)

INTRODUCTION

The Civil War was the largest undertaking in American history. Prior to the start of the war in the spring of 1861, the regular army numbered only 16,000 officers and men. Most of these soldiers were stationed in scattered outposts along the western frontier, rarely coming together in units that numbered more than a few hundred men. Yet, by the end of the fighting in 1865, the Union had raised 2.1 million men and the Confederacy between 850,000 and 900,000 men. Local recruitment efforts made these numbers possible. Individual communities raised companies of 100 soldiers through patriotic rallies, speeches, and other public activities. In turn, state officials grouped 10 companies from neighboring towns and villages into a regiment, the standard building block of American armies since the colonial era. Regiments received numerical designations in the order that they had mustered into service. Thus, the 22nd Massachusetts, the 7th Indiana, and the 19th Virginia all served during the war, amid hundreds of other infantry and cavalry regiments and artillery batteries. Members of each regiment elected their officers upon completing their recruitment, a long-standing practice by that time among American volunteers. Some officers had previous military experience. This knowledge might have been gained during the Mexican War, the nation's last major conflict, or at a military school, most notably West Point in the North and the Citadel and Virginia Military Institute in the South. Many officers, however, were lawyers, merchants, and other prominent community leaders. These men had to learn their newfound trade through experience, with its accompanying cost in battlefield casualties. John Billings, a volunteer in 1861, remembers the recruitment process across the northern states at the start of the war.

KEEP IN MIND AS YOU READ

1. Soldiers often received a state flag stitched by their wives and sweethearts to carry into battle alongside the national flag. The two banners made possible the identification of regiments amid the noise and confusion of Civil War combat. The flag presentation ceremony was public, and often featured speeches and banquets. The ladies presenting the flag encouraged soldiers to "sustain this banner" until

victory won. In turn, the men accepting pledged "their lives and their honor" to never give up or disgrace the flag.

2. Soldiers often left in an assortment of uniforms early in the war, amid the rush to get to the front. The federal government quickly took up the slack, issuing a standard uniform of light blue trousers and dark blue blouse. Lacking the industry and infrastructure of the Union, the Confederacy failed to keep pace in outfitting its troops. Officers received gray uniforms, while enlisted men generally wore homespun clothes dyed with the oil of walnut or butternut trees. The resulting yellow-brown color earned Confederate soldiers the generic name Butternuts.

Document: "Enlisting," an Excerpt from John Billings's Hardtack and Coffee

The methods by which these regiments were raised were various. In 1861 a common way was for someone who had been in the regular army to take the initiative and circulate an enlistment paper for signatures. His chances were pretty good of obtaining a commission as its captain. . . .

War meetings were designed to stir lagging enthusiasm. Musicians and orators blew themselves red in the face with their windy efforts. Choirs sang "Red, White, and Blue" and "Rallied 'Round the Flag" till too hoarse for further endeavor. The old veteran soldier of 1812 was trotted out and worked for all he was worth, and an occasional Mexican War veteran would air his nonchalance at grim-visaged war. At proper intervals the enlistment roll would be presented for signatures. There was generally one old fellow present who, upon slightest provocation, would yell like a hyena and declare his readiness to shoulder his musket and go, if he wasn't so old, while his staid and half-fearful consort would pull violently at his coattails to repress his unreasonable effervescence ere it assumed more dangerous proportions. Then there was a patriotic maiden lady who kept a flag or a handkerchief waving with only the rarest and briefest of intervals, who "would go in a minute if she was a man." Besides these there was usually a man who said he would enlist if fifty others did likewise, when he well understood that such a number could not be obtained. And there was one more often found present who, when challenged to sign, would agree to, *provided* that A or B (men of wealth) would put down *their* names. . . .

Sometimes the patriotism of such a gathering would be wrought up so intensely by waving banners, martial and vocal music and burning eloquence, that a town's quota would be filled in less than an hour. It needed only the first man to step forward, put down his name, be patted on the back, placed upon the platform and cheered to the echo as the hero of the hour, when a second, third, a fourth would follow, and at last a perfect stampede set in to sign the enlistment roll. A frenzy of enthusiasm would take possession of the meeting.

Source: John D. Billings, *Hardtack and Coffee, or the Unwritten Story of Army Life.* Boston: George M. Smith, 1887, pp. 34–41.

AFTERMATH

The local orientation of Civil War regiments reflected the nature of American life at mid-century. Northerners and southerners very often grew up, lived, and died in the community of their birth. They had learned the importance of self-government in local schools, and had practiced it throughout holding public office. When the Civil War began, the strong local connections among Americans meant that they looked first to their neighbors and towns-people to ready for war. By contrast, direct ties to the national government were weak in 1861. Americans living at the time paid no income taxes, and few of them had any contact with federal officials beyond the local postmaster. To the Union and Confederacy alike, an army raised through national recruiting efforts would have been as unfamiliar as it would have been unnecessary.

ASK YOURSELF

1. Would you want to go to war with your friends and neighbors, or with individuals from across the rest of the nation? What are the advantages and disadvantages in going to war, or any other large-scale undertaking, with people you know?
2. Did community pressure encourage men to volunteer at recruitment rallies? Such pressure may have gotten men into the ranks, but would they have made determined soldiers without also believing in why they fought?

TOPICS AND ACTIVITIES TO CONSIDER

ॐ Analyze two different recruitment appeals for black Union soldiers at: "Comparing Civil War Recruitment Posters," National Archives and Records Administration, Washington, D.C.: http://docsteach.org/activities/21.

CONSCRIPTION DURING THE CIVIL WAR

The Civil War saw the first large-scale use of conscription in the nation's history. Conscription requires the compulsory military service of men of a specified age. Americans more often refer to the practice as the draft. The Confederacy turned first to the draft in 1862, given its relatively small population. Eventually, white males between 17 and 50 years of age were required to serve for the duration of the war. The Confederacy made exemptions for plantation owners and overseers, making the draft unpopular. Cries of "a rich man's war but a poor man's fight" circulated widely. Modern-day scholars have demonstrated that slave owners fought in equal proportion to non-slave owners, but this gave little comfort at the time. The Union turned to the draft the next year. Men between 20 and 45 years of age were drafted, although those conscripted might either hire a substitute or pay a commutation fee. A substitute agreed to fight in place of a drafted man, for an agreed-upon price (usually several hundred dollars). Failing this, a commutation fee of $300 exempted the draftee from serving. The draft better served the Union military by encouraging men to volunteer. Serving as a draftee carried a social stigma that few men wanted to endure. Better to fight by choice than to be seen as a coward and shirker. The four Federal drafts netted only about 46,000 men but prompted the enlistment of far more volunteers.

    ~ How does mobilization during the Civil War compare to that during World War II? Explore the contributions made by Americans toward Allied victory in 1945 at "A People at War," National Archives and Records Administration, Washington, DC: http://www.archives.gov/exhibits/a_people_at_war/a_people_at_war.html.

Further Reading

Daniel, Larry J. *Days of Glory: The Army of the Cumberland, 1861–1865.* Baton Rouge: Louisiana State University Press, 2004.

Daniel, Larry J. *Soldiering in the Army of Tennessee: A Portrait of Life in a Confederate Army.* Chapel Hill: University of North Carolina Press, 1991.

Glatthaar, Joseph T. *General Lee's Army: From Victory to Collapse.* New York: Free Press, 2008.

Prokopowicz, Gerald J. *All For the Regiment: The Army of the Ohio, 1861–1862.* Chapel Hill: University of North Carolina Press, 2001.

Wert, Jeffry D. *The Sword of Lincoln: The Army of the Potomac.* New York: Simon and Schuster, 2005.

Woodworth, Steven E. *Nothing But Victory: The Army of the Tennessee, 1861–1865.* New York: Alfred A. Knopf, 2005.

Web Sites

An exceptionally good site on the histories of two communities during the war is found at Edward Ayers, "The Valley of the Shadow: Two Communities in the American Civil War," Virginia Center for Digital History and the University of Virginia, Charlottesville, http://valley.lib.virginia.edu/.

The Library of Congress maintains a list of regimental histories, divided by region and state, at "U.S. Civil War Regimental Histories in the Library of Congress," http://www.loc.gov/rr/main/uscivilwar/.

10. "Valiantly Did the Heroic Descendants of Africa Move Forward . . .": Letter from Captain Elias D. Strunke (1863)

INTRODUCTION

The Union bolstered its ranks after the Emancipation Proclamation went into effect through the recruitment of African American soldiers. By the end of the war, 200,000 black men had served in the Federal military. These numbers represented about 9 percent of total Union manpower. Black soldiers often suffered discrimination, serving in segregated regiments under the command of white officers, working extensively in heavy-labor duties, and earning less pay per month than their white comrades. Yet black soldiers proved that, when given the opportunity, they were as willing to fight for their country as any white soldier. The 54TH MASSACHUSETTS was among the most well-known African American regiments to serve in the Union army. Members of the unit won praise for their battlefield gallantry while leading a failed Union attempt to capture Battery Wagner, a Confederate stronghold outside Charleston, South Carolina, on July 18, 1863. The black soldiers gained Wagner's parapet for an hour before falling back under intense Confederate fire. The bravery of the 54th Massachusetts won wide praise across the Union, although at a high cost. The regiment had lost 227 men killed, wounded, and missing, about one-half of its numbers engaged. Earlier, in the spring of 1863, African American soldiers had participated in a failed Union attempt to capture the Confederate-held PORT HUDSON, Louisiana. Captain Elias Strunke details the battle to Brigadier General D. Ullman, who was in charge of recruiting black soldiers in Louisiana.

KEEP IN MIND AS YOU READ

1. Black soldiers initially received a pay of several dollars less per month than white soldiers, under the argument that they had enlisted as laborers. The disparity in pay provoked much bitter feeling, especially as more and more black regiments went into battle. Only in 1864 did Congress authorize black soldiers to receive the same pay as their white counterparts.

2. Confederate response to the recruitment of black men into the Union army was severe. In late 1862, Jefferson Davis announced that the Confederacy would reenslave or execute any captured black soldiers and their officers. In response, Abraham Lincoln pledged to execute an equal number of Confederate prisoners.

Lincoln eventually backed down, recognizing that "if once begun, there was no telling where [retaliation] would end." Although sometimes still disputed today, ample evidence exists that the Confederates did execute some black prisoners and singled out their officers for especially harsh treatment.

3. The Confederate Congress passed an act in mid-March 1865 to recruit black men as soldiers. The act came after weeks of bitter debate, on the grounds that the entire premise of the Confederacy was based on black inferiority. The act had little practical application, with the effective end of the war with the surrender of the Confederate Army of Northern Virginia in early April.

Document: Captain Elias D. Strunke's Letter to Brigadier General D. Ullman (May 29, 1863)

General,

[F]eeling deeply interested in the cause which you have espoused, I take the liberty to transmit the following, concerning the colored Troops engaged in the recent battles at Port Hudson. I arrived here the evening of the 26th, was mustered and reported to Maj[or] Tucker for duty. During the night I heard heavy cannonading at Port Hudson. Early next morning I obtained permission and went to the front. But was so much detained, I did not reach our lines until the fighting for the day had nearly ceased. . . . My anxiety was to learn all I could concerning the Bravery of the Colored Reg. engaged, for their good conduct and bravery would add to your undertakings and make more popular the movement. . . .

The following is (in substance) a statement personally made to me, by 1st L[ieutenan]t Co[mpany] F 1st R[egiment] La. Native Guard who was wounded during the fighting.

"We went into action about 6 A.M. and was under fire most of the time until sunset.

The very first thing after forming line of battle we were ordered to charge—My company was apparently brave. Yet they are mostly **contrabands**, and I must say I entertained some fears as to their pluck. But I have now none—The moment the order was given, they entered upon its execution. Valiantly did the heroic descendants of Africa move forward cool as if Marshaled for dress parade, under a most murderous fire from the enemies guns, until we reached the main ditch which surrounds the Fort. [F]inding it impassible we retreated under orders to the woods and deployed as skirmishers—In the charge we lost our Capt[ain] and Colored sergeant, the latter fell wrapped in the flag he had so gallantly borne—Alone we held our position until 12 o'clock when we were relieved.

At two o'clock P.M. we were again ordered to the front where we made two separate charges each in the face of a heavy fire from the enemies Battery of seven guns—whose destructive fire would have confused and almost disorganized the bravest troops. But these men did not swerve, or show cowardice. I have been in several engagements, and I never before behold such coolness and daring—

Their gallantry entitles them to a special praise. And I already observe, the sneers of others are being tempered into eulogy—"

> **contrabands:** Escaped and former slaves.

It is pleasant to learn these things, and it must be indeed gratifying to the General to know that his army will be composed of men of almost unequaled coolness and bravery.

Source: Elias Strunke to D. Ullman, May 29, 1863, D. Ullman Papers, Generals' Papers and Books, series 159, Record Group 94, National Archives, Washington, DC. The Strunke letter also is printed in Ira Berlin et al., eds. *The Black Military Experience.* New York: Cambridge University Press, 1982, series 2 of *Freedom: A Documentary History of Emancipation, 1861–1867*, pp. 439–41.

AFTERMATH

ETHNIC SOLDIERS also served in the Union army, although their exact numbers are uncertain. Many historians place the figure as high as one out of every four men. The large numbers of foreign-born soldiers to wear Union blue reflected the massive waves of immigrants who arrived in northern seaports throughout much of the mid-19th century. German and Irish soldiers constituted the most numerous ethnic groups to serve in the Union army, at 350,000 men. Members of both nationalities often went to war in their own regiments, an expression of ethnic pride. The Irish soldiers of the 63rd New York, 69th New York, and 88th New York formed the famed Irish Brigade, among the most hard-fighting units in the Federal army. Ethnic soldiers expressed a strong ideological commitment toward the Union. "This is my country as much as the man that was born on the soil," Sergeant Peter Welsh of the Irish 28th Massachusetts explained after enlisting, "and so it is with every man who comes to this country . . . I have as much interest in the maintenance of the government and laws and integrity of the nation as any other man." Other ethnic regiments widely known throughout the Union included the Scottish 79th New York and the southern and eastern European 39th New York.

ASK YOURSELF

1. How might a unit structured along racial and ethnic lines be received in the military today?
2. Should scholars take a letter like that written by Strunke as completely accurate? Might Strunke have had an interest in overreporting the fighting spirit of Union soldiers at Port Hudson? Why or why not? Are there examples of overreporting in the news today?

TOPICS AND ACTIVITIES TO CONSIDER

↝ How does the experience of black and ethnic soldiers in the Civil War compare to that during World War II? Find out the experiences of Japanese Americans, African Americans, and Latino and Native Americans between 1941 and 1945 at "Fighting for Democracy," Public Broadcasting System: http://www.pbs.org/thewar/at_war_democracy_african_american.htm.

↝ Read a review of the movie *Glory* by Roger Ebert, a nationally known and respected film critic who writes for the *Chicago Sun-Times,* at http://rogerebert.suntimes.com/apps/pbcs.dll/article?AID=/19900112/REVIEWS/1120302/1023. Does the letter written by Strunke seem to support or contradict Ebert's take on the 54th Massachusetts? Why is the battlefield valor of African Americans during the Civil War sometimes overlooked by popular culture?

Further Reading

Berlin, Ira, Joseph P. Reidy, and Leslie S. Rowland, eds. *Freedom's Soldiers: The Black Military Experience in the Civil War.* New York: Cambridge University Press, 1998.

Burton, William L. *Melting Pot Soldiers: The Union's Ethnic Regiments.* New York: Fordham University Press, 1998.

Cornish, Dudley Taylor. *The Sable Arm: Black Troops in the Union Army, 1861–1865.* Reprint. Lawrence: University Press of Kansas, 1987.

Glatthaar, Joseph T. *Forged in Battle: The Civil War Alliance of Black Soldiers and White Officers.* New York: Free Press, 1990.

Lonn, Ella. *Foreigners in the Union Army and Navy.* Baton Rouge: Louisiana State University Press, 1952.

Welsh, Peter. *Irish Green and Union Blue: The Civil War Letters of Peter Welsh, Color Sergeant, 28th Regiment Massachusetts Volunteers,* edited by Lawrence F. Kohl and Margaret Cosse Richard. New York: Fordham University Press, 1986.

Web Sites

For more on the African American military experience during the Civil War, see Freeman, Elsie, Wynell Burroughs Schamel, and Jean West, "The Fight for Equal Rights: A Recruiting Poster for Black Soldiers in the Civil War." *Social Education* 56, 2 (February 1992): 118–20. Also see, "The Fight for Equal Rights: Black Soldiers in the Civil War," National Archives and Records Administration, Washington, DC: http://www.archives.gov/education/lessons/blacks-civil-war/ (revised and updated in 1999 by Budge Weidman).

The Web site "Shotgun's Home of the American Civil War: Civil War Potpourri" lists an essay on foreign-born soldiers serving in the Civil War, with links to different ethnic groups at, Dick Weeks, "Ethnic Composition of Civil War Forces": http://www.civilwarhome.com/ethnic.htm. The Web site bills itself as a "mini Civil War encyclopedia."

11. "I Will Commence Writing You a Letter": Description of Life in Fredericksburg, Virginia (1863)

INTRODUCTION

Civil War soldiers spent the overwhelming majority of their time in camp, fighting boredom and loneliness. The men had ample time to fill, spending about 50 days in camp for every 1 day in battle. Encampments stretched for weeks at a time over the winter, when bad weather made the logistics for launching and sustaining a campaign too difficult an undertaking. Military drill occupied several hours each day over the winter, weather permitting. Otherwise, soldiers were left to entertain themselves. Some men sought pleasures of the flesh. Brothels flourished in large cities and towns, where soldiers on assignment and leave passed through. Many of the customers at the houses of ill repute wore blue and gray. In the Union army, which possessed more detailed medical reports than the Confederate army, between 8 and 9 out of every 100 soldiers suffered from some form of venereal disease. More soldiers, however, filled the time by writing letters, singing songs, thinking about food, and playing baseball, cards, and other sports and games. In the following letter, Union CORPORAL Frederick Pettit describes camp life around Fredericksburg, Virginia. A 20-year-old man living on the family farm, Pettit had enlisted in the 100th Pennsylvania during the late summer of 1862. Pettit was killed by a Confederate sharpshooter outside Petersburg, Virginia, two years later.

KEEP IN MIND AS YOU READ

1. Soldiers generally spent their time in more substantial structures during the winter than in the summer, when they slept in shelter tents. Soon after going into winter quarters, soldiers constructed log huts that slept between two and four men. Roughly furnished on the inside with bunks and a fireplace, log huts provided some protection from the elements. If they had time, soldiers knocked down their houses prior to the start of a spring campaign.

2. In the East, where much of the nation's attention was focused because of the proximity of Washington and Richmond, soldiers stayed in winter quarters through early March 1862 and late April 1863 and 1864. Soldiers did not go into

quarters during the winter of 1864–65, because of the ongoing Union siege of the Confederate transportation hub at Petersburg.

Document: Frederick Pettit's Letter to His Family (February 3, 1863)

Dear parents, brothers, and sisters:

As I am at a loss for employment on this cold day I will commence writing you a letter. Now don't think because it is to all of you that no one need answer it, but all answer it. Let each one write a little at least no difference how poorly. The last letter I received from you was written by mother and Margaret Jan. 23rd. There were several things in it I forgot to mention in Mag's letter, and first I must say I did receive a Christmas present in a letter from you. All I can say of it is that it was small but sweet. I was glad to hear in mother's that Albert had commenced to read small words. I think he will soon be able to write me that letter. You must be taking uncommon interest in the school this winter. I think you are very fortunate in getting a good teacher. How are Wirtenberg, Hope Dale, and the other schools getting along?

Our hardest work is getting wood. We carry most of it half a mile. Though when not too stormy it is good exercise.

Lieutenant Critchlow told me there are 2 pounds of butter on the way for me. He said he received the key of the box Sunday night. He did not say who sent it but I think I can guess. It will be a great luxury for me when I get it.

None of [us] have received any word of our books except what Mag. wrote, but we suppose you intend to send them. We can buy many things at the sutlers here but they are very dear. Butter 50 and 60 cts per lb. Sugar 20 to 30 cts and scarce, ham 25 to 30 cts. Dried Beef 20 cts lb. Air tight peaches and tomatoes in quart cans from 75 cts to $1.00. As a soldiers pay is but $13.00 per month you can calculate how many of the luxuries he can afford to buy. Bread sells at 25 cts per lb., and crackers and cakes about the same. We can get plenty of newspapers here but they cost 10 cts apiece.

I cannot think of anything more that would interest you. Write soon a long letter.

Source: William Gilfillan Gavin, ed. *Infantryman Pettit: The Civil War Letters of Corporal Frederick Pettit*. Shippensburg, PA: White Mane Publishing Co., 1990, pp. 50–52.

AFTERMATH

Debauchery failed to triumph in Civil War encampments because many soldiers turned to religion for inner guidance and strength. Union and Confederate soldiers were overwhelmingly Christian, like the rest of mid-19th American society. Religious revivals occurred often, especially during winter quarters, when there was more time for soldiers to reflect. Soldiers praised the Lord for surviving their most recent campaign and beseeched His protection for their next. Once a campaign started, some soldiers had the benefit of a chaplain. Ministers, priests, and, occasionally, a rabbi, never seemed present in enough numbers, due to continuing demands from their home churches. James Robertson, a nationally known Civil War historian, estimates that by the summer of 1862, only about two-thirds of Union regiments had the service of a chaplain, and only about one-half of Confederate regiments. Still, the work of one minister often went far. Corporal Pettit attended a church service on a Sunday soon after the Union army had again taken the field during the spring of 1863. The meeting bolstered Pettit's spirits for the hard work ahead. "How refreshing and how much like the happy days of yore to listen to the precious words of divine truth as they fall from the lips of the faithful servant of Jesus," Pettit declared. "And how it reminds us of the many pleasant Sabbaths we have spent in other society, to spend one here in peace after a week of toilsome marching. Ah those home influences. They will save many of our brave boys from a fate worse than death on the battlefield."

ASK YOURSELF

1. Civil War soldiers wrote letters, played games, and daydreamed to pass the time. Have text messengers, cell phones, and laptop computers changed the way we spend our leisure time today, and if so, have they for better or worse?
2. Both Union and Confederate soldiers claimed that they were fighting to express the will of God. Peoples on opposing sides of armed conflicts often believe the same. How and why do people fighting one another claim the benefit of the same God?

TOPICS AND ACTIVITIES TO CONSIDER

- ❧ Many modern-day Americans like to reenact the Civil War. How do they attempt to recreate events from almost 150 years ago? How do they remember why the war was fought? Explore these questions and others at the following academic site: Michael O'Malley, "Civil War in Living Memory," Center for History and New Media, George Mason University, Fairfax, Virginia: http://www.chnm.gmu.edu/exploring/19thcentury/civilwar/index.php.
- ❧ Corporal Pettit mentions the availability of newspapers in camp. What are some of the articles that he might have read? Find out by searching newspapers published in Hagerstown, Maryland, at: "150th Anniversary of the Civil War-Hagerstown Newspapers," Western Maryland Regional Library: http://:www.whilbr.org/CW150Hagerstown/index.aspx.

Further Reading

Bates, Samuel P. *A Brief History of the One Hundredth Regiment (Roundheads)*. New Castle, PA: W. B. Thomas, 1884.

Brinsfield, Jr., John W., ed. *The Spirit Divided: Memoirs of Civil War Chaplains: The Confederacy*. Macon, GA: Mercer University Press, 2006.

Maryniak, Benedict R., and John W. Brinsfield Jr., eds. *The Spirit Divided: Memoirs of Civil War Chaplains: The Union*. Macon, GA: Mercer University Press, 2007.

Noll, Mark A. *The Civil War as a Theological Crisis*. Chapel Hill: University of North Carolina Press, 2006.

Rable, George C. *God's Almost Chosen Peoples: A Religious History of the American Civil War*. Chapel Hill: University of North Carolina Press, 2010.

Woodworth, Steven E. *While God Is Marching On: The Religious World of Civil War Soldiers*. Lawrence: University Press of Kansas, 2001.

Web Sites

Corporal Pettit served in the 100th Pennsylvania. Find out more about the regiment and its soldiers at "One-Hundredth Regiment, Pennsylvania Volunteer Infantry, 'The Roundheads'": http://www.100thpenn.com/100TH_PVI_MAIN.

The daily life and experiences of Civil War soldiers is well detailed at The National Museum of the Civil War Soldier at Pamplin Historical Park, near Petersburg, Virginia. Information and a description are posted at: http://www.pamplinpark.org/national_museum.html.

12. "The Balls Make a Very Loud Singing Noise When They Pass Near You ...": An Experience of Battle (1861)

INTRODUCTION

The Union and the Confederacy were only to win the war through fighting, and the experience of battle proved the ultimate test for soldiers. Many new volunteers eagerly had anticipated their first combat encounter, anxious to test their mettle and fight for their country. Many of the volunteers of 1861 had fretted that the war would end before they had a chance to actively participate. The terrors of battle quickly dashed any glorified expectations. The waiting to attack proved the most trying of battlefield moments for many men, especially if they were under enemy fire. Soldiers hugged the ground amid what they variously described as a "hail of shot and shell" and a "storm of fire." The move forward brought temporary relief to many men, who found refuge in action. For other soldiers, advancing into the thick of the action made the horrors of death all too real. The killed and mortally wounded dropped to the ground. The wounded that could move streamed to the rear. Groans from the dead and the dying seemed to permeate the otherwise deafening roar of musket and artillery fire. Amid the confusion, some soldiers ran away. More soldiers persevered. Their training helped, by providing a routine of loading and firing. Yet, in the rush to get to the front, most soldiers had received little training before first going into battle. More important, soldiers persevered through the ordeal of battle because they remained committed to their comrades and to their cause. Soldiers recognized that the fate of their neighbors and friends in their units, as well as the very outcome of the battle, might depend upon their actions. In the following description, a company officer in the 5th Alabama describes his experiences during the battle at MANASSAS, VIRGINIA. The fighting on July 21, 1861, marked the first major combat encounter of the war.

KEEP IN MIND AS YOU READ

1. Soldiers generally went into battle with their regiment formed into two massed and consecutive lines. The linear tactics allowed regimental and company officers to more directly control their units and allowed soldiers to amass their fire. Soldiers marching forward, shoulder to shoulder, and fighting in the open often suffered heavy losses. The attacking army, therefore, generally suffered far more battlefield

casualties than the defending army. Modern military strategists have taken the lesson to heart and try to amass three times the number of attackers for every defender.

2. Soldiers often described going into battle the first time as "seeing the elephant." The origins of the term are debated. Many scholars, however, attribute the phrase to the advent of the traveling circus in the mid-19th century. Often these performances featured an elephant—a creature otherwise seen only in books and drawings. The expression "seeing the elephant" came to mean witnessing any unusual but exciting experience.

Document: Eugene Blackford's Letter to His Father (July 22, 1861)

At last they were driven in, and the firing commenced upon our line. . . . No wound was sustained by our men (in my company) except one pretty badly wounded. The balls make a very loud singing noise when they pass near you, and at first caused me to duck my head, . . .

We then came right about and set off to reinforce our men in the great battle (not yet named) about ten miles from us. This distance we marched at double time and came on the field about five o'clock, too late as I said to do much service, but early enough to smell a little gunpowder and received a little of the enemy's fire. We went over the battlefield several miles in extent. T'was truly awful, an immense **cloud of smoke** and dust hung over the whole country, and the flashing of the artillery was incessant tho none of the balls struck my company. One bomb burst a little above me, and killed and wounded several. This was our only loss. Had we been an hour earlier, many would not have lived to tell of it.

I shan't attempt to describe the appearance of the field, literally covered with bodies, and for five miles before reaching it I saw men limping off, more or less wounded. We met wagon loads of bodies coming off to Manassas, where they are now **piled in heaps**. While we were looking over the field, and order came for us to go back to our batteries ten miles off, and defend them from the enemy who were advancing upon them, so we had to go back, tired as we were, to our holes, where we arrived half dead at twelve o'clock last night, having marched twenty-six miles heavily loaded. We have no protection against the rain, which has been falling all day. I have no blanket, not having seen my baggage since leaving Fairfax; I never was so dirty in my life . . .

I do not complain, nor do my men, tho I never thought that such hardships were to be endured.

Source: Annette Tapert, ed. *The Brothers' War: Civil War Letters to Their Loved Ones from the Blue and the Gray*. New York: Time Books, 1988, pp. 8–11.

cloud of smoke: Gunpowder from musket and artillery often clouded Civil War battlefields, only adding to the confusion. Smokeless gunpowder appeared later, first in Europe.

piled in heaps: Burial of the dead was left to the victorious army. Soldiers tried to inter their own dead as best as possible, but often had to hurry as a campaign continued. Burial of the enemy's dead often was hasty. Since soldiers were recruited locally, they received no identification tags from the government. A shockingly high number of Civil War dead went into the ground as *unknown*, too badly mangled for their friends and comrades to recognize them.

AFTERMATH

The aftermath of a battle often proved as trying as the fighting itself. Survivors had to tend to the wounded as best as they could and bury the dead. Captain David Pierson, whose letter on why he enlisted in the Confederate army runs previously in Document 8, described the aftermath of the fighting at WILSON'S CREEK, MISSOURI, during the late summer of 1861: "The ground was literally strewn with the wounded, dead, and dying; some with their heads shot off, some with bodies torn into with cannon balls, some with their legs shot off, and, in fact, wounds of every description could be seen. The groans of the wounded and cries for water from every side and all around was enough to sicken even the heartiest soldier. . . . [T]he enemy sent in a white flag to bury their dead & take up their wounded which was allowed them, of course, but they did not half finish. We have buried a great many since for them, and the whole battle field stinks with their dead bodies yet." Soldiers held in reserve from the fighting found no reprieve from the horrors, because field hospitals were often set up near their lines. Amputated legs and arms piled up outside doctor's tents, while the stench from infected wounds filled the air. Some soldiers claimed that the sight of the wounded and their sufferings unnerved them more than the battle itself, because they had little else to distract their attention.

ASK YOURSELF

1. Most Americans will not go into battle, as did Eugene Blackford, but how do modern-day Americans cope with stresses in their everyday lives, from school to work to home? Do any of these experiences come close to the stresses experienced by Civil War soldiers going into battle? Why or why not?
2. Why did seeing the dead and wounded after a battle was finished unnerve some soldiers as much as the fighting itself?

TOPICS AND ACTIVITIES TO CONSIDER

- ❧ How did the military experience for Civil War soldiers compare to that of Americans who fought during World War II? Find out by visiting the Web site for the National World War II Museum, located in New Orleans, at: http://www.ddaymuseum.org.
- ❧ How did life at sea compare to life on land during the Civil War? The National Civil War Naval Museum in Columbus, Georgia, provides background on both the Union and Confederate fleets. The Web site is: http://www.portcolumbus.org.

Further Reading

Hess, Earl J. *The Union Soldier in Battle: Enduring the Ordeal of Combat.* Lawrence: University Press of Kansas, 1997.

Linderman, Gerald F. *Embattled Courage: The Experience of Combat in the American Civil War.* New York: Free Press, 1987.

Neff, John R. *Honoring the Civil War Dead: Commemoration and the Problem of Reconciliation.* Lawrence: University Press of Kansas, 2005.

Steiner, Paul E. *Disease in the Civil War: Natural Biological Warfare in 1861–1865.* Springfield, IL: C. C. Thomas, 1968.

Web Sites

An excellent description of the common soldier of the Civil War, including the weapons he fought with, is found at John Heiser, "The Civil War Soldier," Gettysburg National Military Park: http://www.nps.gov/archive/gett/soldierlife/soldiers.htm.

A summary of battles that occurred in each state is found at "Civil War Battle Summaries by State," The American Battlefield Protection Program, National Park Service: http://www.nps.gov/history/hps/abpp/battles/bystate.htm.

13. "Our Dear Boys—Now as Ever—I Commit Them into Thy Hands": A Confederate Woman Supports the War Effort (1862)

INTRODUCTION

The absence of fathers and sons left families to cope across the Union and Confederacy. Soldiers rarely received leave, because of the logistical and administrative strains involved. Families had to cope with the absence of loved ones for several-year stretches. The task was, arguably, more difficult in the Confederacy. Southern women had to cope with the threat of northern invasion, all the while raising their children and running their households. "We who stay behind," Kate Stone, a young diarist in Louisiana admitted after watching her brothers depart for the war, "may find it harder than they who go." Some Confederate women questioned the continued need for self-sacrifice, especially as their cause lurched closer and closer toward final defeat. The decline in morale on the home front may have contributed to the final military collapse of the Confederacy, by encouraging soldiers to desert and place their families first. Yet many other Confederate women rallied enthusiastically behind the war effort. Judith Brockenbrough McGuire was one. McGuire and her husband, a minister turned clerk for the Confederate government, were forced by the war to move to Ashland, Virginia. A small village 12 miles north of Richmond, Ashland sat astride the Richmond, Fredericksburg & Potomac Railroad. McGuire chronicled the war in late 1862, as the Union Army of the Potomac threatened to cross the Rapidan River in northern Virginia, and seize FREDERICKSBURG. From there, the Union offensive to capture Richmond might continue.

KEEP IN MIND AS YOU READ

1. Soldiers in the Union army who reenlisted during the winter of 1863–64 received a 30-day furlough home. The incentive alone might have caused some men to accept, because they otherwise might not have seen their families since they had volunteered in 1861.

2. Disgruntled about time away from home, poor living conditions, and a myriad of other factors, some soldiers deserted. If caught, these men might be executed. High-ranking military officers resorted to executing deserters by firing squad more to serve as a warning to onlookers than to simply carry out policy. Desertion

in the Union army briefly soared during the winter of 1862–63, as soldiers expressed their frustration with recent battlefield setbacks and the broadening of the nation's war aims to include the destruction of slavery. Two years later, men going absent without leave soared in the Confederate army. Rebel soldiers gave way to privations at home and fast-dimming chances for ultimate Confederate victory.

Document: Excerpts from the Diary of Judith Brockenbrough McGuire (late November–mid-December, 1862)

November 29—Nothing of importance from the army. The people of Fredericksburg suffer greatly from the sudden move. I know a family, accustomed to every luxury at home, now in a damp basement-room in Richmond. The mother and three young daughters cooking, washing, etc.; the father, a merchant, is sick and cut off from business, friends, and every thing else. Another family, consisting of a mother and four daughters, in one room, supported by the work of one of the daughters who has an office in the Note-Signing Department. To keep starvation from the house is all that they can do; their supplies in Fredericksburg can't be brought to them—no transportation. I cannot mention the numbers who are similarly situated; the country is filled with them. . . . Luxuries have been given up long ago, by many persons. Coffee is $4 per pound, and good tea from $18 to $20; butter ranges from $1.50 to $2 per pound; lard 50 cents; corn $15 per barrel; and wheat $4.50 per bushel. We can't get a muslin dress for less than $6 or $8 per yard; calico $1.75, etc. This last is no great hardship, for we will all resort to homespun.

30th—The Yankee army ravaging Stafford County dreadfully, but they do not cross the [Rapidan] river. **Burnside**, with the "greatest army on the planet," is quietly waiting and watching our little band on the opposite side. Is he afraid to venture over? His "On to Richmond" seems slow.

December 13th—Our hearts are full of apprehension! A battle is going on at or near Fredericksburg. The Federal army passed over the river on their pontoons the night before last. They attempted to throw the bridges over it at three places; from two of these they were driven back with much slaughter; at the third they crossed. Our army was too small to guard all points. The firing is very heavy and incessant. We hear it with terrible distinctness from our portico. God of mercy, be with our people, and drive back the invaders! I ask not for their destruction; but that they may be driven to their own homes, never more to put foot on our soil; that we may enjoy the sweets of peace and security once more. Our dear boys—now as ever—I commit them into Thy hands.

Burnside: Born in Indiana in 1824, Ambrose Burnside took his degree from West Point 19 years later. Burnside fought well at the Battle of First Bull Run in the summer of 1861, and soon after won promotion to brigadier general. Burnside continued to show military promise during early 1862, leading a Union expedition that captured Roanoke Island in coastal North Carolina. Late that same year, Burnside received appointment to command the Army of the Potomac. The badly managed Union offensive at Fredericksburg, combined with a short-lived attempt to again cross the Rapidan in January 1863, caused Lincoln to remove Burnside from command of the army. In the postwar era, Burnside served as governor of Rhode Island. He died in 1881.

Cobb: Thomas Cobb was born in Georgia in 1823. After graduating from the University of Georgia,

14th, Nine o'Clock at Night—A sad, sad train passed down a short time ago, bearing the bodies of Generals **Cobb**, of Georgia, and Maxcy **Gregg**, of South Carolina. Two noble spirits have thus passed away from us. Peace to their honoured remains! The gentlemen report many wounded on the train, but not severely. I fear it has been another bloody Sabbath. The host of wounded will pass to-morrow; we must be up early to prepare to administer to their comfort. The sound of cannon this evening was much more distant, and not constant enough for a regular fight. We are victorious again! Will they now go from our shores forever? We dread to hear of the casualties. Who may not be among the wounded to-morrow?

Source: James I. Robertson Jr., ed. "Diary of a Southern Refugee during the War, September 1862–May 1863: Judith Brockenbrough McGuire." In *Virginia at War: 1863*, edited by William C. Davis and James I. Robertson Jr. Lexington: The University Press of Kentucky, 2009, pp. 150–53.

AFTERMATH

Civilians went beyond lending morale support to the Union and Confederate war effort by volunteering. At way stations and refreshment saloons, men and women distributed food and clothing to soldiers traveling toward the front lines. The Cooper's Shop in Philadelphia was among the most efficient, claiming to feed 1,000 soldiers an hour when needed. Religious societies published periodicals and leaflets, known by soldiers as *tracts*. The American Bible

Cobb began a distinguished legal career. A staunch supporter of secession, Cobb recruited a legion of infantry and cavalry at the start of the Civil War. Cobb's Legion fought with the Confederate Army of Northern Virginia throughout most of the war. Hit in the leg by a musket ball during the fighting at Fredericksburg, Cobb bled to death in a house located just behind the front lines.

Gregg: Maxcy Gregg, like Cobb, was an outspoken supporter of secession. Born in South Carolina in 1814, Gregg was an accomplished lawyer and politician by the start of the Civil War. Gregg helped to raise the 1st South Carolina and, for battlefield gallantry, won promotion to brigadier general in late 1861. Gregg was hit in the spine during the battle at Fredericksburg and died two days later.

WOMEN SOLDIERS

Women were barred from serving in the Union and Confederate armies, although the legalities did not stop a few enterprising spirits. Medical inspections prior to mustering into national service often were precursory. Potential soldiers usually did not disrobe; the doctor walked up and down the ranks of a regiment. Getting into the army was one thing, staying in was another. Many of the 400 or so women who served in either blue or gray ultimately were exposed. Discovery usually came when the women-turned-soldiers visited the hospital from either illness or wounds. In at least one case, a private's true gender was discovered when she gave birth. Having a baby was, the surprised commanding officer declared, "in violation of all military law and army regulations."

Sarah Emma Edmonds was among the most famous women soldiers because of her length of service. Edmonds volunteered in the 2nd Michigan during April 1861, under the alias "Franklin Thompson." She worked as both a hospital steward and a mail carrier through the regiment's early campaigns. Edmonds deserted during 1863, fearful that an illness she was suffering from might result in a hospital stay—and the likely exposure of her secret. Edmonds served as a nurse for the remainder of the war, and published her tale in *Nurse and Spy in the Union Army* (1865). She applied for and received a veterans' pension, the only woman soldier to do so under her own name. The federal government later dropped the desertion charge against Edmonds, allowing her to receive full military honors at her burial after her death in 1894.

Society and the Confederate Bible Society also distributed Bibles and hymn books to soldiers. Union and Confederate women sewed socks, pants, and shirts for needy soldiers. Equally important, more than 3,000 women served as nurses in army hospitals, an otherwise traditionally male occupation. Female nurses won praise from their soldier patients, despite enduring criticism from many doctors jealous of their professional territory. The Union supplemented the medical work of its doctors and nurses by organizing the U.S. Sanitary Commission in 1861. The Sanitary Commission attempted to reduce the incidence of disease among soldiers in camps and hospitals by advising them on matters of "sanitary and hygienic interests." The organization also donated to soldiers $15 million for various supplies, including medicine, food, and writing paper.

ASK YOURSELF

1. Does morale on the home front influence the way that America wages war today?
2. Why is it important for Judith Brockenbrough McGuire and other civilians to believe they are supporting the war effort? Are sacrifices on the home front necessary for victory on the battlefield?

TOPICS AND ACTIVITIES TO CONSIDER

- ✍ How did activities on the home front during the Civil War compare to those during World War II? Explore life at home between 1941 and 1945 at "World War II Remembered: American Home Front," Scholastic Inc., http://teacher.scholastic.com/activities/wwii/ahf.
- ✍ What was life like for women who served as nurses during the Civil War? How did their experiences compare to soldiers? Find out at "Our Army Nurses," Edinborough Press, Roseville, MN, http://www.edinborough.com/Learn/cw_nurses/Nurses.html.

Further Reading

Clinton, Catharine and Nina Silber, eds. *Divided Houses: Gender and the Civil War*. New York: Oxford University Press, 1992.

Faust, Drew Gilpin. *Mothers of Invention: Women of the Slaveholding South in the American Civil War*. Chapel Hill: University of North Carolina Press, 1996.

Freemon, Frank R. *Microbes and Minie Balls: An Annotated Bibliography of Civil War Medicine*. Rutherford: Fairleigh Dickinson University Press, 1993.

Maxwell, William Q. *Lincoln's Fifth Wheel: The Political History of the United States Sanitary Commission*. New York: Longman, 1956.

Rable, George C. *Fredericksburg! Fredericksburg!* Chapel Hill: University of North Carolina Press, 2002.

Rutkow, Ira M. *Bleeding Blue and Gray: Civil War Surgery and the Evolution of American Medicine*. New York: Random House, 2005.

Schroeder-Lein, Glenna R. *The Encyclopedia of Civil War Medicine*. Armonk, NY: M. E. Sharpe, 2008.

Schultz, Jane E. *Women at the Front: Hospital Workers in Civil War America*. Chapel Hill: University of North Carolina Press, 2004.

Stone, Kate. *Brokenburn: The Journal of Kate Stone, 1861–68*, edited by John Q. Anderson. Baton Rouge: Louisiana State University Press, 1955.

Web Sites

An excellent site on the U.S. Sanitary Commission and Civil War medicine in general is "Sanitary Commission Pennant Proclaimed Improved Conditions," AmericanCivilWar.com: www.americancivilwar.com/sanitary_commision.html.

An outstanding site for the wartime roles of women is "Civil War Women: Primary Sources on the Internet," sponsored by the Sallie Bingham Center for Women's History and Culture at Duke University, North Carolina. The address is: http://library.duke.edu/special collections/bingham/guides/cwdocs.html.

14. "We Now Are in Indian Country . . .": Life Near a Reservation (1867–1868)

INTRODUCTION

Americans continued to spill westward in even greater numbers following the end of the Civil War. Missouri, led by the growth of St. Louis, emerged by 1870 as the fourth most populous state in the Union. Over the same five years, the population of Nebraska increased by nearly one-half (to almost 124,000 people). A newspaper reporter traveling westward claimed that although the prairies might be largely unoccupied, the trails were as busy as any road in the East. The steady flow of American settlers westward brought increasing contact with Native Americans. By the late 19th century, the great majority of Native Americans lived on the Great Plains—or the region stretching west from the Mississippi River and across the Rocky Mountains. Hoping to clear lands for the transcontinental railroad and other transportation routes, the federal government attempted to group Native Americans onto RESERVATIONS. The logistics often worked poorly, as much from haphazard planning in Congress as corruption among individual agents assigned to administer the reservations. Native American tribes often had little access to herds of elk and buffalo for food, and their lands suffered frequent reductions. Tensions soared, and warfare between Native Americans and the American army became more frequent during the late 1860s. Elizabeth Haas Canfield was the wife of an army officer stationed in the Montana Territory during the same years. Canfield details in her diary her journey from Iowa to join her husband.

KEEP IN MIND AS YOU READ

1. Many Native American tribes living west of the Mississippi had suffered removal from the East during the 1830s, under orders from President Andrew Jackson. Poor logistical planning on part of the federal government plagued the "Trail of Tears," resulting in many deaths from disease and hunger.
2. The American army in the late 1860s numbered only about 25,000 men. Making up for these small numbers, the army fielded advanced military technology and drew upon leadership from officers who had fought in the Civil War. Still, Native Americans proved adept at small-unit tactics. One American general grumbled that 50 Native American warriors often "checkmated" 3,000 soldiers.

3. Conflict between Native Americans and settlers also had occurred during the Civil War. The Santee Sioux attacked white settlements in Minnesota in 1862, angered over the continued influx of immigrants and pioneers into the region. Hastily assembled militia soldiers, who might otherwise have been sent east to fight Confederates, helped to put down the uprising. In the fall, 307 Sioux were sentenced to hang for their role in the violence. President Abraham Lincoln commuted the sentences of all but 38 Native Americans, who were executed in December. Two years later, in the Colorado Territory, hostilities briefly flared between the Arapaho and Cheyenne tribes and white settlers. While awaiting negotiations, members of the two Native American tribes encamped at Sand Creek, 40 miles northeast of Fort Lyons. Here they suffered a surprise, and unprovoked, attack by volunteer troops under the command of Colonel John Chivington. The American soldiers massacred about 500 of the 1,000 or so Native Americans at Sand Creek, including women and children. Chivington received condemnation in the East for his butchery, but was widely praised in the West for his decisive action.

Document: Excerpts from Elizabeth Haas Canfield's Diary

April 3rd—Had our first view of a Fort today, Fr. Randall [near Yankton, South Dakota] which seems to be on the edge of civilization. . . . The Fort itself is a rude affair. The buildings are placed around a square of ground called the Parade. One side is occupied by the officers. On each side are quarters for the soldiers and on the fourth side is the Hospital and buildings for clothing and **commissary** stores. Outside of all this is a stockade of logs, squared and set very close together, with frequent small loop holes for musketry firing while at opposite corners is a square projection called a Bastion two stories high, the lower containing a swivel gun which could on occasion rake the sides of the fort. The upper room is the lookout where a soldier is stationed all day with a powerful field glass watching for Indians, for we are now in Indian country and they are very hostile.

April 13—This is a worse country than I ever dreamed of. Nothing but hills of dry sand, with little streaks of shriveled grass in the hollows and on the river bottoms. We saw several large droves of Antelopes today. I suppose several hundred in all, and just before night a large gray wolf came down to the river bank to see us pass. We saw three Indians yesterday but nothing like a human being today.

May 10th—Saw a very imposing sight today. A large herd of Buffalo, several, probably eight or ten thousand, swam the river just ahead of the boat. The boat stopped until they had passed. One of the deck hands lassoed a half grown calf and we had fresh meat for dinner. It was very nice with a wild flavor.

May 22nd—I spent some time in the lookout today. The location of the Fort [Berthold, in the Dakota Territory] on a bluff on the river bank is very fine. . . . The country is very rough but would be rather nice if there were more signs of civilization. What interests me most is the [Sioux] Indian village of about two thousand inhabitants. It is made up of the remnants of three tribes and they are supposed to be friendly having asked the protection of the soldiers.

. . . Looking down on the village there are no streets nor plans in its arrangement. Looks as if the tepees had been dropped from a height and landed anywhere they happened to. They are built by driving a row of poles in the ground in a circle, then drawing the tops almost together, leaving a small opening for the escape of smoke. Brush is piled over the poles, then covered with dirt, except in one place which is left open with a buffalo skin hung for a door. All the light is from the smoke hole in the center.

May 5th [1868]—We have had great excitement today. About 3 P.M. Indians in great numbers were seen coming over the hills south of the Fort [Cooke, in the Montana Territory]. The alarm was sounded and soon every man at his post at a loop hole. Our swivel gun in the bastion was manned. . . . The officers and ladies watched the coming of the Indians from the **sally-port**. . . . We saw they were painted and mounted for war, having no women or children with them. They circled round three sides of the Fort (the river being the fourth). The commanding officer took ten men and rode out to parley but was met by a volley of arrows and returned in hot haste. As soon as they were inside, the Sally-port was closed. The Indians were so near that both Artillery and Infantry fire was opened on them which scattered them in short order. They made for the mountains rapidly as possible. We do not know their losses as each man is tied to his pony which will carry him away.

When we ladies saw what might happen, we . . . decided if the Fort could not be held that we preferred to be shot by our own officers rather than be taken captive. . . . but while it would have been done if necessary we are still spared to tell about the attack of the Fort by three thousand Indians.

commissary: A store operated on a military post, selling food, clothing, and other related supplies. Soldiers and their families paid for items bought at the commissary, although often at a reduced rate.

sally-port: A door in a fort or defensive wall allowing for quick entrance and exit. Defending troops might launch a raid on an attacking force through a sally-port, without weakening their position

Source: Marsha C. Markman, Jonathan Boe, and Susan Corey, eds. *The American Journey: United States History Through Letters and Diaries*, vol. 2. St. James, NY: Brandywine Press, 1997, pp. 3–8. A typescript of the Elizabeth Haas Canfield diary, April 30, 1866, to June 14, 1868, is located at the Minnesota Historical Society, St. Paul, Minnesota.

AFTERMATH

The American army initially had trouble in the Native American wars that occurred more frequently after 1865. Native American tribes proved elusive in the vast stretches of the West, often staging hit-and-run tactics. One high-ranking government official estimated that the nation spent several million dollars a year for each army regiment stationed on the frontier, without achieving any decisive results. The military finally had the idea of killing the buffalo as a way to break Native American resistance through starvation. Soldiers did not have to pursue and fight Native American to force them onto reservations, they only had to slaughter the buffalo. American soldiers and civilians began to hunt the animals with abandon. Perhaps as many as 15 million buffalo roamed the American West by the late 1860s, divided into a northern herd and a southern herd by the transcontinental railroad. The southern herd was hunted first, because it was accessible by more railroad routes. As many as one million buffalo a year were killed during the early 1870s. Buffalo fur became a fashion rage in the East, creating for many years a nearly insatiable demand. The northern herd suffered a similar fate in the early 1880s, following the opening of the Northern Pacific line. By the late 19th century, hunters had pursued buffalos to near extinction. Confronted by the food shortages and the very real specter of starvation, Native Americans had little choice but to submit to American rule. By 1890, the Sioux, the last to offer military resistance to the American army, had moved onto a reservation. The western frontier, which had been a factor in American life since the colonial era, had closed.

ASK YOURSELF

1. Would you have liked to travel alongside Elizabeth Canfield, sharing the dangers and the excitements of the western frontier?
2. Does Canfield seem to hold a positive or negative outlook toward the people and land of the American West? What diary entries offer support for your position?

TOPICS AND ACTIVITIES TO CONSIDER

- African American soldiers served on the western frontier, earning distinction as "Buffalo soldiers." What were their experiences like? Find out at the Web site for the Buffalo Soldiers National Museum in Houston, Texas, at: http://www.buffalosoldiermuseum.com.
- Would you have liked to live along the western frontier? Find out what the West was like at "The American West": http://www.vlib.us/americanwest/.

Further Reading

Coffman, Edward M. *The Old Army: A Portrait of the American Army in Peacetime, 1784–1898*. New York: Oxford University Press, 1986.

Nichols, Roger L. *American Indians in U.S. History*. Norman: University of Oklahoma Press, 2003.

Quay, Sara E. *Westward Expansion*. Westport, CT: Greenwood Press, 2002.

Utley, Robert M. *Cavalier in Buckskin: George Armstrong Custer and the Western Military Frontier*. Norman: University of Oklahoma Press, 1988.

Utley, Robert M. *The Indian Frontier, 1846–1890*. Albuquerque: University of New Mexico Press, 2003.

Web Sites

The National Museum of the American Indian, in Washington, DC, hopes to advance "knowledge and understanding of the Native cultures of the Western Hemisphere, past, present, and future, through partnership with Native people and others." The museum's Web site is: http://www.nmai.si.edu/.

The Museum of the American West, in Lander, Wyoming is the "only institution which celebrates the different groups of people who utilized the critical geography of what is now central Wyoming to shape the American West." The Website is: http://www.amwest.org.

ECONOMICS

15. "The Soil Is All the Best Quality . . .": Results of the Homestead Act (1872)

INTRODUCTION

America in the mid-19th century primarily was an agricultural nation. Industrialization and urbanization were occurring at near break-neck speed, and would continue to do so over many decades. But most Americans still made their living from the land. Millions of new acres were put under the plow each year, most often in the West. The opening of new lands pulled the center of gravity of the American population ever inland. In 1790, when the federal government first conducted the CENSUS, the center of population was located just outside of Baltimore, Maryland. Fifty years later, it was in western Virginia. The beginning of the Civil War saw the center of the American population in southern Ohio, where it would remain for the remainder of the decade. The Homestead Act of 1862 played a major role in the westward pull. The Homestead Act granted 160 acres of surveyed public lands to any adult head of household. Claimants were required at least to begin making improvements on their plots by building a dwelling and cultivating the land. After five years, the original filer was entitled to receive the property for no charge, other than a minimal filing fee. The claimant might also acquire the plot after a six-month residence, by paying the government $1.25 per acre. Uriah Oblinger, a Union veteran, moved to Nebraska to acquire a Homestead plot. He wrote to his aunt and uncle in Indiana, detailing his initial experiences.

KEEP IN MIND AS YOU READ

1. There were exceptions to the land-owning policies dictated by the Homestead Act. Any person who had borne arms against the federal government—meaning Confederate veterans—were disqualified from participation. In general, however, the Homestead Act was generous. Union veterans might deduct their military service against the five-year tenancy requirement. Additionally, any immigrant who declared his intention to become a citizen might receive a Homestead plot.

2. Congress had earlier discussed passing the Homestead Act, only to stall over sectional and economic tensions. Southerners feared that a government-sponsored land program would benefit small farmers and free labor. Northern factory owners

had their own worries, fearing that a homestead act would result in a massive drain on their labor force.

3. The 160 acres granted by the Homestead Act were sizeable. On average, farms in Europe were several times smaller.

Document: Letter from Uriah Oblinger to Eliza and John Cook (December 3, 1872)

Dear Aunt and Uncle,

I guess I had better write pretty soon or you will think I have forgotten you, but I have not. The reason I have not written sooner is because I have been on the go almost ever since I left Ind[iana] till recently. . . . At present my health is good & has been ever since I left Ind, just now I have a sore leg. One of the mares fell on it two weeks ago Sunday & hurt it pretty bad as the ground was frozen. And Sunday evening I was feeding a man's oxen for him as I went in the stable to give them the feed one kicked me on the sore leg so it is quite sore again. Well I suppose the first question you would ask me know would be how do you like Nebraska. Well I like it for the greater part of what I have seen can nearly all be cultivated here if we are a mind to. . . . There is less waste land here than I ever saw in so large a body and the soil is all the best quality and very even all being about alike. . . . For beauty I do not think Neb can be excelled by any country.

The piece I have taken . . . is in the **Lincoln** District and I have to go there to get it. It has been taken by another man but he has been away from it more than six months and has never done anything on it so I **jumped** his claim the trial comes off the 20th of this month I have to prove by 2 witnesses that he has never done anything on it & his claim will be set aside and then I can Homestead it. . . . Every foot of it can be plowed I can plow round the entire 160 acres and not find a stone on the whole piece and can stand almost any where on and see a rabbit run all over it.

> **jumped:** In this context, to move in on someone else's land claim. Oblinger had the law on his side in *jumping* the claim. Settlers had to begin making improvements on their property within a specified time period or forfeit title to the land.
>
> **Lincoln:** The second most populous city in Nebraska today and the state capital. The city was established in 1856 as Lancaster. The city was renamed to honor President Lincoln when Nebraska became a state in 1867.

Source: Uriah W. Oblinger Collection, Nebraska Historical Society, from Prairie Settlement: Nebraska Photographs and Family Letters, American Memory, Library of Congress: http://memory.loc.gov/ammem/award98/nbhihtml/pshome.html.

AFTERMATH

Through the Homestead Act, the federal government hoped to populate the West with small farmers like Oblinger. There certainly were bumps in the process. Much of the land went to speculators, railroad officials, miners, and cattlemen. While non-farmers exploited the loopholes, land prices in the East fell. Still, the Homestead Act worked. Families went west to farm, and common people became landowners. Settlers far removed from the authority of the national government now had a vested interest in its upkeep. Theodore Roosevelt, himself a future president, judged that the Homestead Act achieved an unprecedented level of stability across an otherwise vast region because "it fills the state with homes, it builds up communities and lessens the chance of social and civil disorder by giving ownership of the soil, in small tracts, to the occupants thereof." In addition to promoting political and social continuity, the Homestead Act helped to physically expand the United States. Nevada and Nebraska joined the Union in the mid- and late1860s. The Arizona, Idaho, Wyoming, and Montana Territories were organized soon after, all on their way toward eventually achieving statehood. Because of its many long-lasting influences, modern-day scholars rank the Homestead Act as one of the most important pieces of Congressional legislation in the nation's history.

ASK YOURSELF

1. Would you move far across the country today, if the government offered a land program similar to the Homestead Act? What would influence your decision?
2. Does property ownership help to ensure political and social stability? Are there any modern-day examples?

TOPICS AND ACTIVITIES TO CONSIDER

- Read other letters from Uriah Oblinger and his wife Mattie. What was life like for a Homestead family? The letters are posted at Uriah W. Oblinger Collection, Nebraska Historical Society, from Prairie Settlement: Nebraska Photographs and Family Letters, American Memory, Library of Congress: http://memory.loc.gov/ammem/award98/nbhihtml/pshome.html.
- Laura Ingalls Wilder and her family, celebrated in *Little House on the Prairie* and the popular television series by the same name, are perhaps some of America's most famous homesteaders. How does the life of a Homestead family compare to family life today? Visit the Laura Ingalls Wilder Historic Home and Museum, located in Mansfield, Missouri, at: http://www.lauraingallswilderhome.com.

Further Reading

Cross, Coy F. *Go West, Young Man!: Horace Greeley's Vision for America*. Albuquerque: University of New Mexico Press, 1995.

Ellis, David M., ed. *The Frontier in American Development: Essays in Honor of Paul Wallace Gates*. Ithaca, NY: Cornell University Press, 1969.

Lee, Lawrence B. *Kansas and the Homestead Act, 1862–1905*. New York: Arno Press, 1979.

Stephenson, George Malcolm. *The Political History of Public Lands from 1840 to 1862; From Preemption to Homestead*. New York: Russell and Russell, 1967.

Web Sites

For more information on the Homestead Act, see "Frontier Life: Homestead History," Public Broadcasting System: http://www.pbs.org/wnet/frontierhouse/frontierlife/essay1.html.

The Homestead National Monument of America, a National Park Service site, is located in Beatrice, Nebraska. The Web site is: http://www.nps.gov/home/.

View a photograph of the Homestead Act and read more historical detail at "Our Documents," National Archives: http://www.ourdocuments.gov.

16. The Completion of the Transcontinental Railroad: An Eyewitness Observance (1869)

INTRODUCTION

"Americans have a perfect passion for railroads" one European observer judged during the early 1850s. He was right, with the United States constructing 30,000 miles of railroads by the end of that decade. The total was more than all of the track mileage combined in Western Europe, where railways had originated. Yet no network stretched across the United States, and business leaders recognized the opportunity. If a transcontinental railroad existed, the United States might link together trade between Asia and Europe. Sectional tensions about where to place the eastern hub of a coast-to-coast rail line prevented the project from going forward. Only after the start of the Civil War did Congress approve LEGISLATION granting land and funding for the building of a transcontinental route. The Central Pacific Railroad began building eastward from California, while the Union Pacific Railroad began building westward from Nebraska. The challenges surmounted over the 2,000-mile stretch were marvels of engineering, with mountain ranges tunneled through and vast stretches of prairie land built across. On May 10, 1869, the two lines met at PROMONTORY SUMMIT, Utah. Governor Leland Stanford of California, representing the Central Pacific, Thomas Durant, president of the Union Pacific, and many other dignitaries were present. Stanford and Durant took turns tapping a ceremonial golden spike in the tie that united the two lines. Alexander Toponce, a businessman, also was on the scene.

KEEP IN MIND AS YOU READ

1. Prior to the completion of the transcontinental railroad, the fastest way to go from the east coast to the west coast was by ship. The journey took several weeks, having to go around the southern tip of South America. By rail, the trip across the United States took six days.

2. Fares on the transcontinental railroad, from Omaha to San Francisco, ran from $110, for a first class ticket, to $40, for a third class ticket. In 2009 the fare for a standard ticket between the two cities cost $158.

3. The completion of the transcontinental railroad was tremendously exciting to most Americans. Some modern-day scholars have compared the level of enthusiasm to

that of Americans first landing on the moon in 1969. Perhaps in the future, a similarly exciting event might be when Americans land on Mars.

Document: Alexander Toponce Remembers the Completion of the Transcontinental Railroad, May 10, 1869

I saw the Golden Spike driven at Promontory, Utah, on May 10, 1869. I had a beef contract to furnish meat to the construction camps of Benson and West . . .

On the last day, only about 100 feet were laid, and everybody tried to have a hand in the work. I took a shovel from an Irishman, and threw a shovel full of dirt on the ties just to tell about it afterward.

A special train from the west brought Sidney Dillon, General Dodge, T. C. Durant, John R. Duff, S. A. Seymour, a lot of newspaper men, and plenty of the best brands of champagne. Another train made up at Ogden carried the band from Fort Douglas, the leading men of Utah Territory, . . .

It was a very hilarious occasion; everybody had all they wanted to drink all the time. Some of the participants got "sloppy," and these were not all Irish and Chinese by any means.

California furnished the Golden Spike. Governor Tuttle of Nevada furnished one of silver. General Stanford presented one of gold, silver, and iron from Arizona. The last tie was of California laurel.

When they came to drive the last spike, Governor Stanford, president of the Central Pacific, took the sledge, and the first time he struck he missed the spike and hit the rail.

What a howl went up! Irish, Chinese, Mexicans, and everybody yelled with delight. "He missed it. Yee." The engineers blew the whistles and rang their bells. Then Stanford tried it again and tapped the spike and the telegraph operators had fixed their instruments so that the tap was reported in all the offices east and west, and set bells to tapping in hundreds of towns and cities. . . . Then Vice President T. C. Durant of the Union Pacific took up the sledge and he missed the spike the first time. Then everybody slapped everybody else again and yelled, "He missed it too, yow!"

It was a great occasion, everyone carried off souvenirs and there are enough splinters of the last tie in museums to make a good bonfire.

When the connection was finally made the Union Pacific and the Central Pacific engineers ran their engines up until their pilots touched. Then the engineers shook hands and had their pictures taken and each broke a bottle of champagne on the pilot of the other's engine and had their picture taken again.

The Union Pacific engine, the, "Jupiter," was driven by my good friend, George Lashus, who still lives in Ogden.

Both before and after the spike driving ceremony there were speeches, which were cheered heartily. I do not remember what any of the speakers said now, but I do remember that there was a great abundance of champagne.

Source: "Completing the Transcontinental Railroad, 1869," EyeWitness to History: http://www.eyewitnesstohistory.com.

AFTERMATH

The influence of the transcontinental railroad on the United States was significant, although not perhaps as significant as many of its early visionaries had imagined. Tea from Japan was the first cargo to receive shipment, leaving California for the East on May 11. Yet the opening of the Suez Canal in Egypt in 1869 linked Europe more directly to Asia than did the transcontinental railroad. Still, the route brought together American producers and customers like never before. By the late 1870s, $50 million worth of freight moved every year from coast to coast. The surge helped the United States to become the world's strongest manufacturing power by the start of the 20th century.

ASK YOURSELF

1. Would you have wanted to travel right away along the transcontinental railroad? If offered a trip to the moon today, would you go?
2. Are public ceremonies like the one organized to mark the completion of the transcontinental railroad important to help focus national attention? Have you attended any public ceremonies? And what do you remember about them?

TOPICS AND ACTIVITIES TO CONSIDER

≈ Writing in 1868 about the soon-to-be completion of the transcontinental railroad, one observer claimed that "Already centres [sic] of population dot its length from Omaha to San Francisco, and it seems certain that a chain of great cities must grow up in its path, swelling the volume of trade and travel to dimensions which baffle all present estimate." Explore some of the cities that boomed because of their location along the railroad at " 'Wedding of the Rails,' " American Memory Collection, Library of Congress: http://memory.loc.gov/ammem/today/may10. html.

THE GOLDEN AGE OF THE RAILROAD

The completion of the transcontinental railroad helped to spur the construction of other lines. By 1890, the rail network in the United States stretched for 164,000 miles. This was more than four times the mileage in operation only 25 years earlier. Much of the new construction occurred west of the Mississippi River, including several Pacific routes. Amid the expansion, railroads became more efficient and uniform in their operations. Engines became more powerful, allowing train loads to increase by five fold, on average, between 1870 and 1915 (to 500 tons). Standing schedules became possible in 1883, when the United States adopted standard time zones. Passengers traveling in the late 19th century enjoyed a more comfortable ride. Dining cars first went into operation in 1868, steam heat in 1881, and, six years later, electric lights. The golden age of the American railroad began to come to an end in the early 20th century. By the 1920s, railroads were losing both commercial and passenger traffic to cars, trucks, and airplanes. Although the decline in traffic by comparison to other forms of transportation continues through the present day, railroads are efficient. The nation's iron rails carries far more freight per employee than ever before, at about four million tons per worker.

  Was the completion of a coast-to-coast railroad an unqualified success? Native Americans certainly lost much in the process. To find out more, go to Kerry Brinkerhoff, "Native Americans and the Railroads," ParkNet, National Park Service: http://www.nps.gov/archive/gosp/history/Native_American_RR.html.

Further Reading

Ambrose, Stephen E. *Nothing Like It in the World: The Men Who Built the Transcontinental Railroad, 1863–1869*. New York: Simon and Schuster, 2000.

Bianculli, Anthony J. *Trains and Technology: The American Railroad in the Nineteenth Century*. Newark: University of Delaware Press, 2001.

Clark, John E. *Railroad in the Civil War: The Impact of Management on Victory and Defeat*. Baton Rouge: Louisiana State University Press, 2001.

Turner, George E. *Victory Rode the Rails: The Strategic Place of the Railroads in the Civil War*. Indianapolis, IN: Bobbs-Merrill, 1953.

Ward, James A. *Railroads and the Character of America, 1820–1887*. Knoxville: University of Tennessee Press, 1986.

Web Sites

For discussion and analysis of the transcontinental railroad, as well as several interactive features, visit "American Experience: The Transcontinental Railroad," Public Broadcasting System: http://www.pbs.org/wgbh/amex/tcrr/timeline/index.html.

For the story behind what happened to the ceremonial spikes, read "The Last Spikes," ParkNet, National Park Service: http://www.nps.gov/archive/gosp/history/spike.html.

17. "The Chinese Must Go": Article in *The Illustrated Wasp* (1878)

INTRODUCTION

Chinese immigrants had come to America's West Coast in increasing numbers during the 1850s, hoping both to escape poverty and violence and to find employment. With construction on the transcontinental railroad in full swing only a few years later, Chinese immigrants provided much of the labor (as Alexander Toponce noted). Some estimates place as many as 12,000 Chinese working for the Central Pacific Railroad, or almost 90 percent of its workforce. The Chinese worked for lower wages than their white counterparts, in part helping to explain their large numbers. But the Chinese also worked hard. One foreman protested that the Chinese could not possibly cut stone as well as his Irish workers. Another foreman reportedly shot back "Did they not build the Chinese Wall, the biggest piece of masonry in the world?" The muscle and skill of Chinese laborers hastened the completion of the railroad in 1869. Yet, in the aftermath, many native-born Americans questioned the continuing need for the Chinese in America. Legislators in California placed the Chinese in segregated neighborhoods and schools, and attempted to limit their economic opportunities and legal protections. Some protest emerged from white Americans, on grounds of fairness. More whites argued that the Chinese question needed an even more severe response. *The Illustrated Wasp*, a weekly paper published in San Francisco, was one of these voices.

KEEP IN MIND AS YOU READ

1. The American economy took a downturn in the mid-1870s. Sparked by a panic on Wall Street and rippling outward, the economic hard times saw banks and business go bankrupt. Unemployment soared to 14 percent. Many native-born Americans saw immigrants as competition for all-too-scarce jobs. Economic growth and prosperity only returned later in the decade.
2. MARK TWAIN traveled through the West during the early and mid-1860s, both as a tourist and a newspaper reporter. Twain later detailed his experiences in *Roughing It*, published in 1872. Twain weighed in on the side of Chinese immigrants, declaring,

They are a harmless race when white men either let them alone or treat them no worse than dogs; in fact they are almost entirely harmless anyhow, for they seldom think of resenting the vilest insults or the cruelest injuries. They are quiet, peaceable, tractable, free from drunkenness, and they are as industrious as the day is long. A disorderly Chinaman is rare, and a lazy one does not exist. So long as a Chinaman has strength to use his hands he needs no support from anybody; white men often complain of want of work, but a Chinaman offers no such complaint; he always manages to find something to do. He is a great convenience to everybody—even to the worst class of white men, for he bears the most of their sins, suffering fines for their petty thefts, imprisonment for their robberies, and death for their murders. Any white man can swear a Chinaman's life away in the courts, but no Chinaman can testify against a white man. Ours is the 'land of the free'—nobody denies that—nobody challenges it. (Maybe it is because we won't let other people testify.) As I write, news comes that in broad daylight in San Francisco, some boys have stoned an inoffensive Chinaman to death, and that although a large crowd witnessed the shameful deed, no one interfered.

3. Irish immigrants provided much of the labor for the completion of the Union Pacific Railroad.

Document: "The Chinese Must Go" (May 11, 1878)

As a shibboleth the above expression is very alluring. Probably there are not a thousand people in California, outside of the Chinese themselves, who do not wish to see the last **pigtail** sail west through the **Golden Gate**. When labor was scarce in California there might have been a shade of necessity of the employment of the Chinese; but now, when thousands of men and women are out of work, there is no good reason why the **celestials** should be retained. . . . The presence of the Chinese in California intensifies the distress of our industrial population. Every Chinaman who is employed, practically makes one tramp or loafer. The poor man is driven to the wall by the unnatural competition of the cheap Mongolians. The rich are daily getting richer—the poor are getting poorer. The bone and sinew of the land is being quietly crushed out of existence in California. Our government is theoretically founded on the popular will, but the tendency to-day is to destroy the populace and create two distinct classes—masters and serfs. . . . For the sake of our institutions, our government and our society, "the Chinese must go."

Source: "The Chinese Must Go," *The Wasp* 2, no. 93 (Aug. 1877–July 1878): 642. The Bancroft Library, University of California, Berkeley, in "The Chinese in California, 1850–1925," at: http://www.memory.loc.gov/ammem/award99/cubhtml/.

---

celestials: Another derogatory term used to describe Chinese immigrants. The name derives from the Chinese as subjects of the Emperor, referred to as the Son of Heaven.

Golden Gate: The strait that connects San Francisco Bay to the Pacific Ocean. The Golden Gate Bridge was not constructed until the 1930s.

pigtail: A derogatory name given to Chinese immigrants, based on the custom of wearing their hair in a long braid down the back.

AFTERMATH

Anti-immigrant sentiment ultimately carried the day, when Congress passed the Chinese Exclusion Act. The 1882 law was the first in the nation to ban immigration by race or nationality. Virtually no Chinese were allowed to enter the United States. Some exceptions were made for travelers, teachers, merchants, and students. No Chinese resident was allowed to become a naturalized citizen, regardless of how long he or she had lived in the United States. The Exclusion Act was loosened during World War II, when China fought as an ally alongside the United States against Japan.

ASK YOURSELF

1. Do economic hard times foster anti-immigrant sentiment? Or, is anti-immigrant sentiment almost always present regardless of economic conditions?
2. Twain makes Chinese immigrants look almost all good, while *The Wasp* makes Chinese immigrants look almost all bad. Is there a middle ground to most debates, or are issues generally all one way or the other?

TOPICS AND ACTIVITIES TO CONSIDER

- How does the experience of Chinese immigrants compare to other immigrants? Read modern-day immigration stories, and search for immigrant ancestors, at "Ellis Island" The Statue of Liberty-Ellis Island Foundation: http://www.ellisisland.org.
- Does the debate over Chinese immigration in the late 19th century echo in the debate over illegal immigration today? Find articles related to the current debates over illegal immigration at "Illegal Immigrants": http://topics.nytimes.com/top/reference/timestopics/subjects/i/illegal_immigrants/index.html.

IMMIGRATION WORRIES

Many native-born Americans worried about immigrants from regions of the world other than Asia. They especially feared the arrival of immigrants from southern and eastern Europe by the end of the 19th century. Individuals and families fleeing Italy, Russia, and Austria-Hungary spoke a seeming babble of languages and, often, worshipped in synagogues and Catholic churches. Nativist fears helped to found the Immigration Restriction League in 1894. Based in Boston, the League called for foreigners to take and pass literacy tests before gaining admission into the United States. The League argued that immigrants who could not read could not understand the workings of American democracy. The idea established the basis for literacy tests requiring American citizens to demonstrate their ability to read and interpret the Constitution before exercising the right to vote. Such exams, adjusted to nearly impossible difficulty as needed by local officials, later excluded large numbers of African Americans in the South from the ballot box. Worries over the continuing arrival of immigrants from southern and eastern Europe culminated in 1924, with the passage of the Johnson-Reed Act. The legislation curtailed immigration from all regions but northern Europe to all but a trickle. More people were leaving the United States than entering by the 1930s, a first in the nation's history. The discriminatory quotas on immigration remained largely intact until the passage of the Immigration Act of 1965.

Further Reading

Bailyn, Bernard. *The Peopling of British North America: An Introduction.* New York: Knopf, 1986.

Bodnar, John E. *The Transplanted: A History of Immigrants in Urban America.* Bloomington: Indiana University Press, 1985.

Gyory, Andrew. *Closing the Gate: Race, Politics, and the Chinese Exclusion Act.* Chapel Hill: University of North Carolina Press, 1998.

Jones, Maldwyn A. *American Immigration,* 2nd ed. Chicago: University of Chicago Press, 1992.

Yung, Judy. *Chinese American Voices: From the Gold Rush to the Present.* Berkeley: University of California Press, 2006.

Web Sites

"The Chinese in California, 1850–1925," posts thousands of primary sources. Photographs, images, letters, and other source materials are available. The site is part of the American Memory Collection, through the Library of Congress. The address is: http://www.memory.loc.gov/ammem/award99/cubhtml/cichome.html.

The Chinese Historical Society of America, located in San Francisco, is listed at: http://www.chsa.org.

18. "A Farmer's Life": Article in The Atlantic Monthly (1877)

INTRODUCTION

More Americans worked in agriculture than in any other economic pursuit by the early 1870s. The vast majority of these nearly seven million people were landowning farmers and hired hands, who labored primarily east of the Mississippi River. Tremendously hard work and little margin for error and mishap was a constant on American farms. Otherwise, the type of crops grown and the seasonal routine varied widely by (and within) region. In the South, cotton still was the chief CASH CROP, as it had been in the antebellum era. Preparing the fields through picking the cotton consumed almost all of the year, but for a few weeks in the late summer as the plants came into bud. Tobacco, rice, and sugar rounded out the most eagerly sought southern corps. By contrast, northern farmers grew a range of foodstuffs. They increasingly concentrated, however, on the profit found in wheat, hay, and dairy. Harvesting and planting on northern farms generally ran from April through October. The work over these seven months stretched into 14 and 15 hours a day, every day of the week but Sunday. "The world always seemed a little darker at sunset on Sunday night than a Saturday night," one farmer's son lamented. "The week ahead . . . seemed hopelessly long and profitless." Although no typical American farm existed, the routine of a dairy farmer described in THE ATLANTIC MONTHLY gives insight into the rhythms of agricultural life.

KEEP IN MIND AS YOU READ

1. The size of the average farm in the United States in 1870 was 153 acres. This includes some homestead farms, thereby slightly pulling up the average acreage. Farming was not an inexpensive undertaking. To operate a small farm, the costs for tools, supplies, and other equipment might run up to $700 a year.
2. Sharecropping was widespread throughout the South. Sharecroppers rented land from a large farmer in return for a percentage of their agricultural output. Sharecroppers often went into debt to local bankers and merchants, who often charged inflated prices and high interest. Mired in poverty, sharecroppers remained tied to the land.

3. Almost all farmers planted at least some acres with corn. In the South, corn actually was the most widely grown crop. Humans and livestock consumed corn, while its upkeep, once growing, was minimal.

Document: "Life and Work of the Eastern Farmer" (May 1877)

The milk-selling farmer . . . is one of the most wide-spread in Eastern farming and is more regularly employed than any other. Winter and summer his cows must be milked twice a day. Evenings milk must be cooled and safely kept until morning; and mornings milk must be ready for early delivery. It is usual for the farmer to rise at three every morning, winter and summer, to milk his cows, with one assistant, and to start as early as five o'clock to deliver his milk. Returning about the middle of the forenoon, he is able to attend to the details of barn work in winter and field work in summer until half past two or three o'clock in the afternoon, less the brief interval needed for the consumption of food. Early in the afternoon the cows must be again milked, and the cans of milk must in summer time be set in spring water for cooling. Then comes the feeding of the stock and the greasing of axles, the mending of harness, the repairing of tools, and the thousand and one odds and ends of the farmer's irregular work. In the winter, save for the early rising and the work of cold mornings, life is by no means hurried, and after a very early supper there is often a stroll to the corner store or to a neighbors house for a little wholesome idleness and gossip, the latter not invariably wholesome. At about the hour when the average reader of *The Atlantic* has finished his after-dinner cigar, all lights are extinguished and the farm household is wrapped in heavy slumber, for such early rising as the milkman is condemned to must needs trench upon the valuable evening hours for the requisite rest and sleep.

In summer, the conditions of life are immeasurably hardened. The farmer himself is necessarily absent several hours every morning with his milk wagon; but although he cannot lend a hand at the early field work, this work must go on with promptness, and he must arrange in advance for its proper performance. From the moment when he has finished his late breakfast until the last glimmer of twilight, he is doomed to harrowing and often anxious toil. There is no wide margin of profit that will admit of a slackening of the pace. Land must be prepared for planting; planting must be done when the condition of the ground and the state of the weather permit. Weeds grow without regard to our convenience, and they must be kept down from the first; and well on into the intervals of the hay harvest the corn field needs all of the cultivation that there is time for. Regularly as clock-work, in the late hours of the night and the early hours of the afternoon, the milking must be attended to, and the daily trip to town knows no exception because of heat, rain, or snow. At rigidly fixed hours, this part of the work must be done, and all other hours of the growing and of the harvest seasons are almost more than filled with work of imperative need. These alone seem to make a sufficient demand on the patience and endurance of the most industrious farmer; but, aside from these, he is loaded with the endless details of an intricate business, and with the responsibility of the successful management of a capital of from fifteen to twenty thousand dollars, upon the safety and the economical management of which entirely depend his success; he must avoid leakage and waste, and make every dollar paid for labor, or seed, or manure, or live stock, bring its adequate return.

Source: George E. Waring Jr., "Life and Work of the Eastern Farmer." *The Atlantic Monthly* 39, no. 235 (May 1877): 584–95, in "The Nineteenth Century in Print: Periodicals," American Memory Collection, Library of Congress: http://memory.loc.gov/ammem/ndlpcoop/moahtml/snchome.html.

AFTERMATH

In terms of work and tools, a farmer in the mid-1860s would recognize the farm operated by his grandfather or, even, great-grandfather. The same might not be said only a few years later, as new technologies began to rapidly change the farming routine. The McCormick Reaper already was in existence, to harvest wheat. Beginning in the 1870s, a self-binding harvester, that cut and bound hay and wheat, appeared widely on the market. Soon after came combines. Pulled by 20 to 40 horses and manned by several workers, combines reaped and bagged grains. The efficiency of American farms soared, but so did their costs and complexities. Farms became larger, in terms of acres planted and laborers employed, and specialized in individual crops. Add in railroad networks that shipped foodstuffs to nearly anywhere in the nation, and farming became increasingly modern and capitalistic. As one farmer advised, those who worked the land had to "understand farming as a business; if they do not it will go hard with them."

ASK YOURSELF

1. The life of farmers sometimes is romanticized, as an individual controlling his or her own time and surroundings. Does this seem more myth or reality, based on the reading? How does the daily routine of the dairy farmer described here compare to that of modern-day Americans? How does it compare to your daily routine?
2. Farmers often pooled their resources, to buy a new piece of equipment that they all might use. The farmers had access to the technology as a group that they might not have had on their own. But carelessness or accident on part of one person might hurt the entire group. Was the practice of sharing resources a good idea? Why?

TOPICS AND ACTIVITIES TO CONSIDER

    ❧ How have inventors and inventions, whether related to agriculture or other pursuits, influenced American life? Search for answers at "American Inventors and Inventions," Smithsonian Institute, Washington, DC: http://www.150.si.edu/150trav/remember/amerinv.htm.

    ❧ How have artists depicted the American farm in the 19th and 20th centuries? Find out at "The American Farm as Portrayed by Artists," Illinois State Museum, Springfield: http://www.museum.state.il.us/ismdepts/art/sadorus/FarmArtistsLesson.html.

Further Reading

Danhof, Clarence H. *Change in Agriculture: The Northern United States, 1820–1870.* Cambridge, MA.: Harvard University Press, 1969.

Gates, Paul W. *Agriculture and the Civil War.* New York: Knopf, 1965.

Livesay, Harold C. *American Made: Shapers of the American Economy.* New York: Pearson-Longman, 2007.

McMurry, Sally Ann. *Transforming Rural Life: Dairying Families and Agricultural Change, 1820–1885*. Baltimore: Johns Hopkins University Press, 1995.

Web Sites

The Farmers' Museum in Cooperstown, New York, attempts to cultivate an "understanding of the rural heritage that has shaped our land, communities and American culture." The Web site is: http://www.farmersmuseum.org/.

For a discussion of the sharecropping system, as well as images and primary documents, see "Reconstruction: The Second Civil War," American Experience, Public Broadcasting System: http://www.pbs.org/wgbh/amex/reconstruction/sharecrop/index.html.

19. "The Old Chisholm Trail": A Cowboy Ballad (1870s)

INTRODUCTION

There are few images that conjure up the idea of the western frontier to most modern-day Americans as a cowboy. Far more settlers moved west to take advantage of the Homestead Act, but few farmers might match cowboys for sheer dash and excitement. Truth be told, much of the cowboy's year was occupied by drudgery and boredom. Ranch buildings and fences needed mending, horses needed grooming and feeding, and cattle needed herding. The spring and early summer saw the pace quicken into a near frenzy of activity. Cowboys *broke* or *gentled* new horses for riding. When they were not busy bronco-busting, cowboys branded new calves for easy identification. Cowboys next began the several-month process of herding cattle northward from Texas to rail heads in Kansas, Nebraska, and Wyoming. These long drives saw herds that generally numbered around 2,500 cattle. Ten or 12 cowboys oversaw the operation, and each man had a distinct role. The most experienced cowboy served as the foreman, who led the long drive. Other veteran cowboys rode on either side of the massive herd, prohibiting strays. The least experienced men brought up the rear, keeping the herd closed up. Massive clouds of dust churned up by thousands of hooves made the job of catching stragglers the dirtiest and most disagreeable on the journey. The cook and his chuck wagon rode between the foreman and the cattle herd. Food for the evening meal was plentiful and hot, although the standard fare of bacon and beans and coffee perhaps grew monotonous after so many weeks. The payoff for completing the long drive was enormous. Each head of cattle might fetch up to $40. This was several times more than the monthly pay of a Union private throughout most of the Civil War. Cowboys pocketed their share of the profit and returned to Texas the following spring for the start of the next long drive. A song like "The Old Chisholm Trail" gives some insight into the difficulties and hardships encountered on the northward ride.

KEEP IN MIND AS YOU READ

1. The Chisholm Trail stretched from southern Texas to Kansas. The trail is named after Jesse Chisholm, who built several trading outposts in western Oklahoma that eventually serviced the long drive. Joseph McCoy was the first to mark the

Chisholm Trail, in the late 1860s. A businessman and promoter, McCoy built stockyards in Abilene, Kansas, to ship cattle to the East. Some five million cattle eventually traveled along the Chisholm Trail, making the route one of the most heavily used.

2. The westward extension of the railroad after the conclusion of the Civil War made the long drive possible. Cattle towns at Abilene, Dodge City, and Topeka served as transit points. From these cattle towns, trains shipped to stockyards in Kansas City and Chicago. With the invention of the refrigerated rail car in the late 19th century, fresh beef shipped to almost anywhere in the nation.

3. Riding herd as a cowboy was one of the few color-blind occupations in late-19th-century America. Scholars estimate that Hispanics and blacks comprised up to one-third of the cowboys who participated in the long drives.

4. The lyrics for the "The Old Chisholm Trail" might vary from long drive to long drive, as cowboys swapped lyrics and created others. The free exchange sometimes shortened a song. More often the new lyrics expanded songs to, as one cowboy music scholar claims, "interminable length."

Document: "The Old Chisholm Trail"

Come along, boys, and listen to my tale, / I'll tell you of my troubles on the old Chisholm trail.

Coma ti yi youpy, youpy ya, youpy ya, / Coma ti yi youpy, youpy ya.

I started up the trail October twenty-third, / I started up the trail with the **2-U herd**.

Oh, a ten dollar hoss and a forty dollar saddle,—/ And I'm goin' to punchin' Texas cattle.

I woke up one morning on the old Chisholm trail, / Rope in my hand and a cow by the tail.

I'm up in the mornin' afore daylight / And afore I sleep the moon shines bright.

Old Ben Bolt was a blamed good boss, / But he'd go to see the girls on a sore-backed hoss.

Old Ben Bolt was a fine old man / And you'd know there was whiskey wherever he'd land.

My hoss threw me off at the creek called Mud, / My hoss threw me off round the 2-U herd.

Last time I saw him he was going cross the level / A-kicking up his heels and a-running like the devil.

It's cloudy in the West, a-looking like rain, / And my damned old **slicker**'s in the wagon again.

Crippled my hoss, I don't know how, / Ropin' at the horns of a 2-U cow.

We hit Caldwell and we hit her on the fly, / We bedded down the cattle on the hill close by.

No **chaps**, no slicker, and it's pouring down rain, / And I swear, by God, I'll never night-herd again.

Feet in the stirrups and seat in the saddle, / I hung and rattled with them long-horn cattle.

Last night I was on guard and the leader broke the ranks, / I hit my horse down the shoulders and I spurred him in the flanks.

The wind commenced to blow, and the rain began to fall, / It looked, by grab, like we was goin' to loss 'em all.

I jumped in the saddle and grabbed holt the horn, / Best blamed **cow-puncher** ever was born.

I popped my foot in the stirrup and gave a little yell, / The tail cattle broke and the leaders went to hell.

I don't give a damn if they never do stop; / I'll ride as long as an eight-day clock.

Foot in the stirrup and hand on the horn, / Best damned cowboy ever was born.

I herded and I hollered and I done very well, / Till the boss said, "Boys, just let 'em go to hell."

Stray in the herd and the boss said kill it, / So I shot him in the rump with the handle of the skillet.

We rounded 'em up and put 'em on the cars, / And that was the last of the old Two Bars.

Oh it's bacon and beans most every day,—/ I'd as soon be a-eatin' prairie hay.

I'm on my best horse and I'm goin' at a run, / I'm the quickest shootin' cowboy that ever pulled a gun.

I went to the wagon to get my roll, / To come back to Texas, dad-burn my soul.

I went to the boss to draw my roll, / He had it figgered out I was nine dollars in the **hole**.

I'll sell my outfit just as soon as I can, / I won't punch cattle for no damned man.

Goin' back to town to draw my money, / Goin' back home to see my honey.

With my knees in the saddle and my seat in the sky, / I'll quit punching cows in the sweet by and by.

Coma ti yi youpy, youpy ya, youpy ya, / Coma ti yi youpy, youpy ya.

Source: John A. Lomax, comp. *Cowboy Songs and Other Frontier Ballads*. New York: The MacMillan Company, 1929, pp. 58–61. The text is posted online by Project Gutenberg Literary Archive Foundation: http://www.gutenberg.org/etext/21300.

AFTERMATH

The long drive did not have a long history, and sputtered to a close by the early 1890s. A series of bitterly cold winters helped to do in the undertaking, killing off large numbers of cattle through exposure and starvation. Barbed wire, however, proved the main nemesis to the cowboy. Cheaply produced and widely available by the mid-1870s, barbed wire allowed ranchers to mark off their territory. The grasslands that the long drive had crossed were less and less open, depriving cattle of food. The cost of the journey became increasingly prohibitive, if cowboys had to bring forage for the cattle. The nation had not lost its taste for beef. Rather, by the late 19th century, rail lines pushed almost to the door of cattle ranchers. The days of the cowboy and the long drive had ended.

ASK YOURSELF

1. Would you have wanted to participate in a long drive? What might be the pros and cons of this type of occupation and lifestyle?
2. Do the lyrics of "The Old Chisholm Trail" dispel some of the romance often associated with cowboy life? Why or why not?

chaps: Leggings worn by cowboys, to protect from briars.

cow-puncher: A slang, if long-lasting, name given to cowboys who helped to herd cattle onto waiting trains. Cowboys and rail yard workers used a prod to poke cattle in the flanks, to guide them onto the cars.

hole: Some cowboys had money withheld from their pay, to compensate for food, clothing, and other supplies issued.

slicker: Rain poncho. Cowboys often carried no tents in order to travel lightly. The slicker served as some protection from bad weather and the nighttime cold.

2-U herd: Probably a reference to the brand marking the particular herd of cattle.

TOPICS TO CONSIDER

- What was the experience of black cowboys like? Find out at Gracia, Socorro, Ramon Gomez and Desiree Crawford, "Black Cowboys Rode the Trails Too," *Borderlands*, vol. 21 (2002–03): 5, *Borderlands*, El Paso Community College Libraries, Texas: http://dnn.epcc.edu/nwlibrary/borderlands/21_black_cowboys.htm.
- The long drive and westward expansion helped to alter the habitat and ecosystems of the United States. Explore efforts to protect America's natural world by the Sierra Club, America's oldest conservation group. The Web site is posted at: http://www.sierraclub.org.

Further Reading

Branch, Douglas. *The Cowboy and His Interpreters*. New York: Cooper Square Publishers, 1961.

Green, Douglas B. *Singing in the Saddle: The History of Singing Cowboy*. Nashville, TN: Country Music Foundation Press and Vanderbilt University Press, 2002.

Lee, Katie. "*Ten Thousand Goddam Cattle*": *A History of the American Cowboy in Song, Story and Verse*. Flagstaff, AZ: Northland Press, 1976.

McCracken, Harold. *The American Cowboy*. Garden City, NY: Doubleday, 1973.

Slatta, Richard W. *The Cowboy Encyclopedia*. Santa Barbara, CA: ABC-CLIO, 1994.

Web Sites

Explore the history of the Chisholm Trail at the Chisholm Trail Heritage Center, posted at: http://www.onthechisholmtrail.com.

The American Cowboy Museum on the Taylor-Stevenson Ranch in Houston, Texas, is listed at: http://www.americancowboymuseum.org.

20. "Regulations to Be Observed by All Persons Employed in the Lewiston Mills" (1867)

INTRODUCTION

Most Americans lived in the countryside during the mid-19th century, but the gap was narrowing. Between 1820 and 1870, city populations increased at a faster rate than at any other time in American history. New York City, Philadelphia, and Chicago were the largest cities, each with 300,000 people or more. Urban populations swelled in numbers because cities, in addition to providing excitements and experiences not found on the farm, offered jobs. American manufacturing power had soared throughout much of the first half of the 19th century, due to the TRANSPORTATION AND MARKET REVOLUTIONS. By 1860, the United States possessed one of most vibrant economies in the world. Cotton textiles, lumber products, boots and shoes, and flour milling were the leading American industries. These four economic sectors needed workers on site, to take advantage of new technologies and transportation networks. The workday often was long and monotonous, with workers focusing on only one part of the production process. Yet, common laborers were relatively easy to find (one might today term this a buyer's market, with factory owners as the buyers). Workers fit in, or found themselves replaced by someone else who would. The rules and regulations for a textile mill in Maine in the late 1860s give some insight into the expectations that employers held for their workers.

KEEP IN MIND AS YOU READ

1. New England dominated the American textile industry due to the region's ready access to rivers for steam power and population centers for labor. Nearly all of the nation's textiles came from New England mills.
2. Women provided much of the labor in textile mills. Factory owners argued that women were more attentive to detail, and more easily controlled, than men. Women also worked for less pay. Men generally earned about $1 per day, while women might earn as little as 50 cents.
3. Children made up a significant amount of the work force in textile mills. Employers often worked children in seasonal shifts, to get around mandatory school attendance. Children had to go to school for so many weeks, but often no starting and ending

date was specified. One group of children, therefore, might work for four months before going to school for four months. A second group of children would pick up the slack.

4. The workday at a mill generally ran from 7:00 in the morning until 6:00 in the evening, six days a week.

Document: Lewiston Mills Regulations

1. The Overseers are required to be in their rooms at the starting of the Mills, and not to be absent unnecessarily during working hours. They are to see that all those employed under them are in their places in due season; they may grant leave of absence to those employed under them, when they can do so without stopping the machinery.

2. All persons employed in the Lewiston Mills are required to observe the regulations of the room in which they work; they are not to be absent without the consent of their Overseer, except in cases of sickness, and then they are required to send him word of the cause of their absence.

3. All persons employed in the Lewiston Mills, excepting minors under the age of sixteen years, are considered as agreeing to labor as many hours each day, and for each and every day's work, as the Company may require, not exceeding eleven hours each day.

4. No person who drinks intoxicating liquors, will knowingly be employed by the Lewiston Mills. . . .

8. Payment, including board and wages, will be made up to the last Saturday of every month, and will be made due on the third Thursday of the following month.

9. All persons in the employ of the Lewiston Mills are earnestly requested to attend public worship on the Sabbath.

10. Any person who may take from the Mill or yard, or any other portion of the Company's premises, any property belonging to the Company, without leave, will be considered guilty of stealing, and prosecuted accordingly.

11. Sewing, Reading, Knitting, &c., are not allowed during working hours.

12. The foregoing Rules and Regulations are considered as an express contract between the Company and all persons in its employ, particularly those referring to the use of intoxicating liquors, [and] the hours of labor, . . .

Source: Lewiston Mills Regulations, Lewiston, Maine, 1867, American Textile History Museum, Lowell, Massachusetts. Posted at: http://invention.smithsonian.org/centerpieces/whole_cloth/u2ei/u2images/act9/Lew_rules.html.

AFTERMATH

The late 19th century ushered in an era of big business in the United States. American manufacturing would continue to soar, surging the nation to the strongest industrial economy in the world by 1900. The oil industry and steel industry turned enormous profits, ranging into the tens of millions of dollars. At the same, many workers sweated through long hours, low pay, and unsafe working conditions. The resulting tensions raised new questions between business and labor that still are discussed and debated today. Some of these include, Should there be a minimum wage, and if so, what should it be? How many hours should comprise a standard work week? What rights do workers have if they are injured on the job? What obligations do business owners have to their workers and the larger community, if any?

ASK YOURSELF

1. Why do you think mill owners prohibited employees from "Sewing, Reading, Knitting," in Regulation 11? How do you think workers overcame the tedium of working at one task and one machine for 11 hours every day, week after week?
2. Do you think that you could work by the above rules, if you needed the employment?

TOPICS AND ACTIVITIES TO CONSIDER

- ⇴ The textile mill in Lowell, Massachusetts, was one of the first in the nation. Established in the 1820s, the Lowell textile mill became a major employer. The National Park Service operates the mill today as a historic site. What was life like in the early mill? Explore the answer at: http://www.nps.gov/lowe.
- ⇴ Do arguments that women and children worked for fewer wages, and therefore were more cost-efficient, echo in arguments today over the use of immigrant labor? The point is explored in Laura Parker, "USA Just Wouldn't Work without Immigrant Labor," *USA Today*: http://www.usatoday.com/news/washington/july01/2001-07-23-immigrant.htm.

Further Reading

Dawley, Alan. *Class and Community: The Industrial Revolution in Lynn*. Cambridge, MA: Harvard University Press, 1976.

Licht, Walter. *Industrializing America: The Nineteenth Century*. Baltimore: Johns Hopkins University Press, 1995.

Meyer, David R. *The Roots of American Industrialization*. Baltimore: Johns Hopkins University Press, 2003.

Web Sites

The American Labor Museum/Botto House National Landmark, located in Haledon, New Jersey, is detailed at: http://www.labormuseum.org.

The American Textile History Museum in Lowell, Massachusetts, is listed at: http://www.athm.org.

DOMESTIC LIFE

21. "This Morning We Have Heard That [Father] Is Safe and I Can Take up My Journal Again": Diary Entries of Emma LeConte (January–February 1865)

INTRODUCTION

The world of American youth was in transition by the mid-19th century. Families increasingly were child-centered, with sons and daughters seen as individuals with their own needs and wants. Yet never before in the nation's past did children (defined by the census as any person 14 years of age and younger, but more broadly by scholars as including older teenagers living at home) experience such a tumultuous period as during the four years of the Civil War. Almost every family had a father, brother, or cousin away in the military. Children still played games between 1861 and 1865, including dolls, checkers, and dress-up. But the war intruded into all, and, in a sense, childhood was lost. Sons and daughters had to help the rest of the family shoulder the workloads, as much as possible, of their departed fathers. This might be in the field or, sometimes, in the factory. While children toiled, their families received letters from the war front. These writings often came with souvenirs from the battlefield, including spent bullets and bits of uniforms and flags. Fathers usually attempted to sanitize their description of the war, but sometimes the enormity of the carnage broke through. One Confederate soldier detailed to his youngsters that in a recent battle he had seen "Some with one eye shot out, nose shot off mouth shot off side of their fact shot off shot in the arms hand & legs." Children sometimes had the war literally sweep past their home, as armies marched back and forth and battle lines ebbed and flowed. A few intrepid youngsters sought out the fighting. Most of these children served as drummer boys, to sound calls for daily duties and parades and drill. A handful managed to escape detection and actually enlist. One study of the Union army estimated that almost 1,000 soldiers were between 13 and 15 years of age. Emma LeConte did not serve in the military, but the 17-year-old South Carolinian worried about her father, who was fighting for the Confederacy. She also witnessed the ravages of war first hand, after the Federal army captured Columbia in early 1865.

KEEP IN MIND AS YOU READ

1. In 1860, 12.7 million Americans were 14 years of age and younger. The figure indicates that 41 percent of Americans were children.

2. Johnny Clem is perhaps the most famous drummer boy to serve in the Union army. Clem ran away from home and began to follow along with the 22nd Michigan during the spring of 1861, when he was nine years old. Clem came under Confederate fire in northern Georgia two years later, earning him the nickname across much of the Union as the "drummer boy of Chickamauga." Clem won promotion to officer in the postwar era, and eventually retired in 1916 as a major general.

Document: Diary Entries of Emma LeConte

January 4, 1865

What a budget of bad news this morning! Four letters. One from Father, who writes from camp at Doctortown only fifteen miles from Halifax, but he cannot get there. He had sent word to Aunt Jane by some scouts to try to reach him with the girls, but how can they when every mule and horse has been taken—they could only walk, and that, of course, would be impracticable. Father said the Yanks made a clean sweep of everything, and we have lost all our worldly possessions except the few negroes here. Perhaps Aunt Jane's family and Sallie are almost starving! Oh, it is dreadful to think of! . . .

And Father—I cannot bear to think of him. Every day I tremble with the fear that I may hear he is a prisoner or killed. Killed—oh, no—God would not be so cruel as that—I could not think of that—my darling, precious father, if you were only safe at home again! . . .

I am constantly thinking of the time **Columbia** will be given up to the enemy. The horrible picture is constantly before my mind. They have promised to show no mercy in this **state**. Mother wants to send me off, but of course I would not leave here. I can only hope their conduct in the city will not be so shocking as it has been through the country. Yet no doubt the **college** buildings will be burned, with other public buildings, and we will at least lose our home.

February 22, 1865

I meant last night to write down some description of what I had seen, but was too wretchedly depressed and miserable to even think of it. This morning we have heard that [Father] is safe and I can take up my journal again. Yesterday afternoon we walked all over the town in company with Miss Ellen LaBorde. Yes, I have seen it all—I have seen the "Abomination of Desolation." It is even worse than I thought. The place is literally in ruins. The entire heart of the city is in ashes—only the outer edges remain. On the whole length of Sumter Street not one house beyond the first block after the Campus is standing, except the brick house of Mr. Mordecai. Standing in the center of the town, as far as the eye can reach, nothing is to be seen but heaps of rubbish, tall dreary chimneys and shattered brick walls, wile "in the hollow windows, dreary horror's sitting." Poor old Columbia—where is all her beauty, so admired by strangers, so loved by her children! She can only excite the pity of the former and the tears of the latter. I hear several Yankee officers remarked to some of the citizens on the loveliness of their town as they first saw it by sunrise across the river.

Source: Emma LeConte, diary entries, January 4 and February 22, 1865, in *When the World Ended: The Diary of Emma LeConte*, edited by Earl Schenck Miers. New York: Oxford University Press, 1957, pp. 7–8 and pp. 60–61.

AFTERMATH

The Civil War influenced children in later years in different ways. Most directly, some sons and daughters who had lost their fathers ended up in orphanages. These institutions were more numerous in the North, because they generally received state support. Other children looked back at the Civil War as the defining moment in their youth. The material scarcity and worry over loved ones in the military dominated whatever other memories they might have held about growing up. For yet some youth, Emma LeConte included, the war initially left feelings of bitterness and loss. Although grateful that her father had survived the struggle, LeConte could not bring herself to accept that the Confederacy was defeated. Time healed at least some of the rawer emotions. When the United States entered World War I in 1917, LeConte, then in her early 70s, eagerly volunteered in war drives to help raise supplies for American soldiers.

ASK YOURSELF

1. Some scholars argue that war might be harder on families at home, rather than soldiers at the front, because civilians have to wait on events, rather than helping to shape them. Do you agree with the argument?
2. How does one reconcile sharing the worry expressed by LeConte over the well-being of her father with disapproval over her reference to slaves as property? Does the tension between the two statements help to illustrate the point that historians study the past in an attempt to explain and understand it, rather than to necessarily agree or disagree with it?

TOPICS AND ACTIVITIES TO CONSIDER

- What role did the capture of Columbia play in helping the Union to win the war? Explore the history behind Sherman's march, as well as interactive features, at "Sherman's March," The History Channel: http://www.history.com/civilwar/shermansmarch/.
- Want to find out more about Emma LeConte and her family? Go to Lester D. Stephens, "LeConte Family," The New Georgia Encyclopedia: http://www.georgiaencyclopedia.org/nge/Article.jsp?id=h-791.

college: South Carolina College, established in 1801. The College closed during the Civil War, due to declining enrollment. The College opened and closed at various times throughout the remainder of the 19th century, due to political and economic issues. In 1906 the school was rechartered as the University of South Carolina.

Columbia: The capital of South Carolina; fell to the Union army on February 17, 1865. Retreating Confederate soldiers set ablaze cotton bales that winds and drunken soldiers and stragglers helped to spread into the night. By the time the fire was brought under control, much of the city was in ruins. The Union army left Columbia on February 20 to again march north.

state: Union soldiers vowed to take special revenge on South Carolina, the first state to secede from the Union in late 1860. One Indiana soldier judged that "Poor South Carolina must suffer now. Her deluded people will . . . reap the full reward of all their folly and crimes." Union soldiers left behind many towns battered, but they acted with perhaps a less heavy hand than many Confederate civilians expected from them.

THE CAROLINAS CAMPAIGN

Under the command of Major General WILLIAM T. SHERMAN, Union forces had marched from Atlanta and captured the Confederate port city of Savannah, Georgia, in late 1864. Early the next year, the Union army marched into South Carolina. Sherman hoped that his offensive would cut Richmond, Virginia, off from the interior and thereby demonstrate the futility of continued Confederate military resistance. Sherman's soldiers met little opposition on the northward march, and sometimes roamed widely in search of plunder. The Union columns crossed into North Carolina before suffering a Confederate counterattack at Bentonville on March 19. In vicious fighting, the Union defenders smashed several desperate Confederate assaults. The battle at Bentonville marked the end of any effective resistance to the Union offensive. Confederate General JOSEPH E. JOHNSTON surrendered the remnants of his army to Sherman at Durham Station, near Raleigh, on April 26.

Further Reading

Marten, James A. *The Children's Civil War*. Chapel Hill: University of North Carolina Press, 1998.

Marten, James A. *Children for the Union: The War Spirit on the Northern Home Front*. Chicago: Ivan D. Dee, 2004.

Werner, Emmy E. *Reluctant Witnesses: Children's Voices from the Civil War*. Boulder, CO: Westview Press, 1998.

Web Sites

For photographs and discussion of children during the Civil War, go to "The Civil War through a Child's Eye," The Library of Congress: http://www.nylearns.org/module/content/search/item/3526/viewdetail.ashx.

For discussion and analysis of *Across Five Aprils,* by Irene Hunt, one of the most popular fictional accounts of childhood during the Civil War, visit "Across Five Aprils Book Notes Summary," BookRags: http://www.bookrags.com/notes/afa/.

22. "Perhaps a Courtship of Generous Length …": A Columnist's Advice to Couples (1871)

INTRODUCTION

Memories of the Civil War did not preclude everything else, and many young men and women eventually turned their attention to courting. Earlier social restrictions on displays of affection in public had begun to slip way by the late 19th century. Couples now strolled with hands clasped and arms locked to church and to various social functions. Boyfriends and girlfriends also increasingly saw one another without the presence of a chaperone. Some social commentators sniped that the lack of reserve between couples led to dangerous flirtations. Statistics, at least, fail to support the claim. Unwed women accounted for about 10 percent of all pregnancies, a drop since earlier in the 19th century. For far more couples instead, a brief period of courtship led to marriage. The overwhelming majority of Americans married, and most did so at a relatively young age. Men usually married during their mid-20s, while women usually married in their early 20s. These are roughly the same ages as when their parents and grandparents had married. An advice writer in *The Overland Monthly* suggested that perhaps a longer period of courting would serve couples better, to get to know one another in good times as well as bad times. Too many newly married couples otherwise failed to realize that in the days, weeks, and, even years to come, "real life has just begun."

KEEP IN MIND AS YOU READ

1. Fidelity formed the basis for many, if not most, marriages during the Civil War and Reconstruction era. Sexual intercourse seemingly remained for the marriage bed, not before. A desire for closer physical intimacy, however, perhaps prompted some couples to marry sooner rather than later.
2. Wedding ceremonies had undergone considerable change by the late 19th century, growing increasingly formal and public. Engagement rings, wedding invitations, and white bridal gowns were nearly standard features by the mid-1870s.

Document: Sarah Cooper's "Ideal Womanhood," Overland Monthly (October 1871)

But when the **honey-moon** is over! What then? Why, *then* the film of unreality begins to wear away, and the picture stands out in bold relief in its true colors; free from the glamour of the star-lit eye, and the incandescent light of nuptial splendor. And then, too, often the skies darken and weep out their agony; . . . The skies, the birds, the trees, the flowers, and the very air, seem to have entered into a combination for the manufacture of misery; to have leagued together for the dispensing of wretchedness. Leaden-footed, the hours drag on. . . .

And wherefore all this? Is there no way to prevent this canker of disappointment? . . . Can no fortunate compromise-ground be discovered between the domain of turtle-doves and snapping-turtles? This little heavenly dispensation of billing and cooing is all well enough; none but frostbitten, snarling old bachelors, or grimly prudish old maids would ever be churlish enough to get squeamish over an occasional dash of irrepressible, passionate adoration, even though a kindly curtain should fail to interpose in behalf of the ardent enthusiasts. Perhaps a courtship of generous length would be a sort of antidote to such immoderate "lovingness." It would, undoubtedly, be a most impertinent humiliation for a dainty, exquisite little lady, to be unconsciously caught by her "sweetheart," divested of the many artful decorations and appliances in which she is wont to be decked out, while in all the threadbareness of a neat, plain, calico wrapper, she was energetically cleaning the silver, and setting the dinning-room to rights. But, then, such an onslaught could be made the happy occasion for some healthy, wholesome courting; all the more spicy, were the sagacious explorer to seize the **chamois,** whether or not, and put on the finishing touches. We would not fear to wager slight odds that the polish would transcend in brilliancy all ordinary polish. This would be a capital initiation into the homelier phases of domestic industry. A fortunate thing, also, would it be for the husband prospective, if, as a plighted lover, he were compelled, or rather permitted, to stand the crucial test of the sick-room; to see if his affianced petulant with pain, or nervously fretful with fever; to see her face woefully distorted with toothache; or, what is worse still, with her false teeth loosed from their moorings and entirely thrown aside. A lover who can stand these heroic tests, will not be apt to fail in the day of calamity.

chamois: In this context, a towel or cloth.

honey-moon: Many couples in earlier generations had embarked on a postwedding trip, similar to newlyweds in the late 19th century. The difference was that couples in the 1860s and 1870s often embarked on these trips on their own, without family and friends in tow. Honeymoons had become increasingly private.

Source: Sarah Cooper, "Ideal Womanhood." *Overland Monthly* 7 (October 1871): 358–69; listed at "Making of America Journals," University of Michigan, Humanities Text Initiative: http://quod.lib.umich.edu/cgi/t/text/text-idx?c=moajrnl&idno=ahj1472.1-07.004.

AFTERMATH

Most marriages lasted permanently, although an increasing number ended in divorce. In the early 1860s, the rate of divorce was very low across the nation. The numbers increased dramatically in the aftermath of the Civil War. In the 11 years between 1867 and 1878, the number of divorces skyrocketed from 9,900 to 16,000. Women initiated many of the break-ups, seemingly more unhappy with their choice of husbands than with the institution of marriage. Most women granted divorces during this time period cited their husbands for physical and mental cruelty, desertion, drunkenness, and neglect. But men also expressed unhappiness with their choice of spouse. Men receiving divorces most often claimed that their wife had "acted in an unwife-like manner." Husbands winning divorce on these grounds charged that their wives had failed to do everything from washing their clothes to bearing their children. Husbands and wives having trouble obtaining divorces in their home states often moved to Indiana, which possessed the most liberal divorce laws in the nation. The Hoosier state permitted individuals seeking divorce only to inform their spouse of their decision if they chose to do so, a far less formal and public proceeding than was used throughout the rest of the nation. The loosening of divorce laws perhaps as much as any other factor explains the rising American divorce rate.

ASK YOURSELF

1. Does marrying for romance rather than economics, societal obligations, or other reasons perhaps lead to more unhappiness between husbands and wives? Meaning, are people who expect more from marriage sometimes disappointed?
2. Is the advice in "Ideal Womanhood" correct? Do people who know one another in good times and bad make for better spouses? If so, does this rule out the notion of love at first sight?

TOPICS AND ACTIVITIES TO CONSIDER

- Want to know more on the history behind St. Valentine's Day? Find out at "Valentine's Day," History.Com: http://www.history.com/content/valentine.
- Want to know more about the history of weddings? See Matt Jacks, "The History of Weddings—Tying the Knot Through the Ages," TheHistoryOf.net: http://www.thehistoryof.net/history-of-weddings.html.

Further Reading

Coontz, Stephanie. *Marriage, A History: How Love Conquered Marriage.* New York: Penguin Books, 2006.

Kett, Joseph F. *Rites of Passage: Adolescence in America, 1790 to the Present.* New York: Basic Books, 1977.

Lystra, Karen. *Searching the Heart: Women, Men, and Romantic Love in Nineteenth-Century America.* New York: Oxford University Press, 1989.

Rothman, Ellen K. *Hands and Hearts: A History of Courtship in America.* New York: Basic Books, 1984.

Web Sites

Gone with the Wind (1939), a tremendously popular if oversimplified film depiction of the Civil War and Reconstruction years ranks as the second most romantic film in American movie history. Find out the other historically themed films on the list at "American Film Institute's 100 Years . . . 100 Passions," AFI.com: http://www.afi.com/100years/passions.aspx.

Some Civil War reenactors extend their interest in history even to their wedding ceremonies. Find out more at Ashley Andyshak, "Re-Enactment for Real," July 16, 2007, FrederickNewsPost.com (Maryland): http://www.fredericknewspost.com/sections/news/display.htm?storyID=62554; and, Erica Kritt, "Couple Wed at Gettysburg Re-Enactment," July 6, 2008, *Carroll County Times* (Maryland): http://www.carrollcounty times.com/couple-wed-at-gettysburg-re-enactment/article_8548769e-1e25-58c9-9291-d0ca7f155d48.html.

23. A Manual for New Mothers: Domestic Advice from Catharine E. Beecher and Harriet Beecher Stowe (1869)

INTRODUCTION

Soon after marriage, about 18 months to be exact, most newlyweds became first-time parents. Expectant mothers had little time to quietly reflect on the changes occurring within their bodies, because all but the most well-to-do women continued to perform household chores until the big moment occurred. That moment usually happened in the bedroom, because public hospitals existed only to provide aid to the indigent. Americans viewed childbirth as a natural experience so, when labor started, they often believed no specific medical tools were needed. Physicians generally came to a woman's house to help in the birthing process in urban areas, if called to assist at all. Doctors were less numerous in the countryside, where most mid-19th-century Americans lived, and neighbors and family members often helped mothers-to-be through their labor. With the new babe in arms, the work for the mother became almost nonstop. Some social commentators believed that too few women understood the day-to-day demands of motherhood. Most children had likely seen someone in their family give birth by the time they had reached adulthood. Understanding the ins and outs of taking care of an infant, however, was an entirely different question. Catharine Beecher and Harriet Beecher Stowe devoted a chapter in *The American Woman's Home* to taking care of a new baby. The book was one of the most popular domestic advice manuals in the 1870s.

KEEP IN MIND AS YOU READ

1. Competition between midwives and physicians about the oversight of the birthing process had raged fiercely into the early 19th century. Midwives were women who relied on observation and experience to assist in birthing. They gradually fell out of favor, especially in cities, as obstetricians frowned on their activities.
2. Regardless of whether it was overseen by a midwife or a physician, the birthing process carried significant risk to the child (and the mother). Infant mortality in Massachusetts averaged about 150 per 1,000 births. The rate of death was nearly 10 times higher than today.

Document: *"The Care of Infants"*

Every young lady ought to learn how to take **proper care** of an infant; for, even if she is never to become the responsible guardian of a nursery, she will often be in situations where she can render benevolent aid to others, in this most fatiguing and anxious duty. . . .

In order to be prepared for such benevolent ministries, every young lady should improve the opportunity, whenever it is afforded her, for learning how to wash, dress, and tend a young infant; and whenever she meets with such a work as Dr. Combe's, on the management of infants, she ought to read it, and *remember* its contents.

There is no point on which medical men so emphatically lift the voice of warning as in reference to administering medicines to infants. It is so difficult to discover what is the matter with an infant, its frame is so delicate and so susceptible, and slight causes have such a powerful influence, that it requires the utmost skill and judgment to ascertain what would be proper medicines, and the proper quantity to be given. . . .

After it is a month or two old, take an infant out to walk, or ride, in a little wagon, every fair and warm day; but be very careful that its feet, and every part of its body, are kept warm; and be sure that its eyes are well protected from the light. Weak eyes, and sometimes blindness, are caused by neglecting this precaution. Keep the head of an infant cool, never allowing too warm bonnets, nor permitting it to sink into soft pillows when asleep. Keeping an infant's head too warm very much increases nervous irritability; and this is the reason why medical men forbid the use of caps for infants. But the head of an infant should, especially while sleeping, be protected from draughts of air, and from getting cold.

It is better for both mother and child, that it should not sleep on the mother's arm at night, unless the weather be extremely cold. This practice keeps the child too warm, and leads it to seek food too frequently. A child should ordinarily take nourishment but twice in the night. A crib beside the mother, with plenty of warm and light covering, is best for the child; but the mother must be sure that it is always kept warm.

Never cover a child's head, so that it will inhale the air of its own lungs. In very warm weather, especially in cities, great pains should be taken to find fresh and cool air by rides and sailing. Walks in a public square in the cool of the morning, and frequent excursions in ferry or steamboats, would often save a long bill for medical attendance.

In hot nights, the windows should be kept open, and the infant laid on a mattress, or on folded blankets. A bit of straw matting, laid over a feather bed and covered with the under sheet, makes a very cool bed for an infant. . . .

Cool bathing, in hot weather, is very useful; but the water should be very little cooler than the skin of the child. When the constitution is delicate, the water should be slightly warmed. Simply sponging the body freely in a tub, answers the same purpose as a regular bath. In very warm weather, this should be done two or three times a day, always waiting two or three hours after food has been given. Do not allow a child to form such habits that it will not be quiet unless tended and amused. A healthy child should be accustomed to lie or sit in its cradle much of the time; but it should occasionally be taken up and tossed, or carried about for exercise and amusement. An infant should be encouraged to *creep,* as an exercise very strengthening and useful. If the mother fears the soiling of its nice dresses, she can keep a long slip or apron which will entirely cover the dress, and can be removed when the child is taken in the arms. A child should not be allowed, when quite young, to bear its weight on its feet very long at a time, as this tends to weaken and distort the limbs. . . .

Many mothers, with a little painstaking, succeed in putting their infants into their cradle while awake, at regular hours for sleep; and induce regularity in other habits, which saves much trouble. During this training process a child may cry, at first, a great deal; but for a healthy child, this use of the lungs does no harm and tends rather to strengthen than to injure them, unless it becomes exceedingly violent. A child who is trained to lie or sit and amuse itself, is happier than one who is carried and tended a great deal, and thus rendered restless and uneasy when not so indulged.

Source: Catharine E. Beecher and Harriet Beecher Stowe. *The American Woman's Home: Or, Principles of Domestic Science.* New York: 1869. Listed online at Project Gutenberg: http://www.gutenberg.org/etext/6598.

AFTERMATH

Some married couples found the thought of parenthood either too daunting or not convenient. Wives especially took the lead in the matter. Modern-day scholars have coined the term *domestic feminism* to describe women attempting to gain control over their bodies and family circumstances. According to reports from contemporary druggists, women chose to avoid expanding their families through abortion more often than through contraception, at least through the late 1860s. Some women attempted to induce accidental miscarriages through the ingestion of abortive drugs, including iodine,

proper care: In some aspects, Beecher and Stowe give poor advice from a modern-day perspective. Infants should not sleep with pillows and blankets, for fear of suffocation. And parents should place infants to sleep on their backs, to reduce the chance of sudden infant death syndrome. In the main, however, Beecher and Stowe offer advice that still is relevant today. Infants never should receive adult medicines, even for colds and fevers. Infants also develop better in all aspects with love, play, and attention from parents and caregivers, as Beecher and Stowe suggest.

NINETEENTH-CENTURY SELF-HELP BOOKS

The plethora of advice manuals and how-to guides that crowd American book shelves today dates back to the late 19th century and earlier. Much of the literature surrounded adolescent teenagers and the convertibility of energy. Many medical practitioners held that as teenagers went through puberty and gained in sexual capacity, they also gained in spiritual energy and physical energy. Young men and women had to be on guard, because anything that decreased one of their three energies also lowered the other two energies. Masturbation was a chief danger to guard against. Many physicians believed that spinal marrow directly connected the brain to the sexual organs. The spinal connection drained vital brain fluids whenever one experienced sexual climax. The rising sexual energy of young people made them especially at risk to self-harm. Masturbation indulged in too often placed teenagers "in imminent danger of becoming Insane, or at least of weak Intellect." Other dangers to the health and well-being of teenagers seemingly lurked around every corner. Isaac Ray, a psychiatrist, warned that a host of actions could lead young people to disease and illness. Some of these behaviors included drinking coffee, which stimulated the urge to masturbate, to worrying over school, which diminished vital nervous fluids. Orson Fowler, another advice writer, shifted the blame for adolescent woes from teenagers to parents. Fowler argued that parents who urged their children toward perfection in daily activities risked wearing them out. Parents should let their children be children "if you have [them] live to be a hundred," rather than push them too quickly into becoming "young ladies and gentlemen."

cotton root, and oil of tansy. Other women visited abortionists, although many of these practitioners reportedly had little more medical knowledge than their patients. Beginning in the 1870s, as talk about family planning crept more into public conversation, women increasingly turned to contraceptive devices and were able to choose from approved medical devices, such as diaphragms and contraceptives. Less knowledgeable women might resort to popular superstitions, such as the belief that if women engaged in vigorous exercise—horseback riding and dancing, among other forms—after intercourse, she would avoid conception. Together, abortions and contraception helped to cause the American birthrate to fall. By the end of the 19th century, fertility rates had dropped to about 3.5 children per family. The decline in family size continued a trend that first had began in the early 1800s. As the nation became more urbanized, children were no longer seen as the economic necessity (as laborers on the family farm) that they had been previously.

ASK YOURSELF

1. What seems the most practical advice in raising infants offered by Beecher and Stowe? What seems the least practical advice?
2. Beecher and Stowe suggest that young adults learn early on how to take care of infants, so they have first-hand experience when they become parents. Is the advice still applicable today? Or, do most modern-day parents learn as they go?

TOPICS AND ACTIVITIES TO CONSIDER

- How does the parental advice offered in the 1870s compare to advice offered today? Check out the wide-range of tips and pointers for today's new moms and dads at "Parenting Articles on Raising Infants, Toddlers, Preschoolers & School-Age Kids," Parenthood.com: http://www.parenthood.com/parenting/yourchild. php.
- Interested in learning more about midwives and their craft? Check out *A Midwife's Tale: The Life of Martha Ballard, Based on Her Diary, 1785–1812,* by Laurel Thatcher Ulrich. A three-part interview with Ulrich is listed at "Interview with Laurel Ulrich," DoHistory, developed and maintained by the Film Study Center at Harvard University, Boston, Massachusetts, and hosted by the Center for History and New Media, George Mason University, Fairfax, Virginia: http://dohistory.org/ book/100_interview.html.

Further Reading

Degler, Carl N. *At Odds: Women and the Family in America from the Revolution to the Present.* New York: Oxford University Press, 1981.

Gordon, Linda. *The Moral Property of Women: A History of Birth Control Politics in America.* Urbana: University of Illinois Press, 2002.

Haller, John S., Jr., and Robin M. Haller. *The Physician and Sexuality in Victorian America.* Urbana: University of Illinois Press, 1974.

Leavitt, Sarah. *From Catharine Beecher to Martha Stewart: A Cultural History of Domestic Advice.* Chapel Hill: University of North Carolina Press, 2002.

Sklar, Kathryn K. *Catharine Beecher: A Study in American Domesticity.* New Haven: Yale University Press, 1973.

White, Barbara Anne. *The Beecher Sisters.* New Haven: Yale University Press, 2003.

Web Sites

Harriet Beecher Stowe is widely known today for her authorship of *Uncle Tom's Cabin.* For discussion of Stowe and her literary work, see "The American Novel: Harriet Beecher Stowe," Educational Broadcasting Corporation: http://www.pbs.org/wnet/american novel/timeline/stowe.html.

The experience of motherhood in the 1880s and 1890s is detailed at "Late 19th Century America Advice for Women," American Studies Department, University of Virginia, Charlottesville, Virginia: http://xroads.virginia.edu/~MA02/rodriguez/GildedAge/ home.html.

24. "She Bore the Yoke and Wore the Name of Wife": In Praise of Domesticity (1872)

INTRODUCTION

The number of women who worked outside the family home continued to climb in the aftermath of the Civil War. By 1870, women comprised about 15 percent of the nation's workforce. Still, to many Americans, the proper place for women was in the home. One labor union official argued in the late 1860s that there was no need to try to organize women to push for higher wages and better working conditions. This was because the proper sphere for married women, at least, was "to be the presiding deity of the home circle . . . to guide the tottering footsteps of tender infancy." The demands at home were heavy, even though the invisible labor of housekeeping rarely received much public credit. Elizabeth Akers Allen attempted to call attention to the often overlooked role that women played as wives, mothers, and homemakers in her poem "Her Sphere."

KEEP IN MIND AS YOU READ

1. The first public political meeting in the United States dealing with women's rights had met in 1848 at Seneca Falls, New York. In the "Declaration of Sentiments," participants called for the full rights of citizenship for women. These rights included the right to vote and equal access to economic and educational opportunities. The platform became a focus for an increasingly growing and vocal women's rights movement.

2. The idea of women reigning over a domestic sphere gained momentum during the 19th century. Women, due to their supposedly superior capacity to nurture and influence, helped to support American democracy by supplying stability and morality at home. Women might be a force for the national good, through their example of self-sacrifice, moral values, and devotion to family.

Document: "Her Sphere," by Elizabeth Akers Allen

No outward sign her angelhood revealed, / Save that her eyes were wondrous mild and fair,—

The aureole round her forehead was concealed / By the pale glory of her shining hair.

She bore the yoke and wore the name of wife / To one who made her tenderness and grace

A mere convenience of his narrow life, / And put a **seraph** in a servant's place.

She cheered his meager hearth—she blessed and warmed / His poverty, and met its harsh demands

With meek, unvarying patience, and performed / Its menial tasks with stained and battered hands.

She nursed his children through their helpless years,—/ Gave them her strength, her youth, her beauty's prime,—

Bore for them sore privation, toil, and tears, / Which made her old and tired before her time.

And when fierce fever smote him with its blight / Her calm, consoling presence charmed his pain;

Through long and thankless watches, day and night, / Her fluttering fingers cooled his face like rain.

With soft magnetic touch, and murmurs sweet, / She brought him sleep, and stilled his fretful moan,

And taught his flying pulses to repeat / The mild and moderate measure of her own.

She had an artist's quick, perceptive eyes / For all the beautiful; a poet's heart

For every changing phase of earth and skies, / And all things fair in nature and in art.

She looked with all a woman's keen delight / On jewels rich and dainty drapery,

Rare fabrics and soft hues,—the happy right / Of those more favored but less fair than she;

On pallid pearls, which glimmer cool and white, / Dimming proud foreheads with their purity;

On silks which gleam and ripple in the light, / And shift and shimmer like the summer sea;

On gems like drops by sudden sunlight kissed, / When fall the last large brilliants of the rain;

On laces delicate as frozen mist / Embroidering a winter window-pane;—

Yet, near the throng of worldly butterflies, / She dwelt, a chrysalis, in homely brown;

With costliest splendors flaunting in her eyes, / She went her dull way in a gingham gown.

Hedged in by alien hearts, unloved, alone, / With slender shoulders bowed beneath their load,

She trod the path that Fate had made her own, / Nor met one kindred spirit on the road.

Slowly the years rolled onward; and at last, / When the bruised reed was broken, and her soul

Knew its sad term of earthly bondage past, / And felt its nearness to the heavenly goal,

Then a strange gladness filled the tender eyes, / Which gazed afar beyond all grief and sin,

And seemed to see the gates of Paradise / Unclosing for her feet to enter in.

Vainly the master she had served so long / Clasped her worn hands, and, with remorseful tears,

seraph: Angel; or, also, a celestial being.

Cried: "Stay, oh, stay! Forgive my bitter wrong; / Let me atone for all these dreary years!"
Alas for heedless hearts and blinded sense! / With what faint welcome and what meager fare,
What mean subjections and small recompense, / We entertain our angels unaware!

Source: Elizabeth Akers Allen. "Her Sphere." *Scribner's Monthly* 4, no. 2 (June 1872): 218–20. Listed at "The Nineteenth Century in Print: Journals," American Memory Collection, Library of Congress: http://memory.loc.gov/ammem/ndlpcoop/moahtml/snchome.html.

AFTERMATH

Women attempted to expand their sphere in public life, pushing for the right to vote in the aftermath of Seneca Falls. The movement received delay during the sectional crisis and the Civil War. The push for women's suffrage became bumpy when it was more actively resumed during the Reconstruction era. Some supporters argued that the right to vote first needed to be extended to African American men. Other activists claimed that white women, at least, should gain the right to vote before black men and newly arriving immigrants. Supporters of women's right to vote also argued about whether the push should be made through state legislatures, one at a time, or through the federal government. Taking a broader view, Susan B. Anthony and Elizabeth Cady Stanton formed the National Woman Suffrage Association (NWSA) in 1869. Anthony and Stanton were dedicated reformers, having since the prewar era supported abolition and women's rights. The NWSA pushed not only for extending the franchise to women though a Constitutional amendment but also supported a range of other women's issues such as property rights and greater educational and economic opportunities. The NWSA merged with the American Woman Suffrage Association in 1890. The resulting National American Woman Suffrage Association continued to push for the franchise into the early 20th century, when women gained the right to vote under the 19th Amendment.

ASK YOURSELF

1. Is the value of housework still underappreciated today? Is it still an invisible labor?
2. Is the work of parents still sometimes taken for granted today, whether helping with homework or driving to and from doctor's appointments and sports practice?

TOPICS AND ACTIVITIES TO CONSIDER

- Want to compare the push for women's suffrage in the United States to the rest of the world? Check out Jone Johnson Lewis, "Women Suffrage Timeline International-Winning the Vote around the World," About.com: http://womenshistory.about.com/od/suffrage/a/intl_timeline.htm.
- How does housework today compare to the 1880s and 1890s? Find out at Steven Mintz, "Housework in Late 19th Century America," Digital History: http://www.digitalhistory.uh.edu/historyonline/housework.cfm.

Further Reading

Cutter, Barbara. *Domestic Devils, Battlefield Angels: The Radicalism of American Womanhood, 1830–1865*. DeKalb: Northern Illinois University Press, 2003.

Jones, Martha S. *All Bound Up Together: The Woman Question in African American Public Culture, 1830–1900*. Chapel Hill: University of North Carolina Press, 2007.

Scott, Anne Firor and Andrew MacKay Scott. *One Half the People: The Fight for Woman Suffrage*. Philadelphia: Lippincott, 1975.

Silber, Nina. *Gender and the Sectional Conflict*. Chapel Hill: University of North Carolina Press, 2008.

Vacca, Carolyn S. *A Reform Against Nature: Woman Suffrage and the Rethinking of American Citizenship, 1840–1920*. New York: Peter Lang, 2004.

Web Sites

For discussion and interactive features on women's suffrage, visit "Women's Suffrage," Scholastic: http://www.teacher.scholastic.com/activities/suffrage/.

On the lives and careers of Susan B. Anthony and Elizabeth Cady Stanton, see "Not for Ourselves Alone: The Story of Elizabeth Cady Stanton and Susan B. Anthony," a Film by Ken Burns and Paul Barnes, Public Broadcasting System: http://www.pbs.org/stantonanthony/.

25. "Our Household Servants": Article in *The Galaxy* (September 1872)

INTRODUCTION

Many wives in the late 19th century turned to domestic servants for help in keeping house. In part, hiring a servant indicated a level of middle-class status. One had the family resources to look for outside assistance. But some families saw hiring domestic servants as almost a necessity, given the rigors of housework. Cleaning, polishing, and cooking occurred almost nonstop. Add in children to watch after, and many housewives felt nearly overwhelmed. Washing day probably elicited the most groans. Women had to create their own cleaning compounds, haul water for the hand-cranked washing machine (or, still in many homes, a large washing vat), and wring and hang the wet garments and fabrics. Soiled and dirty clothes piled high again by the start of the next work week, and wash day earned sobriquet in many households as "blue Monday." By the early 1870s, about one out of every eight American families had domestic help. The demand seemed insatiable, and more women worked as domestic servants than in any other form of outside employment. The demographics began to shift later in the century, with the advent of new economic and educational opportunities. Fewer and fewer domestic servants were to be found, at least those who willing toiled year after year for the same family. Grace Ellis, a wealthy New Englander, bemoaned the trend in *The Galaxy*.

KEEP IN MIND AS YOU READ

1. Families that hired domestic servants tended to break along geographic and economic lines. Urban families tended to hire outside help more frequently than rural families, while more prosperous families hired more help than less prosperous families (that rarely hired any domestic servants, if ever at all).
2. Spring cleaning was an annual ritual in the American home by the 1870s. Everything, and every nook and cranny, received a thorough going over. Historian Daniel Sutherland declares of spring cleaning, "What horror that phrase held for housekeepers!" Everywhere but in the simplest homes, "spring cleaning meant one or two weeks of upheaval, chaos, and pronounced indigestion."
3. Domestic servants generally lived with the family and were on call nearly around the clock, almost every day of the week.

Document: "Our Household Servants"

There is an odd and pithy old proverb which runs thus, "God sends meat and the Devil sends cooks;" and in these later days of housekeeping this adage comes pointedly to our notice as having at least a grain of truth in it. We must have servants, for, in spite of **Dryden**'s line, "Ere the base laws of servitude began," we know of no condition of the world since the expulsion of Adam and Eve from Paradise where menial labor was not a duty for some one. . . .

In this country our corps of servants is composed at the North of mainly Irish; at the South black servants are the rule. We may add that a few Swedes are being introduced into New England; but housekeeping with a dictionary supplemented by signs may be amusing, but cannot be recommended for comfort. . . . We do not ask for the cringing servility of bygone times; in this modern day it would be disgusting, and in our republican country impossible; but there is great need of honest and skilled labor. Now literally "a man's foes are of his own household," and we look upon an old, tried servant as one of the seven wonders of the age, so rare and exceptional are they. . . .

> **Dryden:** Born in England in 1631, John Dryden achieved great literary fame as a poet. Some of the more famous works by Dryden are "Annus Mirabilis" (1667), a historical poem about an English naval victory over the Dutch and the Great Fire of London, and "The Hind and the Panther" (1687), about Dryden's conversion to Roman Catholicism. Dryden died in 1700 and received burial in Westminster Abbey.

There must always be people willing, able, and suited to be hewers of wood and drawers of water, or to do what is equivalent to those duties in a modern household. Unfortunately there still exists the demand for such a class; but the tendency of civilization, culture, and education, though good and beautiful, is to advance and elevate so much that we are in danger of being left without any class of persons whose intellect and capacity render them efficient in the humbler duties of life. We would not for an instant decry or depreciate the education and elevation of mankind, but it is evident that nothing which unsettles and disturbs the material for a good servant, and makes him or her an inferior craftsman or poor domestic, can truly improve the happiness or welfare of the community or household.

Source: Grace A. Ellis. "Our Household Servants." *The Galaxy* 14, no. 3 (September 1872): 349–55. Listed at "The Nineteenth Century in Print: Periodicals," American Memory Collection, Library of Congress: http://memory.loc.gov/ammem/ndlpcoop/moahtml/snchome.html.

AFTERMATH

The days of devoted domestic servants were on the wane by the late 19th century, despite Ellis's hope otherwise. Many women looked for employment elsewhere, because of the long hours, drudgery, and tedium associated with domestic work. If long work weeks and little excitement were not enough to doom taking a job as a household servant, many women recoiled from the low status associated with the position. LOUISA MAY ALCOTT was a popular novelist of the day, especially for her publication of *Little Women* in the late 1860s. Alcott details some of the indignities suffered by domestic help in *Work: A Story of Experience,* published in 1873. The youthful and bright Christie Devon is the heroine of the novel. Devon wins a position as a domestic servant, and she initially enjoys the experience. Devon "loved luxury, and was sensible enough to see the value and comforts of her situation, and to wonder why more girls placed as she was did not choose a life like this rather than the confinements of the sewing-room, or the fatigue and publicity of a shop." Devon soon changes her mind. "She did not learn to love her mistress," Alcott explains, "because Mrs. Stuart evidently considered herself as one belonging to a superior race of beings, and had no desire to establish any of the friendly relations that may become so helpful and pleasant to both mistress and maid. She made a royal progress through her dominions every morning, issued orders, found fault liberally, bestowed praise sparingly, and took no more personal interest in her servants than if they were clocks, to be wound up once a day, and sent away the moment they got out of repair." Many native-born white women identified with Devon. By 1900 black women and immigrant women dominated the ranks of domestic servants, in terms of percentage of the total. The overall numbers of domestic servants began to steadily decline in the early 20th century due to the increasing number of labor-saving household technologies coming onto the market.

ASK YOURSELF

1. Ellis criticizes universal education in the United States for planting ambition in people otherwise destined for "humbler duties." Should all Americans have the opportunity to attend college, if they desire to go?
2. Some scholars suggest that the advent of new household technologies has made domestic work more demanding, if more efficient. For example, the vacuum cleaner became widespread by the early and mid-20th century. Individuals might now thoroughly clean their rugs and carpets, but outside visitors now expect to see freshly vacuumed carpets, thereby not saving the household much, if any, time. Is this a fair assessment of the interaction between technology and housework?

TOPICS AND ACTIVITIES TO CONSIDER

- ❧ How does working as a domestic servant in the United States compare to in England? Find out at Wayne Schmidt, "Victorian Domestic Servant Hierarchy and Wage Scale": http://www.waynesthisandthat.com/servantwages.htm.
- ❧ Will low-paying jobs always find takers, similar to domestic servants in the 1860s and 1870s? Read more at Barbara Hagenbaugh and Barbara Hansen, "Low-wage jobs rise at faster pace," *USA Today*: http://www.usatoday.com/money/economy/employment/2004–06–29-jobs_x.htm.

LITTLE WOMEN

A novel written by Louisa May Alcott and one of the more widely known pieces of 19th-century literature. Published in two parts in 1868 and 1869, the book is based loosely on the childhood experiences of Alcott and her three sisters. Meg, Jo, Beth, and Amy, the fictional sisters, each struggle to overcome different character flaws. Meg is vain, Jo (the character based on Alcott) is high strung, Beth is shy, and Amy is selfish. The novel has many heart-warming scenes, such as the girls receiving oranges for Christmas (no small wonder in Massachusetts during the 1860s) and the father returning home from the Union army. But Alcott also deals with the restrictions confronting young women at the time, such as few opportunities for higher learning and peer and family pressure to find a husband. *Little Women* has appeared as a play, a musical, and an opera. The novel also appeared several times in film, most recently in 1994 (starring Susan Sarandon, Winona Ryder, Kirsten Dunst, and Christian Bale).

Further Reading

O'Leary, Elizabeth L. *At Beck and Call: The Representation of Domestic Servants in Nineteenth-Century American Painting*. Washington, DC: Smithsonian Institution Press, 1996.

Sutherland, Daniel E. *Americans and Their Servants: Domestic Service in the United States from 1800 to 1920*. Baton Rouge: Louisiana State University Press, 1981.

Web Sites

Explore women's work from the Colonial era through the Industrial Revolution at "A Woman's Work Is Never Done," American Antiquarian Society, Worcester, Massachusetts: http://www.americanantiquarian.org/Exhibitions/Womanswork/.

Find out more about Louisa May Alcott and her times at "Louisa May Alcott's Orchard House: Home of 'Little Women,'" Louisa May Alcott Memorial Association, Concord, Massachusetts: http://www.louisamayalcott.org.

MATERIAL LIFE

26. "... The Air of Substantialness": A Plan for Home Ownership (1866)

INTRODUCTION

Many Americans living in the late 19th century dreamed about owning their own home, just as they do today. No national figures on home ownership exist prior to 1890, when about 50 percent of Americans owned the home they lived in (by 2007, the figure had risen to about 70 percent). Perhaps a greater percentage of Americans owned their house during the Reconstruction era than later in the century, when a massive influx of poor European immigrants likely pulled down the figures. Finances proved a key issue in making the switch from renting to owning. The average income for a lower to middle class family during the 1870s ranged between $750 and $2,000 per year. Over the same years, the average price for a house was slightly under $5,000. J. W. Perkins, a columnist for *Harper's Magazine,* argued that newlyweds might as easily afford a mortgage as a rent. The stakes went beyond mere dollars and cents. If a husband and wife did not early on make the move to home ownership, they might never establish a stable domestic life. Only married couples possessing the "liveliest imagination conceivable" might find anything even remotely acceptable about raising a family and growing old "within the walls of a boarding-house." In the excerpt below, Perkins establishes a plan for a mid-level clerk to become a homeowner.

KEEP IN MIND AS YOU READ

1. Home owners during the late 19th century paid interest on their home loans, often at a higher rate than Americans pay today. Perkins, the author of the article on paying for a new home, calculated a $2,500 loan with 7 percent interest. By comparison, interest rates today might range as low as 5 percent. However, Perkins estimated a five-year loan. Mortgages today might take upward of 30 years to pay off.

2. Literature on building a home became increasingly popular during the late 19th century. Floor plans and house patterns appeared in books and magazines. The cost and style ranged widely, from a few hundred dollars to tens of thousands of dollars.

3. Home ownership remained only a dream for many Americans. In the South, sharecroppers often lived in small, drafty, one-room structures. In cities, unskilled laborers often came home to poorly ventilated and overcrowded tenement buildings. On the treeless prairies of the West, settlers constructed their houses of sod.

Document: *"Cost of a Home,"* Harper's New Monthly Magazine *(October 1866)*

Giving our observations a direct application, let us assume $2,000 to be the income of a man desirous of enjoying life in the true sense of the word, and let us likewise suppose him, through rigid economy, to have laid up that amount during the eighteen months previous to his marriage. He will then desire to invest his money in a manner calculated to render him, in time, independent of the precarious condition of house-holders in general, to say nothing of the *unproductive* demands which are annually made upon his income in the form of house rent. The possession of even a modest building site in a city gives a man the air of substantialness that justly belongs to the owner of real estate; and possessing a lot in a respectable neighborhood, free from all liabilities, the proprietor will experience no difficulty in finding persons willing to advance $2,500 on a mortgage upon the lot and upon the house which is to be built. Along some of the **car routes** of Brooklyn, within an hour's ride of the city of New York, lots of 25 x 100 feet can be purchased for the cash price of $500 per lot; and granting the house owner to spend $1,500 on furniture (such as is denominated "cottage furniture"), the following statement would be an exhibit of the outlay of his $2,000 and of the money raised for building purposes:

> **car routes:** Horse-drawn trolley cars served as a major source of transportation in many eastern cities. Carrying between 30 and 40 passengers, trolley cars traveled along steel rails and made possible the outward expansion of cities. By the 1870s, New York City, the focus of Perkins's article, boasted a fleet of 800 trolley cars, pulled by nearly 8,000 horses.

Cash paid for building lot $500
   "   "   " furniture 1500
Mortgage on house and lot for 5 years, renewable for 3 years 2500

This statement shows the entire property to be worth $1,500 more than the mortgage calls for, should the furniture be included; and inasmuch as $400 per annum is regarded as a rent so low that many persons are anxious to take a lease for a considerable number of years upon a dwelling at this figure, it is most reasonable to apply the same amount toward the canceling of the mortgage suggested—which, indeed, can be very nearly accomplished within the time above specified.

Source: J. W. Perkins. "Cost of a Home." *Harper's New Monthly Magazine* 33, no. 197 (October 1866): 661–64. Listed at "The Nineteenth Century in Print: Periodicals," American Memory Collection, Library of Congress: http://memory.loc.gov/ammem/ndlpcoop/moahtml/snchome.html.

AFTERMATH

For those many Americans planning to build their own home, the widespread adoption of balloon-frame construction helped to make the process much less expensive. The balloon frame had originated in the Midwest during the 1830s but became popular nationally only after the end of the Civil War. The balloon frame substituted inexpensive, light-weight nailed wooden frames and panels for the more substantial, hand-pegged timber, brick, and masonry construction used in higher quality houses. Mail-order companies delivered pre-cut materials to the owner's lot for substantially less than the cost of buying a finished home. Once the structure was completed, home owners often added distinctive touches. Brown, gray, green, and other dark colored paints were popular. Gingerbread scrollwork, either carved from wood or cut from tin, was also commonly used to decorate rooftops and porches.

ASK YOURSELF

1. Does home ownership convey domestic stability and public stature, as Perkins suggests? Why or why not?
2. Perkins claims that home owners might live outside their city of employment, where property rates are cheaper. How long might you be willing to commute each way to buy a bigger house or more property? Thirty minutes? Two hours?

TOPICS AND ACTIVITIES TO CONSIDER

- ☙ Americans today seem less sure of Perkins's financial advice, and debate whether it is better to buy a house or to rent a house. Compare how mortgage rates, down payments, and other factors all affect the answer at "Is It Better to Buy or Rent?" *New York Times*, June 2, 2008: http://www.nytimes.com/interactive/business/buy-rent-calculator.html.
- ☙ How does the middle-class home envisioned by Perkins compare to living conditions in Five Points, a rough-and-tumble immigrant neighborhood in New York? Explore life in Five Points during the 19th century at Rebecca Yamin, "The Five Points Site: Archaeologists and Historians Rediscover a Famous Nineteenth-Century New York Neighborhood," U.S. General Services Administration Public Building Service, New York: http://r2.gsa.gov/fivept/fphome.htm.

HOME OWNERSHIP AND THE MAIL

Home ownership also facilitated the receipt of mail, with street addresses and numbers becoming increasingly common by the early 1870s. Fifty-one cities also had instituted free carrier service, saving the letter recipient a trip to the post office. Letter writers who wanted to send mail across the country turned to the Railway Mail Service, instituted in 1869. Postal employees dug through stacks of mail as their specially designed cars rolled along. Letters had to be ready for drop off as each city was reached, and postal workers boasted that they sorted 600 pieces of mail every hour. Standard postage during the Reconstruction era ran three cents. For those with less to say, or who might be traveling, postcards first appeared in the United States in 1873.

Further Reading

Clark, Clifford Edward, Jr. *The American Family Home, 1800–1960*. Chapel Hill: University of North Carolina Press, 1986.

Handlin, David P. *American Architecture*. 2nd ed. London: Thames and Hudson, 2004.

Handlin, David P. *The American Home: Architecture and Society, 1815–1915*. Boston: Little, Brown, 1979.

Smeins, Linda E. *Building an American Identity: Pattern Book Homes and Communities, 1870–1900*. Walnut Creek, CA: AltaMira Press, 1999.

Web Sites

"A Digital Archive of American Architecture," Jeffery Howe, Fine Arts Department, Boston College: http://www.bc.edu/bc_org/avp/cas/fnart/fa267/2ndempire.html.

For a history of construction on the Capitol Building during the Civil War era, see "U.S. Capitol Virtual Tour: A 'Capitol' Experience": http://www.senate.gov.vtour/.

27. "Home to Thanksgiving": A Currier and Ives Lithograph (1867)

INTRODUCTION

LITHOGRAPHS proved popular in decorating new homes, especially those produced by Currier and Ives. Families often decorated their front parlors and dining rooms with artwork, but the habit was expensive through the mid-19th century. Color prints might run between $5 and $15, a relatively hefty sum. Prices dropped dramatically during the 1850s, when NATHANIEL CURRIER and JAMES IVES began to produce black-and-white lithographs for only a few pennies and hand colored lithographs for only a few dollars. Concentrated production was the key to turning out the inexpensive prints. Based on Spruce Street in New York, Currier and Ives put under the same roof printing presses, artists, and lithographers. The Currier and Ives building also boasted a coloring department. Staffed by young women, many of them immigrants, the coloring department required members to add a single color to a designated spot on each print. The print was passed to the next young woman, who was responsible for adding her color. A touch up artist stood at the end of the line, checking each print for quality. Business boomed. By the 1870s, Currier and Ives printed catalogues advertising nearly 3,000 print titles. Subjects ranged from historical portraits and home scenes to natural landscapes and ships and trains. "Home to Thanksgiving" was a popular print available in both black and white and in color. A man welcomed at the front door by parents and family amid a backdrop of well-tended farm buildings and animals creates an idealized image of American home life. Even the snow, seemingly newly fallen and pristine, adds to the emotional warmth of the scene.

KEEP IN MIND AS YOU READ

1. Currier and Ives sent out a handful of prints to contract artists. The going rate generally was one penny for each small image painted and eight cents for each large image painted.
2. Prints from Currier and Ives received approval from CATHARINE BEECHER and HARRIET BEECHER STOWE, the popular domestic advice writers of the day. Beecher

and Stowe appreciated the wide range of subject matter that Currier and Ives printed. This was because artwork should reflect the interests of the family and "not the tyrannical dicta of some art critic or neighbor." Today, a similar level of endorsement to that offered by Beecher and Stowe might occur if Martha Stewart or Oprah Winfrey praised a line of home furnishings.

Document: *"Home to Thanksgiving"*

"Home to Thanksgiving."

Source: "Home to Thanksgiving," LC-DIG-pga-00780, Library of Congress, Prints and Photographs Division, Washington, DC.: http://loc.gov/pictures/resource/pga.00780/.

AFTERMATH

Advances in the printing of images during the late 19th century eventually helped to shift public demand away from lithography. Nathanial Currier and James Ives also had begun to slow down physically, with Currier dying in 1888 and Ives dying seven years later. Their company survived only a few years longer and finally shut its doors in 1907. The company had achieved enormous success. During its 50-year history, Currier and Ives had produced 7,500 titles and printed 1 million copies. The company's influence on American culture remains through today. In "Sleigh Ride," a seasonally popular orchestra piece (by Leroy Anderson), runs the lyric (by Mitchell Parish) that a party at a farm will "nearly be like a picture print by Currier and Ives."

ASK YOURSELF

1. How do decorations in your room reflect your tastes? How do decorations in public spaces reflect the values of the community?
2. Does art lose its value when it is mass produced? Meaning, do frequently seen images lose some of their inspiration as they become commonplace?

TOPICS AND ACTIVITIES TO CONSIDER

- Many 19th-century Americans expected some display of art in middle-class homes. What rights should today's college students have to display material in their residence halls? Find out at least one answer in Bryan Painter's article, "In Oklahoma College Dorms, Signs of Free Speech," *NewsOK*, October 17, 2008: http://newsok.com/in-oklahoma-college-dorms-signs-of-free-speech/article/3312263.
- How do ideas for home decoration in the 19th century compare to decorating ideas today? Find current design trends and styles at the Home and Garden Network Web site: http://www.hgtv.com.

ROGERS GROUP OF STATUARY

Small groups of inexpensive statuary also were popular in decorating American home interiors, and those crafted by John Rogers were the most popular. Born in 1829, Rogers worked a variety of jobs before going to Europe for artistic training. Returning to the United States on the eve of the Civil War, Rogers gained national attention for "Slave Auction," "Picket Guard," and "Union Refugees." Rogers followed with statuettes that emphasized daily life and pleasures, including sports, school, and children. "Weighing the Baby," depicting a newborn put on the scales for perhaps the first time, was one of Rogers's more well-known creations. A popular anecdote later ran that a man down on his luck told a kindly benefactress, "You can realize how poor we were, ma'am, when I tell you that my parents could never afford to buy Rogers's 'Weighing the Baby.'" By the time Rogers died in 1904, his 86 statuary groups had sold tens of thousands of copies. Rogers's work studio in New Canaan, Connecticut, is now a museum open to the public.

Further Reading

LeBeau, Bryan F. *Currier and Ives: America Imagined.* Washington, DC: Smithsonian Institution Press, 2001.

Leopold, Allison Kyle. *Victorian Splendor: Re-Creating America's 19th Century Interiors.* New York: Stewart, Tabori and Chang, 1986.

Peterson, Harold L. *Americans at Home: From the Colonists to the Late Victorians.* New York: Scribner, 1971.

Winkler, Gail Caskey and Roger W. Moss. *Victorian Interior Decoration: American Interiors, 1830–1900.* New York: Henry Holt, 1986.

Web Sites

Learn more about Currier and Ives and see many of the shop's prints at "Currier and Ives," The Currier and Ives Foundation: http://www.currierandives.com.

Visit the studio where John Rogers worked at "Rogers Studio," New Canaan Historical Society, New Canaan Connecticut: http://www.nchistory.org/rogers_studio.html.

28. Improving Mealtime: Recipes from *The National Cook Book* (1866)

INTRODUCTION

Mealtime in the United States gave many late-19th-century observers a shudder. In part, table manners were often nonexistent. Americans seemingly could not take their mind from work, chores, and school. They hurried through dinner and supper, generally served at 12 noon and 6 o'clock. Slurping and gulping allowed little opportunity for conversation. One social critic bemoaned in 1872 that some meals passed with barely a word spoken, serving as a poor example for future generations. Mealtime also gave many observers pause because the food was poorly prepared. CATHARINE BEECHER, the domestic advice writer widely followed during the late 19th century, scoffed that even though American tables often were abundantly filled, the food "has been so spoiled in the treatment that there is really nothing to eat! Green biscuits with acrid spots of alkali; sour yeast-bread; meat slowly simmered in fat till it seemed like grease itself, and slowly congealing in cold grease; and above all, that unpardonable enormity, strong butter! How one longs to show people what might have been done with the raw material out of which all these monstrosities were concocted!" Hannah Peterson sought to change American culinary skills in *The National Cook Book*. First published in 1850, Peterson's work was republished 16 years later. Peterson came from a family that had gained fame for, according to Robert Peterson, Hannah's husband's "skill in all that pertained to the Culinary art." Bettering the food served at mealtime was only one of the goals of the book. Conversation and companionship might increase if dinner and supper became more leisurely affairs, to the benefit of manners and culture. These instructions detail picking the freshest meats and vegetables, and preparing boiled ham and potatoes (both widely popular dishes).

KEEP IN MIND AS YOU READ

1. The need to obtain water for cooking, drinking, and cleaning was one of the great inconveniences of domestic life. Indoor plumbing was not yet widely available outside of cities, and households in towns and villages had to rely on wells and pumps. Every drop of water needed had to be hauled in a bucket, while dirty water had to be carried back out.

2. Canned foods were becoming commonplace during the 1860s. Fruits, vegetables, milk, jams and jellies, and other perishables all sold on the market. Gilbert Van Camp won an army supply contract during the Civil War and soon became famous for his canned beans. By 1870, Americans bought 30 million canned goods (up from only five million canned goods in 1860).

3. Canned goods might be purchased at Atlantic and Pacific Tea Company, the first chain grocery store in the United States. Established in 1864 and based in New York, Atlantic and Pacific Tea Company opened over 100 stores across the country over the next 15 years. Jones Brothers Tea Company, which opened in Brooklyn in 1872, was the nation's second chain grocery store. The operation soon became known as Grand Union Company and still is in business today.

Document: Recipes from The National Cook Book *by Hannah Mary Bouvier Peterson*

Meats

The finest grained **beef** is the best, the flesh is of a fine red, and the fat a light cream color, but not yellow; the fat, too, is solid and firm. The lean of mutton should be of a red color, and the fat white. The skin of pork should be of a light color, and if young it is tender. The fat should appear firm. A tender goose is known by taking hold of the wing and raising it; if the skin tears easily, the goose is tender, or if you can readily insert the head of a pin into the flesh, it is young. The same remarks will hold good with regard to ducks. Young chickens may be known by pressing the lower end of the breast bone; if it yields readily to the pressure they are not old, for in all animals the bones are cartilaginous when young. The breast should be broad and plump in all kinds of poultry, the feet pliable, and the toes easily broken when bent back.

beef: Americans had much more intimate contact with their food in the late 19th century, as Peterson's discussion of selecting fresh cuts of meat suggests. Late 19th-century shoppers handled freshly cut pieces of beef and lamb and recently slaughtered pigs and chickens. Cut and packaged pieces of meat that are widespread in supermarkets today were unknown during the Civil War and Reconstruction era.

flavor: Nutritionists today point out that not only do raw vegetables lose their flavor over many days, they also lose much of their nutritional content.

Boiled Ham

Wash and scrape your ham; if it is not very salty it need not be soaked; if old and dry, let it soak twelve hours in lukewarm water, which should be changed several times. Put in a large vessel filled with cold water. Let it simmer, but be careful not to let it boil, as it hardens and toughens the meat. Allow twenty minutes to cook each pound of meat.

When it is done, take it out of the water, strip off the skin, and serve it. Twist scalloped paper round the shank, or ornament it with sprigs of green parsley neatly twisted round it. If it is not to be eaten whilst hot, as soon as it is taken from the pot, set it away to get cold, then skin it, by which means you preserve all the juices of the meat. It may be garnished as above, or, if you choose, you may glaze it; the recipe for which see under its proper head.

Vegetables

All vegetables are better freshly gathered, when left to stand long, they lose much of their **flavor**. Late in the season, when turnips, parsnips, carrots, &c., begin to lose their sweetness, they may be greatly improved by adding a tea spoonful or two of sugar to the water they are boiled in.

Boiled Potatoes

Select the potatoes as nearly as possible of the same size. Wash and boil with the skins on.

Throw a little salt in the water. When they are soft, peel them and send them to the table hot. Or they may be mashed with butter, salt to taste, and milk or cream in proportion of an ounce of butter and half a gill of milk or cream to ten potatoes. They should be sent to the table immediately, as they spoil if they stand after they are done.

Put them over the fire, in cold water, or they will be likely to burst before they are cooked.

Source: Hannah Mary Bouvier Peterson, *The National Cook Book.* Philadelphia: T. B. Peterson and Brothers, 1866. Listed at "Making of America," University of Michigan Library, Ann Arbor, Michigan: http://name.umdl.umich.edu/AEK7304.0001.001.

AFTERMATH

The American diet remained too centered around meat dishes, often fried in lard before served. Catharine Beecher argued that Americans should reduce their intake of chicken, pork, beef, and veal to just one meal a day. The result would be the lessoning of "fevers, eruptions, headaches, bilious attacks, and the many other ailments which are produced or aggravated by too gross a diet." Beecher fought an uphill battle. Americans continued to eat meat at nearly every meal. Peterson acknowledged as much in her cook book, devoting forty pages to cooking and preparing meats. This was more than twice the page length given to chapters on fish, vegetables, breads, and desserts. Modern-day health experts often wage the same battle as Beecher. To avoid a range of health-related issues from a diet high in fat and calories, the Surgeon General recommends that Americans consume no more than five ounces of red meat per week.

ASK YOURSELF

1. How does food preparation and handling differ today than from how it was described by Peterson? Do at-home cooks still have to worry about skinning ham

COFFEE

Mid-19th-century Americans enjoyed coffee as much as their descendants do today. The Union had a ready supply to the beverage, with the beans imported from overseas. Soldiers usually received ground beans as a part of their daily rations. The men boiled water in a tin can, or any other container at hand, before mixing in the beans. Sugar and milk sometimes were added, but most often soldiers drank their coffee black. Coffee became increasingly rare in the Confederacy, as the Union blockade tightened. Caffeine-deprived soldiers and civilians sometimes turned to roasted and ground corn kernels, but never to the same results. Given a chance to trade with their Union counterparts, Confederate soldiers eagerly swapped tobacco for coffee. In the postwar era, several coffee companies that are well known today began operations. In 1874, Caleb Chase and James Sanborn partnered to form Chase and Sanborn. On the West Coast, 14-year-old Jim Folger entered the coffee business in 1850. After several false starts and a bankruptcy, Folger was thriving in the coffee business 25 years later.

they have cooked and bursting potatoes they are boiling? Do they still worry about the visual presentation of a meal, by adding parsley to the serving plate?

2. What are some foods that you eat that help to define your family, your community, and your region?

TOPICS AND ACTIVITIES TO CONSIDER

- ❧ How does diet and food preparation in the Civil War and Reconstruction era compare to other historical eras? To other cultures? Explore the answers at "The History of Food and . . . ?", International Guild of Hospitality and Restaurant Managers: http://www.hospitalityguild.com/History/history_of_food10.htm.
- ❧ How do cookbooks reflect the historical eras in which they are published? Read descriptions of important cookbooks, as well as of foodstuffs, in American and world history, at Lynn Olver, "The Food Timeline," International Association of Culinary Professionals: http://www.foodtimeline.org.

Further Reading

Grover, Kathryn, ed. *Dining in America, 1850–1900*. Amherst: University of Massachusetts Press, 1987.

Jones, Evan. *American Food: The Gastronomic Story*. Woodstock, NY: Overlook Press, 1990.

Kiple, Kenneth F., and Kriemhild Conee Ornelas. *The Cambridge World History of Food*. New York: Cambridge University Press, 2000.

Mariani, John F. *The Dictionary of American Food and Drink*. New York: Hearst Books, 1994.

Williams, Susan. *Food in the United States, 1820s–1890*. Westport, CT: Greenwood Press, 2006.

Web Sites

Food History News maintains a Web site with links to historic recipes and museums that explore the history of food and drink. The address is: http://www.foodhistorynews.com.

For information on American cookbooks, visit "Feeding America: The Historic American Cookbook Project," The Michigan State University Library: http://digital.lib.msu.edu/projects/cookbooks/.

29. Women's Fashion in an Advertising Lithograph (1869)

INTRODUCTION

Late-19th-century Americans found the world of fashion captivating. They poured over fashion plates that had become standard features in popular women's magazines like *Harper's Bazaar* and *Godey's Lady's Book*. Many of these images highlighted the latest designs from Paris. The French capital city had become a center of women's fashion by the 1850s, with the emergence of many internationally known designers. Some social critics grumbled that American women spent too much money chasing after the latest European styles. More commentators praised the new fashion look. Gone were the days of hoops and crinoline petticoats, which had combined to hold skirts into a fashionable shape. By the 1870s, women instead opted for the bustle. Generally made from wire, bustles swept dress fabric out in the rear. The new fashion lines drew the eye backward, from the bust to the rear. A corset that clinched in the waist by several inches only accentuated the look. The women in this 1869 advertisement for soap are wearing bustled dresses (then—as now—advertisements often featured the latest styles, in hopes of making the product look more chic). Commentators at the time raved that the form-clinging lines of the bustle were "charming" and "elegant." These descriptions might today read as "sexy" and "revealing." Modern-day fashion historians agree, with one well-known scholar declaring the bustle style the "most erotic" look of the 19th century.

KEEP IN MIND AS YOU READ

1. Women might wear high heels with the bustle look, the better to accentuate their body shape. Otherwise, men and women generally wore high-topped shoes with leather soles. Shoes by the 1870s usually buttoned on the side, but laces were becoming more common. Footwear also increasingly came in left and right shoes, rather than the uniform cut prevalent before the Civil War.
2. The waterfall hairstyle was popular in the 1870s. Women swept their hair up on top of the head, and let it flow over the back.
3. Corsets helped to mold women's bodies to fit the bustle style. The corset covered much of the upper torso, and either laced or buttoned, depending on the style, from the front. The tight-fitting corset pushed up at the bust and in at the waist. Some critics charged that the corset caused long-term health issues for women,

including deformation of the rib cage and internal organs. The corset remained widely worn into the early 20th century. The design is still sometimes worn or tailored into dress tops.

Document: Advertising Lithograph for Dobbins' Medicated Toilet Soap

"Dobbins' Medicated Toilet Soap."

Source: "Dobbins' Medicated Toilet Soap," LC-DIG-ppmsca-08126, Library of Congress, Prints and Photographs Division, Washington, DC.: http://www.loc.gov/pictures/item/99472760/.

AFTERMATH

Change came more slowly to men's fashion. Most styles continued to originate from England—a reflection of the influence of the British Empire and its entrepreneurs—as they had since the 18th century. Men still wore hats while in public, but broad-brimmed slouch hats and sporty-looking derby hats increasingly replaced top hats. Suit coats, usually cut from wool, increasingly were squared off at the bottom (rather than tapered). The so-called box coat came in a range of colors and, often, sported understated stripes and checks. Pants usually were fairly baggy, and held up by suspenders. Cowboys and miners along the western frontier, however, often opted for Levi Strauss's copper-riveted denim trousers. Originally offered only in brown, denim pants increasingly appeared in blue (the beginning of the uniquely American blue jean). East or west, a clean-shaven man was rare in the 1870s. Instead, facial hair ranged from handle-bar mustaches to lamb-chop sideburns and full beards. This was not because men did not like to shave; rather, according to the thinking of the day, facial hair very visibly indicated a certain level of vitality and energy.

ASK YOURSELF

1. Do you think the full-bustle style is an attractive look? Why or why not?
2. What do your favorite outfits and accessories say about you? What do they say about American culture in the early 21st century?

TOPICS AND ACTIVITIES TO CONSIDER

- Fashion sometimes enters into the classroom, leading to a debate about whether grade schools and high schools should require uniforms. What are the arguments made? Find out more detail on the topic at "Pros and Cons of School Uniforms," Articlesbase.com: http://www.articlesbase.com/advice-articles/pros-and-cons-of-school-uniforms-182.html.

THE CURVES WERE IN!

For women, a weightier look became more common in the late 19th century. A voluptuous figure was the ideal, with large bust and hips. The move toward fleshiness was in contrast to the style earlier in the century, when a small and thin body shape was the desired image. Several theories exist to why the change in women's images occurred, including a worry that women were becoming too skinny to withstand the rigors of pregnancy. Another widely accepted theory is that the more weight a woman carried, the more she conveyed a level of economic prosperity and material comfort. The thinking ran that weightier women had more food to eat, as well as many servants to help with domestic work. A fleshier body frame also played into the full-bustle style by putting more curve into the bosom and the bottom. The full-figured look remained popular until near the end of the 1800s.

  ∽ Celebrities garner much national attention, from what they wear to what they eat. Is this good? Read more at "Are Hollywood's Bad Girls a Bad Influence on Teens?" *Good Morning America*, December 12, 2006: http://abcnews.go.com/GMA/story?id=2718991&page=1.

Further Reading

Corson, Richard. *Fashions in Makeup from Ancient to Modern Times*. New York: Universe Books, 1972.

Gorsline, Douglas. *What People Wore: A Visual History of Dress from Ancient Times to Twentieth-Century America*. New York: Bonanza Books, 1952.

Perrot, Philippe. *Fashioning the Bourgeoisie: A History of Clothing in the Nineteenth Century*. Princeton, NJ: Princeton University Press, 1994.

Setnik, Linda. *Victorian Costume for Ladies, 1860–1900*. Atglen, PA: Schiffer, 2000.

Summers, Leigh. *Bound to Please: A History of the Victorian Corset*. New York: Berg, 2001.

Wilcox, R. Turner. *Five Centuries of American Costume*. New York: Scribner, 1963.

Web Sites

See images of several thousands of costumes and accessories from across the world at "Works of Art," The Costume Institute, The Metropolitan Museum of Art, New York: http://www.metmuseum.org/works_of_art/department.asp?dep=8.

For a current look into the world of style, visit the Web site of "What Not to Wear," the popular television series on The Learning Channel, at: http://tlc.discovery.com/fansites/whatnottowear/whatnottowear.html.

30. Consumerism Benefits from the "Dailies": A Newspaper Advertisement for Household Goods (1874)

INTRODUCTION

Daily newspapers listed many of the material goods for sale by the late 19th century, a result of their increase in both numbers and circulation. The dailies boomed in number after the invention of the Hoe rotary press during the 1840s. Named after Richard Hoe, a manufacturer of printing equipment in New York, the Hoe rotary press utilized a revolving cylinder to print onto a continuous roll of paper. The result was a dramatic decrease in the time and cost to print newspaper sheets. Publishers took full advantage of Hoe's invention and, between 1840 and 1860, the number of daily newspapers had increased from 138 to 372. Newspapers also proved a sought-after medium for advertisers because they boasted a high circulation. Newspaper readership ran to several million by the early 1860s, their highest total to date. Many readers lived in northern cities, where the penny press scored high subscription levels. The penny press sold at one and two cents a copy, down from the generally set price at six cents a copy. Pictured here is a newspaper advertisement for stoves and other household goods that ran in northern Virginia in 1874.

KEEP IN MIND AS YOU READ

1. Newspapers increasingly fell into the practice of "buyer beware" by the early 1870s. Sellers of patent medicines were the worst abusers, making outrageous claims for their products. The makers of Warner's Safe Kidney and Liver Cure touted that, through the regular use of their medicine, "Bright's Disease, in its worst form, is curable." The makers of St. Jacob's Oil claimed that their product was the "most wonderful pain relieving and healing remedy ever discovered." A single bottle "cures rheumatism, cures neuralgia, cures pain, soreness and stiffness, heals cuts and sores." The claims were outrageous but, without any government oversight, makers and distributors of medicine might claim what they wanted.
2. Magazines began to rival newspapers as the leading advertising medium in the United States following the end of the Civil War. By 1880, there were 2,400 magazines in publication. The total was a three-fold increase from only 15 years earlier. Many of these magazines circulated nationally, giving advertisers a far greater reach than was available in newspapers.

Document: "Stoves! Stoves!" Culpepper (Virginia) Times, 1874

STOVES! STOVES!
OVER 100 AND 30 STOVES
—TO BE—
SOLD LOW FOR CASH!

Now is Your Chance. Call Early and Secure Bargains. A Carload Just Received. The Largest Stock ever Seen in Culpeper, which we are Determined to Sell as Low as they can be Bought anywhere for Cash. Our line of

COOK AND HEATING STOVES

Are so well known throughout the country as not to need comment.

THE "FARMER GIRL" COOK—the Best Constructed Stove in the country—is still in the Lead, giving entire Satisfaction, and selling more rapidly than any other.

"OUR FRIEND" follows in close pursuit, giving universal satisfaction as an Excellent Baker. Next comes the

"JUBILEE COOK," with the late improvements, and acknowledged to be the Neatest and Cheapest Stove in the market.

We could name a number of others we have on hand but for the want of space.

To enumerate the different kinds of Heating Stoves and Grates we have in stock, would require too much time. Suffice it to say we have a large supply of the latest improved, for wood and coal.

Note specially that our Immense Stock of Stoves, Grates, &c., will be sold as LOW as the LOWEST for cash. Prices ranging from $2.50 to $50.00. All can be suited in price and style. Now is the time to buy.

Our stock of the following goods cannot be excelled—such as Fancy Toilet Sets, assortment of Granite Iron Ware, Brass Kettles, Porcelain Kettles and Sauce Pans, Parlor Sets, Muffin Bakers, Coal and Guano Sieves, Extra Heavy Dish Pans, Milk Pans, Retinned Wash Basins, Pat'd Oil Cans, Tea Trays, &c. Also a large supply of Sheet Iron Pans, the "Acme" Fry Pans, Wire Clothes Lines, Best Stove Polish, Basting Spoons, Wire Dish Covers and a great many other articles that we will be glad to show you if you favor us with a call. Remember, these Goods we offer LOW FOR CASH.

OUR SPECIALTIES.

A very heavy supply of Stove Repairs, Sorghum Evaporators made to order, Apple Butter Kettles—Copper, Cast Iron Kettles, Roofing, Gutter, Lightning Rods.

GUN AND LOCK SMITHING executed in the best style at short notice.

☞Your Orders solicited which shall have prompt attention. With many thanks to the public for their liberal patronage in the past we promise to do all we can to merit a continuance of the same. Very Respectfully,

P. L. THOMAS, Culpeper, Va.

Printed at the Office of the "Culpeper Times."

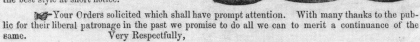

"Stoves! Stoves!"

Source: Emergence of Advertising in America, 1850–1920, Broadsides (1840–1921), B0391, Emergence of Advertising On-Line Project, Duke University Rare Book, Manuscript, and Special Collections Libraries: http://library.duke.edu/digitalcollections/eaa.

AFTERMATH

Newspaper advertisements became more innovate in the 1860s and 1870s, under the leadership of ROBERT BONNER and JAMES GORDON BENNETT JR. Bonner, the editor of *The New York Ledger,* was the first to use eye-catching advertisements. Prior to the Civil War, newspaper editors almost all had printed advertisements in five-and-one-half-point agate type (about the size of today's stock market quotations). The agate rule supposedly marketed each product on its own merits. A former newspaper printer and proofreader, Bonner saw opportunity in breaking the agate rule. Bonner ran ads in different type-faces and fonts, easily capturing the attention of would-be buyers. Bonner found worthy rival in James Gordon Bennett Jr. and the *New York Herald*. Attempting to sell as many copies of the paper as possible, Bennett sent Henry Stanley, one of his correspondents, to find David Livingstone. A well-known Scottish doctor and missionary, Livingstone was last seen alive while on exploration in central Africa. Stanley spent the next eight months describing his adventures to the fascinated readership of the *Herald*. The climax came in 1871, when Stanley, having survived disease, hunger, and battle, greeted the otherwise missing Scotsman with "Dr. Livingstone, I presume?" Stanley's salutation became famous throughout the United States, to the benefit of the *Herald*'s circulation numbers.

ASK YOURSELF

1. Does the way a product is advertised go farther toward gaining a sale than the product itself?
2. What media are the most effective in marketing goods today, and why?

TOPICS AND ACTIVITIES TO CONSIDER

- How have advertisements influenced public warnings about disease? Find out more at Amanda Schaffer, "Grave Warnings of Disease, with the Adman's Flair," *New York Times*, November 3, 2008: http://www.nytimes.com/2008/11/04/health/04post.html.
- Do the media, especially television, have influence on children? For a range of issues on the topic, including "What Are Your Children Learning from Television?" and "What Are the Effects of Television Violence on Children?" go to "Television and Children," Squidoo: http://www.squidoo.com/television_and_children.

Further Reading

Mott, Frank Luther. *A History of American Magazines, 1865–1885*. Cambridge, MA: Harvard University Press, 1938.

Presbrey, Frank. *The History and Development of Advertising*. Garden City, NY: Doubleday, 1929.

Tungate, Mark. *Adland: A Global History of Advertising*. Philadelphia: Kogan Page, 2007.

Turner, E. S. *The Shocking History of Advertising!* New York: Dutton, 1953.

Wood, James P. *The Story of Advertising.* New York: Ronald Press Co., 1958.

Web Sites

An outstanding history of advertising is available through Emergence of Advertising in America, 1850–1920, Emergence of Advertising On-Line Project, Duke University Rare Book, Manuscript, and Special Collections Libraries: http://library.duke.edu/digitalcollections/eaa/.

Several advertising museums have very well-done Web sites, including Pollack Advertising Museum, a virtual museum: http://www.pollackmuseum.com; and, William F. Eisner Museum of Advertising and Design in Milwaukee, Wisconsin: http://www.eisnermuseum.org.

RELIGION

31. An Argument for Slave Ownership: Reverend George Armstrong's *The Christian Doctrine of Slavery* (1857)

INTRODUCTION

One of the more intriguing aspects of the Civil War is that both southerners and northerners used the Bible to bolster their arguments for and against slavery. The passage below turns to the BOOK OF GENESIS to justify the owning of slaves. In fairness, and as discussed later, many Biblical passages seem to directly contradict one person owning another person. The use of Scripture to support slavery seems dishonest to modern-day American sensibilities. But, in the mid-19th century, the argument carried very real credence to many white Americans. George Armstrong, the author of the text cited, was a Presbyterian minister in Norfolk, Virginia. Armstrong hoped that in turning to the divine, he might "do something toward bringing God's people, North and South, to 'see eye to eye' on the much vexed question of slavery."

KEEP IN MIND AS YOU READ

1. The passage in Genesis cited by Armstrong, and many other white southerners, is the first mention of slavery in the Bible. The passage seems to date slavery to very nearly the beginnings of human existence. The text reads,

   The sons of NOAH who came out of the ark were Shem, Ham, and Japheth. These three were the sons of Noah, and from them the whole of the earth were peopled. Now Noah, a man of the soil, was the first to plant a vineyard. When he drank some of the wine, he became drunk and lay naked inside his tent. Ham, the father of Canaan, saw his father's nakedness, and he told his two brothers outside about it. Shem and Japheth, however, took a robe, and holding it on their backs, they walked backward and covered their father's nakedness; since their faces were turned the other way, they did not see their father's nakedness. When Noah woke up from his drunkenness and learned what his youngest son had done to him, he said:

   "Cursed by Canaan! The lowest of slaves shall he be to his brothers."

   He also said:

   "Blessed be the Lord, the God of Shem! Let Canaan be his slave. May God expand Japheth, so that he dwells among the tents of Shem; and let Canaan be his slave." (Gen. 9:18–27)

2. Based on rather loose scientific and archeological evidence, many Westerners in the mid-19th century believed that Africans traced their ancestry to Ham and, thus, to Canaan.

3. Armstrong anticipated the counterarguments that his interpretation of the Bible might raise. Armstrong took these head on, especially the passage from the GOSPEL OF MATTHEW: "Whatsoever ye would that men should do to you, do ye even so to them" (Matt. 7:2). Armstrong countered that interpretation of "general laws," such as that in Matthew, "is delusive." Otherwise, parents could not correct children, nor judges sentence criminals. Ultimately, man had sinned against God from very nearly the beginning of time. "The consequences of sin," Armstrong reminded, "consequences established by God himself, must come upon the sinner." Black Africans, as the descendants of Ham, had to pay the steepest price to achieve redemption.

Document: Excerpts from Armstrong's
The Christian Doctrine of Slavery

The Scriptural theory respecting the origin of slavery may be stated in brief, thus: The effect of sin, i.e., disobedience to God's laws, upon both individuals and nations, is *degradation*. A people under this influence, continued through many generations, sink so low in this scale of intelligence and morality as to become incapable of safe and righteous self-government. When, by God's appointment, slavery comes upon them—an appointment at once punitive and remedial; a punishment for sin actually committed, and at the same time a means of saving the sinning people from that utter extermination which must otherwise be their doom, and gradually raising them from the degradation into which they have sunk.

It was in consequence of sin, in part actually committed, and yet more foreseen in the future, that the first slave sentence of which we have any record, was pronounced by Noah upon Canaan and his descendants—"Cursed be Canaan; a servant of servants shall he be to his brethren"— . . .

Of the remedial operation of slavery, we have a striking illustration in the case of the African race in our own country. In the history of nations, it would be difficult to find an instance in which a people have made more rapid progress, upward and onward, than the African race has made under the operation of American slavery. They have not yet, as a people, attained a point at which they are capable of self-government, is, we believe, conceded by every one personally acquainted with them, and therefore capable of forming an intelligent opinion. That it may take generations yet, to accomplish the gracious purposes of God in inflicting slavery upon them, is very possible. The work which it has taken ages to do, it often takes ages to undo. But nothing is more certain than that God's plan has operated well thus far.

Source: George D. Armstrong, *The Christian Doctrine of Slavery.* New York: Charles Scribner, 1857, pp. 111–13. Listed at Internet Archive: http://www.archive.org/stream/christiandoctrine00arms/christiandoctrine00arms_djvu.txt.

AFTERMATH

Counterattacks using the Bible to condemn slavery did come, perhaps with a greater force than even Armstrong had anticipated. The Beatitudes, drawn from Jesus's Sermon on the Mount, are perhaps the most poignant. The Beatitudes mention nothing about race, gender, ethnicity, or any other distinctions among people. The point is that humans all are created in the image of God. The Beatitudes read as follows:

> Blessed are the poor in spirit, for theirs is the kingdom of heaven. Blessed are they who mourn, for they will be comforted. Blessed are the meek, for they will inherit the land. Blessed are they who hunger and thirst for righteousness, for they will be satisfied. Blessed are the merciful, for they will be shown mercy. Blessed are the clean of heart, for they will see God. Blessed are the peacemakers, for they will be called children of God. Blessed are they who are persecuted for the sake of righteousness, for theirs is the kingdom of heaven. (Matt. 5:3–12)

Another passage from the Gospel of Matthew used to attack slavery reads, "For one is your master, even Christ, and all ye are brethren" (23:8). Enslaved African Americans often drew consolation from the Book of Exodus. Found in the Old Testament, the Exodus story recounts Moses leading the Hebrews out from slavery in Egypt. African Americans believed that if God did not send a leader to directly take them from slavery, freedom and equality awaited them in Heaven as children of God.

ASK YOURSELF

1. Is the Bible used by Americans today to support opposing arguments over abortion, gay marriage, and other controversial issues? How?
2. Does the use of the Bible to support an argument, whether over slavery or modern-day issues, shape opinion or reinforce already existing attitudes? Meaning, do you think the argument by George Armstrong swayed people to defend slavery or did it simply reinforced their already held beliefs?

TOPICS AND ACTIVITIES TO CONSIDER

- A counterpoint to Armstrong's *The Christian Doctrine of Slavery* is an 1862 article by Reverend L. Bacon in *New Englander and Yale Review*. "Noah's Prophecy: 'Cursed by Canaan'" is listed at "The Nineteenth Century in Print: Periodicals," American Memory Collection, Library of Congress: http://memory.loc.gov/ammem/ndlpcoop/moahtml/snchome.html.
- Many American slaves converted to Christianity during the First Great Awakening. A turn toward active religious membership that swept the American colonies in the mid-1700s, the First Great Awakening lead at least some ministers to preach the equality of all peoples. An excellent description of the First Great Awakening, along with various teacher resources, is found at Christine Leigh Heyrman, "The First Great Awakening," Divining America, TeacherServe, National Humanities Center: http://nationalhumanitiescenter.org/tserve/eighteen/ekeyinfo/grawaken.htm.

Further Reading

Goldenberg, David M. *The Curse of Ham: Race and Slavery in Early Judaism, Christianity, and Islam*. Princeton, NJ: Princeton University Press, 2003.

Haynes, Stephen R. *Noah's Curse: The Biblical Justification of American Slavery*. New York: Oxford University Press, 2002.

Lippy, Charles H. *Being Religious, American Style: A History of Popular Religiosity in the United States*. Westport, CT: Greenwood Press, 1994.

Wills, Garry. *Head and Heart: American Christianities*. New York: Penguin Press, 2007.

Web Sites

An excellent discussion of the use of the Bible to justify the practice of slavery is Stephen R. Haynes, "Original Dishonor: Noah's Curse and the Southern Defense of Slavery," *Journal of Southern Religion*, February 2000: http://jsr.fsu.edu/honor.htm.

An online version of the King James Bible is posted at: http://www.kingjamesbibleonline.org. The site is searchable by verse and book. A similar site, but for the New American Bible, and sponsored by the United States Conference of Catholic Bishops, is at: http://www.usccb.org/nab/bible/.

32. THE BATTLE BETWEEN GOOD AND EVIL: AN AFRICAN AMERICAN SPIRITUAL (1872)

INTRODUCTION

Religion remained a constant to many Americans amid the otherwise rapid changes in everyday life. Daniel Sutherland, a historian and leading expert on the Civil War era, estimates that as many as one-half of the 40 million Americans in 1870 attended church on a regular basis. Most Americans counted themselves as Christian, even those who never actually found their way into one of the nation's nearly 70,000 churches. PROTESTANTS formed the largest religious community, led in numbers by Methodists, Baptists, and Presbyterians. Roman Catholics represented the largest single denomination, however, with four million members. Joining white churchgoers, southern blacks had established the Colored Primitive Baptist Church and the Colored Methodist Episcopal Church by 1870. These two independent churches now stood alongside the African Methodist Episcopal Church and the Zion Church, both previously established by African Americans in the North. SPIRITUALS played an important role in black church services, as they had since the antebellum era. The songs often worked at two levels. On the surface, spirituals reminded listeners about the need to work toward gaining eternal salvation. On a deeper level, the songs protested the racial inequities of the day. In "Children, You'll Be Called On," the lyrics call for each Christian, as a "soldier of the cross," to battle earthly evils and temptations. The ills are left unspecified and apply to many situations. The ultimate outcome is never in doubt, with good emerging triumphant. The battle between good and evil might also be linked to the struggle for civil rights. The *jubilee* would occur when the rights granted African Americans as citizens, outlined in the Constitution but fast slipping away in practice, might be realized. The *children* in the song title means youngsters, who, like their elders, would face eternal rights and wrongs. But the use of the terms also serves as a reminder that all people are created in the image of God and, thus, equal before His eyes.

KEEP IN MIND AS YOU READ

1. Prior to the end of the Civil War, black people in the South were not allowed to establish their own churches. They often attended church during the day with the white family, sitting in a segregated area. The message delivered sometimes attempted to reinforce slavery, with biblical injunctions regarding servants and

masters, and accepting one's lot in life. At night, black people might worship in a nearby field or wood. The theme at these invisible churches stressed deliverance from suffering and equality before God.

2. Small towns and villages often lacked the presence of a full-time minister. These rural communities instead relied upon the services of circuit-riders. Traveling between any number of destinations (usually four to six stops was the most common over a two-week period), circuit riders held church services, performed weddings and funerals, and visited the sick.

3. Church attendance has dipped only slightly since 1870, by way of comparison. A 2009 Gallup Poll estimates that 45 percent of Americans had attended church at least once within the past week of being asked. Roman Catholics still form the largest single denomination, with 67 million members.

Document: "Children, You'll Be Called On"

Children, you'll be called on / To march in the field of battle,
    When this warfare'll be ended, Hallelu. / When this warfare'll be ended,
    I'm a soldier of the jubilee, / This warfare'll be ended,
    I'm a soldier of the cross.

Preachers, you'll be called on / To march in the field of battle,
    When this warfare'll be ended, Hallelu. / When this warfare'll be ended,
    I'm a soldier of the jubilee, / This warfare'll be ended,
    I'm a soldier of the cross.

Sinners, you'll be called on / To march in the field of battle,
    When this warfare'll be ended, Hallelu. / When this warfare'll be ended,
    I'm a soldier of the jubilee, / This warfare'll be ended,
    I'm a soldier of the cross.

Seekers, you'll be called on / To march in the field of battle,
    When this warfare'll be ended, Hallelu. / When this warfare'll be ended,
    I'm a soldier of the jubilee, / This warfare'll be ended.
    I'm a soldier of the cross.

Christians, you'll be called on / To march in the field of battle,
    When this warfare'll be ended, Hallelu. / When this warfare'll be ended,
    I'm a soldier of the jubilee, / This warfare'll be ended,
    I'm a soldier of the cross.

Source: "Children, You'll Be Called On," in *Jubilee Songs: Complete. As Sung By The Jubilee Singers of Fisk University, Under the Auspices of the American Missionary Association.* Chicago: Bigelow and Main, 1872. Posted online at "Lit2Go," An online service of Florida's Educational Technology Clearinghouse, Florida Center for Instructional Technology, College of Education, University of South Florida: http://etc.usf.edu/lit2go/contents/4300/4331/4331.html.

AFTERMATH

Black churches played other important roles beyond giving widespread circulation to spirituals. Congregants held christenings, weddings, and funerals. These ceremonies helped to forge bonds of community by bringing people together amid times of shared joy and sorrow. When not holding a religious service, black churches also sometimes doubled as school rooms. These meeting places helped to fill the gap as schools established by the FREEDMEN'S BUREAU were constructed. Last, black churches provided political leadership. Small numbers of African American men had received education at colleges established during the Reconstruction years to train and produce ministers. Fisk University in Nashville, Tennessee, which opened in 1866, and Howard University, in Washington, DC, established the next year, number among these historically black colleges and universities. Many of these college-educated ministers ran for and won political office. The tradition of black ministers actively involved in the public sphere continues into the modern day, most notably under Martin Luther King Jr., Ralph Abernathy, and Jesse Jackson.

TOPICS AND ACTIVITIES TO CONSIDER

- ✍ Elizabeth Harris was born in Georgia in 1867 and wrote her life story when she was 55 years old. A child of former slaves and a mother to nine children, Harris was deeply religious. What does her memoir say about black religious life? Harris's recounting of her religious experiences is posted online, along with the rest of the memoir, at: http://scriptorium.lib.duke.edu/harris/harris-indx.html. The Harris memoir is part of The Digital Scriptorium, Special Collections Library, Duke University, Durham, North Carolina: http://scriptorium.lib.duke.edu/harris/.
- ✍ How do the lyrics and message of "Children, You'll Be Called On" compare to those found in other spirituals? Find the answer, and much more about the Fisk University Jubilee Singers, at "Jubilee Singers: Sacrifice and Glory," The American Experience, PBS Online: http://www.pbs.org/wgbh/amex/singers/.

AMERICAN MISSIONARY ASSOCIATION

Organized and sponsored the Jubilee Singers. Several Protestant antislavery societies founded the American Missionary Association (AMA) in 1846, with the goal of establishing missions for freed slaves overseas. Many of the founders of the AMA had worked to provide legal defense for the slaves seized in 1839 from the Spanish slave ship *Amistad*. By the early 1850s, the AMA had shifted its focus to the abolition of slavery. Over the next decade, the AMA had either established or supported nearly 300 antislavery churches. The AMA expanded its efforts with the start of the Civil War to opening schools for freed slaves. By the late 19th century, several hundred schools supported by the AMA were in operation in the South. The AMA also founded nine historically black colleges, including Fisk University, Dillard University in New Orleans, Talladega College in Alabama, and Tougaloo College in Mississippi. The AMA ended its operations in the 20th century. The organization's papers are housed at the Amistad Research Center at Tulane University, New Orleans.

Further Reading

Giovanni, Nikki. *On My Journey Now: Looking at African-American History Through the Spirituals*. Cambridge, MA: Candlewick Press, 2007.

Hogan, Moses, ed. *The Oxford Book of Spirituals*. New York: Oxford University Press, 2002.

Jones, Arthur C. *Wade in the Water: The Wisdom of the Spirituals*. Maryknoll, NY: Orbis Books, 1999.

Marsh, J.B.T. *The Story of the Jubilee Singers: With Their Songs*. New York: AMS Press, 1971.

Ward, Andrew. *Dark Midnight When I Rise: The Story of the Jubilee Singers Who Introduced the World to the Music of Black America*. New York: Farrar, Straus and Giroux, 2000.

Web Sites

A very good historical overview of spiritual music, with links and many other resources, is sponsored by The Spirituals Project, housed at the University of Denver, at "Sweet Chariot: The Story of Spirituals": http://ctl.du.edu/spirituals. Listen to recordings of spiritual music through the Robert Winslow Gordon Collection, at the American Folklife Center, Library of Congress, "Folk-Songs of America: The Robert Winslow Gordon Collection, 1922–1932": http://www.loc.gov/folklife/Gordon/index.html.

More information about the Jubilee Singers, and the history of Fisk University, is found at: "History of Fisk," http://www.fisk.edu/AboutFisk/HistoryOfFisk.aspx.

33. "… THE HEAT WAS SO INTENSE THAT IT DROVE US DOWN TO THE WATERS …": AN ACCOUNT OF THE CHICAGO FIRE (1873)

INTRODUCTION

Accidents and natural disasters, the latter often labeled as Acts of God—and thus included in this chapter—have occurred throughout American history. Hurricane Katrina, which battered the Gulf Coast and flooded neighborhoods in New Orleans, is perhaps the greatest natural disaster to strike the United States in the modern day. The late 19th century was not immune from fire, floods, and accidental loss of life. The explosion of the steamboat *Sultana* on the Mississippi River in 1865 killed nearly 2,000 passengers, many of them former Union prisoners of war returning home. A fire in Peshtigo, Wisconsin, six years later killed as many as 2,500 people, the deadliest blaze in American history. The fire that consumed much of downtown Chicago in the fall of 1871, however, especially captivated the nation's attention. Starting on Sunday night, October 8, on DeKoven Street, at the time part of a poor neighborhood on the west side of the city, the fire quickly raged out of control. Wood buildings, strong winds, dry conditions, and slow initial reaction from city administrators contributed to the spread of the blaze. The destruction of the city's waterworks, north of the Chicago River, ended all large-scale attempts to battle the fire. By Tuesday morning, diminishing winds and a light drizzle had combined to help slow and extinguish the blaze. Roughly four square miles of the city were destroyed, including much of the downtown business district. Amid the wreckage, 125 bodies were recovered. Almost one-third of the city's 300,000 people were left homeless, including Fannie Belle Becker. A 10-year-old at the time of the fire, Becker recounted her experiences in the "Great Chicago Fire" two years later.

KEEP IN MIND AS YOU READ

1. The *Chicago Tribune* went to press the day after the fire had ended, admitting that "this city has been swept by a conflagration which has no parallel in the annals of history, for the quantity of property destroyed, and the utter and almost irremediable ruin which it wrought." Despite the blow, "no matter how terrible, Chicago will not succumb. Late as it is in the season, general as the ruin is, the spirit of her citizens has not give way, and before the smoke has cleared away, and the ruins are cold, they are beginning to plan for the future."

2. The origins of the Chicago fire still are debated. The *Chicago Tribune* immediately cast blame upon Mrs. Catherine O'Leary, for carelessly allowing a cow to kick over a lantern in the family barn. A popular ditty soon ran:

Late one night, when we were all in bed, / Mrs. O'Leary lit a lantern in her shed,
Her cow kicked it over, / Then winked her eye, and said,
"There'll be a hot time in the old town tonight!"

In later years, Michael Ahern, the reporter who ran the story, recanted. Ahern admitted that the O'Leary cow story made for a colorful, and plausible, explanation. In 2002 Richard Bales, an amateur historian investigating the origins of the fire, pinned blame on a man who ignited some hay while trying to steal milk from the O'Leary barn. Two years later, Robert Wood, an engineer and physicist, argued that falling pieces from Biela's Comet sparked the blaze. Unexplained fires across other parts of the Midwest started the same day as the Chicago fire, lending strength to the theory.

Document: Fannie Belle Becker's Experience of the Chicago Fire

Saturday evening Oct the 8th 1871 there was a large Fire in Chicago it was probably the largest Fire ever in that city . . . there was a great many people out to see it. They stayed until a late hour . . . [I] did not get much rest for Monday morning at three o'clock I was awakened and told to Dress for the Fire was all around us and we would soon be burnt out. My ma put all her valubals into her sewing machine and locked it up and threw some things in to her trunk. I carried ma's fur box (with furs in it), and, account book, and a parasol, and, a little lady called Jennie. And perhaps some of my little friends in Fruit-Port have made her [acquaintance] but some of you may not know who little Jennie is so I will say that she is a little China doll a Christmas present when I was Five years old and I will always keep her as a Relic of the Chicago Fire. We could not save the Sewing Machine but did save the trunk. We had a gentleman friend who helped us; we all went down right away but ma stayed, she said that she would stay as long as she could. So we went around the corner to Monroe street and waited and when she came she brought a large hair Matrass. The air was so full of cinders and was so hot that it almost stifled her. We could not get an express man to carry the things for there were none to be had. So our friend drew our trunk and a trunk that belonged to a friend of his who was out of the city. He lashed the two together and lashed the Matrass on top of the trunks, and then drew them along. The trunks both has castors on. When we got to the corners of Dearborn street ma told me to go Down on Jackson st. a few blocks away to the house of a friend and see if they thought the fire would come there and if not we would go there and stay. And Just as I was about to start a man who had been standing near and heard what ma said told her that he would see me safe there. Ma thanked him and said we would not trouble him but he said it was no trouble and walked along beside me. He said he would take my account book I did not like his looks and so told him that I could carry it myself, and, as we went through a crowd just then I dodged away from him and ran and I have not seen anything of him since. When I got to the house they had all their things packed and out on the side walk and, in a little while ma came and then we went back to Monroe st and then as the Fire came on we went on toward Lake Michigan as we went on we came to our friends brothers house we stayed here until the fire drove us out then the heat was so intense that it drove us down to the waters Edge and then my uncle who was with us (and, had arrived Saturday) took his hat and poured water on the things to keep them from burning but thousands and thousands of dollar's worth of goods were burned right there on the waters Edge. Although our things were saved we sat there until I was almost blind with the dirt and cinders that filled the air I could not open my eyes, so that when I walked ma had to lead me. I did not have anything to eat from Sunday afternoon until Monday afternoon at about four o'clock. Then we went out to the City limits on the South side to the house of a friend I stayed here two days and then I went out in the country with my cousins, and stayed there one week and then I came to Fruit-Port [Michigan]. I shall ever remember with thankfulness my reception by my little friends in Fruit-Port. I almost went barefoot and without any good clothes. I was well treated and one of them even took off her over shoes and let me wear them that I might go out in the cold weather and play. Never while I live will I forget my friends in Fruit Port.

Source: "The Great Chicago Fire and the Web of Memory: An Anthology of Fire Narratives," The Chicago Historical Society: http://www.chicagohs.org/fire/witnesses/library.html.

AFTERMATH

Chicagoans began to rebuild from the fire almost as soon as it had ended. Rubble was cleared away; much of it was pushed into Lake Michigan. Business and city services started back up, often from temporary locations. Stricter building codes were enforced, emphasizing the use of stone and brick. Concrete also became more commonly used, as in other cities across the United States. Some protest occurred during the Great Rebuilding, especially among the city's less affluent residents. Rents went up as living space became premium, and the expense of flame-resistant building materials made purchasing a new home virtually beyond reach. Still, the city moved forward. By 1890, the population topped one million. Commerce boomed, as much as from an optimistic spirit as from the city's position as a transportation hub. In a strong showing of its resurgence, Chicago hosted over 21 million visitors to the World's Columbian Exposition in 1893. In the words of one postfire song, Chicago was "Queen of the West once more."

THE MUNICIPAL FLAG OF CHICAGO

The Municipal Flag of Chicago helps to keep alive the memory of the Great Fire and its aftermath. The flag shows two blue horizontal stripes, on a field of white. In between the blue stripes are four six-pointed red stars, each to mark an especially momentous event in the city's history. The second star represents the fire of 1871, and the rebuilding that followed. The first star represents Fort Dearborn and the eventual founding of the city, while the last two stars represent the World's Columbian Exposition in 1893 and the Century of Progress Exposition in 1933.

ASK YOURSELF

1. How might communities balance the need to improve public service and safety and to maintain affordable costs of living?
2. Why does overcoming adversity, such as that faced by Chicagoans in the aftermath of the Great Fire, help to build community spirit? Does the same apply to sports teams? To individual nations?

TOPICS AND ACTIVITIES TO CONSIDER

- ⮞ How did the Chicago fire start? Research some of the theories at "The Great Chicago Fire and the Web of Memory: The O'Leary Legend," Chicago Historical Society: http://www.chicagohistory.org/fire/oleary/index.html.
- ⮞ One Chicago newspaper compared the fire that raged through the city to a fire that destroyed much of Moscow, the capital of Russia, during the Napoleonic Wars. Is the comparison accurate? Read more at "Fire of Moscow (1812)," Wikipedia.org: http://en.wikipedia.org/wiki/Fire_of_Moscow_(1812).

Further Reading

Bales, Richard F. *The Great Chicago Fire and the Myth of Mrs. O'Leary's Cow*. Jefferson, NC: McFarland, 2002.

Colbert, Elias and Everett Chamberlin. *Chicago and the Great Conflagration*. Reprint of 1871 edition; New York: Viking Press, 1971.

Harvey, Michael T. *The Fifth Floor*. New York: Alfred A. Knopf, 2008. [Historical fiction]

Murphy, Jim. *The Great Fire*. New York: Scholastic, Inc., 1995.

Sawislak, Karen. *Smoldering City: Chicagoans and the Great Fire, 1871–1874*. Chicago: University of Chicago Press, 1995.

Web Sites

Another site maintained by the Chicago Historical Society is "The Chicago Fire": http://www.chicagohs.org/history/fire.html.

A site aimed toward younger children is "The Great Chicago Fire, October 9, 1871": http://www.americaslibrary.gov/jb/recon/jb_recon_chicago_1.html. The site is part of "America's Story from America's Library," Library of Congress: http://www.americaslibrary.gov.

34. "We Sang 'Rock of Ages' as I Thought I Had Never Heard It Sung Before...": Frances Willard's Crusade against Alcohol, from *Glimpses of Fifty Years: The Autobiography of an American Woman* (1889)

INTRODUCTION

The Woman's Christian Temperance Union (WCTU), one of the most powerful women's organizations in American history, traced its origins to the rapid spread of saloons following the end of the Civil War. Americans had always been relatively heavy drinkers, leading many observers to bemoan that the nation fast was becoming an alcoholic republic. By the late 1860s, alcohol became even more readily available through the opening of saloons. Whereas only a small number of dram shops dotted city landscapes in the antebellum era, their numbers exploded after 1865. The reliance of the federal government upon revenue from liquor taxes and the continuing arrival of immigrants in large numbers gave drinking, in the words of one noted social historian, "a new respectability." By 1880, the United States boasted 100,000 liquor establishments, or about one for every 50 Americans. Many social critics believed that with saloons came prostitution, crime, and all sorts of other evils. Women often were the most visible opponents to saloons. Arguing that alcohol threatened the very fabric of the family by luring husbands and fathers into unemployment and crime—to the subsequent ruin of wives and children—women sang hymns and prayed outside saloon doors. These praying crusades caused a number of cities and town to prohibit the sale and consumption of liquor on Sunday, if not all together. From these grass-root beginnings sprang the WCTU in 1874. Frances Willard, who became president of the WCTU in 1879, describes her first experience in the battle against alcohol and drunkenness.

KEEP IN MIND AS YOU READ

1. The per capita (per person) consumption of alcohol in the United States during the 1830s was 7.1 gallons (measured by the alcohol in the drink, rather than by the drink itself). Considering that many people did not drink at all, or only imbided lightly, those who did drink consumed enormous quantities.
2. During the mid-1850s, 13 of the 31 states had prohibited the manufacturing and sale of alcohol. Ten years later, only Maine and Massachusetts maintained such restrictions.

3. Immigrants often opposed Prohibition efforts. Germans, Irish, and Italians saw the effort to close down saloons as a strike against their heritage. In saloons, one might read foreign-language newspapers and discuss on goings in the homeland. Catholic immigrants also feared that Prohibition would prevent the taking of wine along with the host at communion, the central activity of the Mass.

Document: Excerpt from Willard's Glimpses of Fifty Years

The first saloon I ever entered was Sheffner's, on Market street, Pittsburgh, on my way home. In fact, that was the only glimpse I ever personally had of the [Praying] Crusade. [Sheffner's] had lingered in this dun-colored city well nigh a year and when I visited my old friends at the Pittsburgh Female College I spoke with enthusiasm of the Crusade, and of the women who were, as I judged from a morning paper, still engaged in it here. They looked upon me with astonishment when I proposed to seek out those women and go with them to the saloons, . . . However, they were too polite to desire to disappoint me. . . . [I] soon found myself walking down street arm in arm with a young teacher from the public school, who said she had a habit of coming in to add one to the procession when her day's duties were over. We paused in front of the saloon that I have mentioned. The ladies ranged themselves along the curbstone, for they had been forbidden in anywise to incommode the passers-by, being dealt with much more strictly than a drunken man or a heap of dry-goods boxes would be. At a signal from our gray-haired leader, a sweet-voiced woman began to sing, "Jesus the water of life will give," all our voices soon blending in that sweet song. I think it was the most novel spectacle that I recall. There stood women of undoubted religious devotion and the highest character, most of them crowned with the glory of gray hairs. Along the stony pavement of that stoniest of cities rumbled the heavy wagons, many of them carriers of beer; between us and the saloon in front of which we were drawn up in line, passed the motley throng, almost every man lifting his hat and even the little newsboys doing the

same. It was American manhood's tribute to Christianity and to womanhood, and it was significant and full of pathos. The leader had already asked the saloon-keeper if we might enter, and he had declined, else the prayer-meeting would have occurred inside his door. A sorrowful old lady whose only son had gone to ruin through that very death-trap, knelt on the cold, moist pavement and offered a broken-hearted prayer, while all our heads were bowed. At a signal we moved on and the next saloon-keeper permitted us to enter. I had no more idea of the inward appearance of a saloon than if there had been no such place on earth. I knew nothing of its high, heavily corniced bar, its barrels with the ends all pointed towards the looker-on, each barrel being furnished with a faucet; its shelves glittering with decanters and cut glass, its floors thickly strewn with saw-dust, and here and there a round table with chairs—nor of its abundant fumes, sickening to healthful nostrils. The tall, stately lady who led us, placed her Bible on the bar and read a psalm, whether **hortatory**

hortatory or imprecatory: In this context, *hortatory* means strongly encouraging someone, while *imprecatory* means yelling at or cursing someone.

"Rock of Ages": Written in the 18th century, the hymn became very popular both in and out of church. The song is inspired from the Bible verse, "The Lord is my Rock, and my Fortress, and my Deliverer" (Ps. 18:2).

or imprecatory, I do not remember, but the spirit of these crusaders was so gentle, I think it must have been the former. Then we sang **"Rock of Ages"** as I thought I had never heard it sung before, with a tender confidence to the height of which one does not rise in the easy-going, regulation prayer-meeting, and then one of the older women whispered to me softly that the leader wished to know if I would pray. It was strange, perhaps, but I felt not the least reluctance, and kneeling on that saw-dust floor, with a group of earnest hearts around me, and behind them, filling every corner and extending out into the street, a crowd of un-washed, unkempt, hard-looking drinking men, I was conscious that perhaps never in my life, save beside my sister Mary's dying bed had I prayed as truly as I did then. This was my Crusade baptism. The next day I went on to the West and within a week had been made president of the Chicago W. C. T. U.

Source: Frances E. Willard, *Glimpses of Fifty Years: The Autobiography of an American Woman.* Chicago: H. J. Smith & Co., 1889, pp. 339–41.

AFTERMATH

The WCTU increased its national visibility under the leadership of Francis Willard, having 150,000 members by 1890. Willard urged supporters to push elected officials for home protection. The campaign not only called for closing down saloons but also for gaining a limited right to vote for women. The thought was that women would vote saloons out of business in local elections. The call helped to contribute to a growing movement to gain suffrage for women. The WCTU gained a national triumph with the ratification in 1919 of 18th Amendment. The amendment banned across the United States the "manufacture, sale, or transportation of intoxicating liquors." The subsequent failure of Prohibition, and the repeal of the 18th Amendment in 1933, led to a rapid decline in the influence of the WCTU.

ASK YOURSELF

1. Do women, especially older women, make the best advocates for reform, as Willard seems to suggest?
2. Is alcohol the root behind many social problems, as members of the WCTU believed?

TOPICS AND ACTIVITIES TO CONSIDER

- ➣ The WCTU continues to operate today. How has the organization evolved since its initial founding in the 1870s? Does the shift in focus, if any, better reflect the social issues that confront the United States in the early 21st century? Find the answers at the official site of the WCTU, at: http://www.wctu.org.
- ➣ The passage of the 18th Amendment led to the question, Should the government attempt to legislate private behavior? Whether the federal government should legalize marijuana is a topic that comes up often today. What is your position on the question? Find out more on both sides of the issue at Joe Messerli, "Should Marijuana be Legalized under any Circumstances?": http://www.balancedpolitics. org/marijuana_legalization.htm. The site is maintained by BalancedPolitics.org, dedicated to "balanced, non-partisan discussion of important societal issues."

Whether state and local governments have the right to restrict the use of cell phones while driving is another issue that blurs the line between private behavior and public responsibility. To find out more, read Caitlin Crosain, "Driving and Cell Phones—Should Cellular Phones Be Banned while Driving," September 11, 2005, Articlesbase: Free Online Articles Directory: http://www.articlesbase.com/communication-articles/driving-and-cell-phones-should-cellular-phones-be-banned-while-driving-702.html.

Further Reading

Blocker, Jack S. *"Give to the Winds Thy Fears": The Women's Temperance Crusade, 1873–1874.* Westport, CT: Greenwood Press, 1985.

Bordin, Ruth Birgitta Anderson. *Francis Willard: A Biography.* Chapel Hill: University of North Carolina Press, 1986.

Bordin, Ruth Birgitta Anderson. *Women and Temperance: The Quest for Power and Liberty, 1873–1900.* Philadelphia: Temple University Press, 1981.

Mattingly, Carol. *Well-Tempered Women: Nineteenth-Century Temperance Rhetoric.* Carbondale: Southern Illinois University Press, 1998.

Willard, Frances E. *Writing Out My Heart: Selections From the Journal of Frances E. Willard, 1855–96,* edited by Carolyn De Swarte Gifford. Urbana: University of Illinois Press, 1995.

Web Sites

Find more on Frances Willard, the WCTU, and the Prohibition movement at "Temperance & Prohibition," Department of History, Ohio State University, Columbus: http://prohibition.osu.edu.

Explore the history of the antialcohol crusade at "Alcohol, Temperance & Prohibition": http://dl.lib.brown.edu/temperance. The site lists essays and primary sources, through the repeal of Prohibition in 1933. The site is maintained by the Center for Digital Initiatives, Brown University, Providence, Rhode Island.

35. "Baby Looking Out for Me": From Samuel Irenaeus Prime's *Thoughts on the Death of Little Children* (1865)

INTRODUCTION

Infant mortality was shockingly high in the late 19th century, bringing religion into perhaps greater focus than any other family related event. In 1870 there were 110,000 children under the age of one year who died. By comparison, in 2008, the most recent statistics available, 28,000 infants died. The disparity in figures is even more disturbing when one remembers that the population of the United States, at 300 million people today, is nearly eight times as large as it was in 1870. Complications at childbirth, illness, and accidents, among other factors, contributed to the high infant mortality during the Civil War and Reconstruction era. Parents found solace in their faith, but still struggled with their grief. Samuel Irenaeus Prime, a Presbyterian minister in New York, was prompted to address the topic after receiving a summons from a father whose young daughter had just died from influenza. The father was a tough, no-nonsense individual ("One of the iron sort of men," in Prime's description). But, when Prime entered the house, the dad was openly weeping. Prime was at first startled, not believing that "such a man as he had tears to shed." Watching the father cradle the body in his arms, Prime came to believe that only the death of a child could trigger such emotion. The loss bonded people from all backgrounds in a "brotherhood of sorrow." Prime did not attempt to diminish the grief in his book, *Thoughts on the Death of Little Children,* but he did offer hope: "You now have new attractions in the eternal world to draw your hearts higher. Every thing is moving on to higher conditions, and your own hearts should be constantly going upward." Prime offered eleven chapters, among them "He is Not Lost, Though Gone," "The Child is Happier Now," and "We Shall See Him Again." Most of the book, however, was taken up by hymns and poetry (100 of 170 pages). "Baby Looking Out for Me," is one of the poems, penned by Ethel Lynn Beers. One literary critic, writing in 1879, claimed that Beers's lines "must touch any mother's heart."

KEEP IN MIND AS YOU READ

1. The mortality rate among all young children was high in 1870. Among children five years of age and younger, 203,000 died.

2. The life expectancy at birth in late 19th century was low, by modern-day standards. The average life expectancy was 45 years of age. Today, the average life expectancy is 78 years of age.

3. Because of the high infant mortality and low average life expectancy (again, by modern-day standards), under 10 percent of Americans who reached 15 years of age in 1870 had both parents living and all of their younger brothers and sisters living.

Document: "Baby Looking Out for Me," by Elizabeth Beers

Two little busy hands patting on the window / Two laughing, bright eyes looking out at me;
Two rosy-red cheeks dented with a dimple; / Mother-bird is coming; baby do you see?

Down by the lilac-bush, something white and azure, / Saw I in the window as I passed the tree;
Well I know the apron and shoulder-knots of ribbon; / All belonged to baby, looking out for me.

Talking low and tenderly / To myself, as mothers will,
Spake I softly: "God in heaven, / Keep my darling free from ill,
Worldly gain and worldly honors / Ask I not for her from Thee;
But from want and sin and sorrow, / Keep her ever pure and free."

Two little waxen hands, / Folded soft and silently;
Two little curtained eyes, / Looking out no more for me;
Two little snowy cheeks, / Dimple-dented nevermore;
Two little trodden shoes, / That will never touch the floor;
Shoulder-ribbon softly twisted, / Apron folded, clean and white;
These are left me—and these only / Of the childish presence bright.

Thus He sent an answer to my earnest praying, / Thus He keeps my darling free from earthly stain,
Thus He folds the pet lamb safe from earthly straying; / But I miss her *sadly* by the window-pane,
Till I look above it: then, with purer vision, / Sad, I weep no longer the lilac-bush to pass,
For I see her, angel-pure and white and sinless, / Walking with the harpers, by the sea of glass.

Two little snowy wings / Softly flutter to and fro,
Two tiny childish hands / Beckon still to me below;
Two tender angel eyes / Watch me ever earnestly
Through the loop-holes of the stars; Baby's looking out for me.

Source: "Baby Looking Out for Me," in Samuel Irenaeus Prime, *Thoughts on the Death of Little Children*. New York: A.D.F. Randolph, 1865, pp. 162–63. Listed at "The Nineteenth Century in Print: Books," American Memory Collection, Library of Congress: http://hdl.loc.gov/umich.dli.moa/AJG2606.

AFTERMATH

The burial process remained largely a family affair in the 1870s. Family members placed the corpse, washed and dressed, in a front room. A viewing followed, usually lasting for one day. Blocks of ice placed beneath a board that held the body helped to prevent decay, while flowers masked the odor. Family and friends again gathered round the next day, while a minister read a passage from Scripture (although the service might vary, depending upon the family's faith). Once final words were said, the body received transport for burial in a coffin. Most often, this was a pine box lined with a cloth. A local wood worker, if not the family, usually made the coffin. The well-to-do might purchase for the recently deceased a metal or hard-wood coffin. Although costing more, these materials protected the corpse from worms and other insects. Headstones and monuments marked the final resting spot. These markers grew more ornate as families acquired more wealth. Mourners visiting the burial spot found comfort that the dead had passed on to heaven. Loved ones were revived in God's Kingdom, and reunited with friends and family who had preceded them. Death was merely a temporary passage, from the earthly to the spiritual realm.

ASK YOURSELF

1. Might an author like Prime, writing about grief and sadness, find a receptive audience today?
2. Do rituals help families through times of grief? If so, is the funeral process more for the living than the dead?

TOPICS AND ACTIVITIES TO CONSIDER

- ❧ Do statistics distort our view of the past, depending on how they are used? As previously mentioned, the life expectancy in 1870 is disturbingly low from a modern-day perspective. However, the life expectancy in 1850 was 39 years of age for whites and 23 years of age for blacks. Thus, for someone living in 1870, health issues had improved significantly. Depending on the sets of life expectancy figures used by scholars, the Reconstruction era might seem either a good or bad time to be living. For a study of American population trends, see Michael Haines, "Fertility and Mortality in the United States," EH.NetEncyclopeida, edited by Robert Whaples: http://eh.net/encyclopedia/article/haines.demography.
- ❧ Compare the theme of coping with grief found in Prime's book to *Children in Heaven; or, The Infant Dead Redeemed by the Blood of Jesus*, written by William Edward Schenck and also published in 1865. Schenck's book is online at "The Nineteenth Century in Print: Books," American Memory Collection, Library of Congress: http://hdl.loc.gov/umich.dli.moa/AFZ1163.

Further Reading

Farrell, James J. *Inventing the American Way of Death, 1830–1920*. Philadelphia: Temple University Press, 1980.

Faust, Drew Gilpin. *This Republic of Suffering: Death and the American Civil War*. New York: Alfred A. Knopf, 2008.

Frank, Lucy E., ed. *Representations of Death in Nineteenth-Century U.S. Writing and Culture*. Burlington, Vermont: Ashgate, 2007.

Haines, Michael R. and Richard H. Steckel, eds. *A Population History of North America*. New York: Cambridge University Press, 2000.

Prothero, Stephen R. *Purified by Fire: A History of Cremation in America*. Berkeley: University of California Press, 2001.

Schantz, Mark S. *Awaiting the Heavenly Country: The Civil War and America's Culture of Death*. Ithaca, NY: Cornell University Press, 2008.

Web Sites

Find other of Beers's works, as well as those of other late-19th-century writers, at A. A. Hopkins, *Waifs, and Their Authors*. Boston: D. Lothrop and Company, 1879. Full text is online at Internet Archive: http://www.archive.org/stream/waifstheirauthor00hopkuoft/waifstheirauthor00hopkuoft_djvu.txt.

A review of the National Museum of Funeral History in Houston, Texas, is posted by RoadsideAmerica.com at: http://www.roadsideamerica.com/story/2226.

36. "A Buddhist Mission in the United States?": A Satire Highlighting Divisions among Christians (1872)

INTRODUCTION

In addition to providing comfort and inspiration to many late-19th-century Americans, religion also sometimes served as a flashpoint for controversy. By the mid-1870s, the long-standing observance of Sunday as a day of rest was slipping away. Critics claimed that the opening of parks, museums, and theaters drew people away from church. Although these sites might allow opportunity for family outings, they lacked the eternal nature of attending and reflecting upon religious services. Proponents of Sunday outings countered that the more institutions and public sites open, the better. Drinking halls and gambling parlors provided an alternative to church for some individuals anyway, so best to at least offer some opportunity for fresh air and cultural uplift. Questions over who was a true Christian also served as a point for dispute. Suspicions continued to linger among many native-born Protestants that the Catholicism held to by many immigrants was a plot to ROMANIZE the United States. Protestants were by no means a monolithic group, however. Baptists, Presbyterians, Methodists, and Lutherans remained divided into northern and southern churches, a split that had occurred over slavery. The internal divisions within the Christian church served as the starting point for a tongue-in-cheek editorial in *Harper's Magazine*. Written under a column labeled "Editor's Easy Chair," the piece claimed that a Japanese ambassador went around asking as many Americans as he might "What is a Christian?" The response varied greatly, as individuals defined the faith by their region and denomination. Since no one could define Christianity to include all Christians, the ambassador concluded that the religion must not actually exist. In that case, better to send Buddhist missionaries to the United States to teach that "in religion it is not the profession but the practice that is the important point."

KEEP IN MIND AS YOU READ

1. Americans in the 1870s worried more about liberal religious trends coming from Europe than from Asia. The devout worried that immigrants arriving from Europe brought relaxed attitudes toward the strict observance of the Sabbath. They worried that these Continental views might continue to increase the number of nonchurch-related activities taking place on Sunday.

2. Revival meetings remained popular in the late 19th century. Lasting sometimes up to four or five days, attendees sang and prayed. The hope was to claim new converts for the Lord as well as to reenergize less-than-enthusiastic church members. Attendees at revival meetings also socialized, with ample time to eat and talk.

3. The United States first made extended contact with Japan under a naval fleet commanded by Commodore Mathew Perry in 1853. Making a strong show of military force, Perry negotiated a treaty that opened Japanese ports to American trade. Japan after became increasingly subject to Western influences, ending over two centuries of isolation.

Document: "Editor's Easy Chair," Harper's New Monthly Magazine (July 1872)

The Easy Chair gives the alarm. No time is to be lost. It is plain that under the smooth pretense of cultivating friendship with the United States, and becoming their pupils, and sitting at the feet of our sewing machines, the Japanese embassy is engaged in a deep, dark plot to subvert our religion.... If the heathen are to land upon these shores and take to converting us to loving one another, who is safe? If the Japanese are to inundate us with missionaries to convert us before we have fully converted Japan, as at last accounts we had not, then every man, as it were, to the front! Let us all stand by our guns. And as the insidious foe always begins his attack by asking, "What is Christianity?" let the Easy Chair warn the whole line not to fall into the trap of answering, "Wa'al, that depends."

But let every ... man answer—if a Baptist, that Christianity is the Baptist theory; if a Presbyterian, that it is a Presbyterian theory. Do not, above all things, say that the points of difference between the various views are non-essentials, because even the small eyes of the Japanese can see that it is upon the points of difference that we fight the hardest, and that we deny the name of Christian upon sectarian considerations. The only true way to repel the attack is for every body to give a different answer as to what Christianity is; and if that policy confounds the enemy as much as it confounds us, our victory is sure. Meanwhile let us all agree that while it is not only our right but our plain duty to go into other countries and tell the people that their religion is false and their worship foolish, yet that nothing is so plain a proof of heathen degradation as that the people of those countries should come to us to tell us the very same thing.

Source: "Editor's Easy Chair," *Harper's New Monthly Magazine* 45, no. 266 (July 1872): 293–94. Listed at "The Nineteenth Century in Print: Periodicals," American Memory Collection, Library of Congress: http://memory.loc.gov/ammem/ndlpcoop/moahtml/sn chome.html.

AFTERMATH

A more long-running challenge to the authority of the Christian Church came through the theory of evolution. Charles Darwin, a British naturalist, had published his *Origin of Species* in 1859. Darwin argued that living organisms evolved over time, keeping only the characteristics best fitted to their survival. The point challenged traditional religious thought that held God had created humans and animals in their present form. American initially paid little attention to Darwin and his findings, occupied by the Civil War and its immediate aftermath. But as a new generation went to college in the early 1870s, the theory of evolution gained increasing numbers of adherents. Darwin's works became more widely circulated, as did scientific studies on the applications of natural selection (a term coined by the British philosopher Herbert Spencer). The American-born and Harvard-educated John Fiske helped to popularize the theory of evolution outside of college halls by speaking and writing widely on the topic. Some church leaders found a middle ground between science and religion, pointing out that God had provided the spark that made any living life possible. More church leaders went on the attack, claiming that any ideas counter to their own was tantamount to denying the existence of the divine. Science and religion have existed uneasily together ever since, and conflict over how to best teach the origins of the universe and its inhabitants continues to spark debate.

ASK YOURSELF

1. Does the opening of shopping centers, movie theaters, and other public venues detract today from family time?
2. Do internal divisions continue to divide the faithful today—Orthodox and Liberal Jews, Sunni and Shiite Muslims, and Protestant and Catholic Christians—or does a shared religious heritage serve to bind these communities together more than divide them?

TOPICS AND ACTIVITIES TO CONSIDER

- How did religion influence the United States during the 19th century? Find out by reading a range of essays—including "American Abolitionism and Religion," and "Civil War: The Southern Perspective"—written by leading historians, at "Divining America: Religion in American History," National Humanities Center: http://nationalhumanitiesccenter.org/tserve/divam.htm.
- What influence did Sunday school readings have on children? Explore the answer at "Sunday School Books: Shaping the Values of Youth in Nineteenth-Century America," American Memory Collection, Library of Congress: http://memory.loc.gov/ammem/collections/sundayschool/.

Further Reading

Frank, Adam. *The Constant Fire: Beyond the Science vs. Religion Debate.* Berkeley: University of California Press, 2009.

LeBeau, Bryan F. *Religion in America to 1865.* New York: New York University Press, 2000.

Powell, Milton. *The Voluntary Church: American Religious Life, 1740–1865.* New York: Macmillan, 1967.

Robbins, Richard H. and Mark Nathan Cohen, eds. *Darwin and the Bible: The Cultural Confrontation.* Boston: Pearson Education, 2009.

Web Sites

Exploring the "objects, behaviors and people" that combine to give the United States a rich religious history is the goal of "The Material History American Religion Project." The site is maintained by the Divinity School at Vanderbilt University, and is listed at: http://www.materialreligion.org.

"Darwin200" celebrates the 200 Birthday of Charles Darwin with a series of essays and primary sources, at National History Museum, London, England: http://www.darwin200.org.

INTELLECTUAL LIFE

37. FUNDING AGRICULTURAL COLLEGES: THE MORRILL ACT (1862)

INTRODUCTION

The Land-Grant College Act, more commonly known as the Morrill Act, altered the dynamics of higher education in the United States. Relatively few Americans had access to a college or university education throughout the first half of the 19th century, due to high tuition costs and, away from the eastern seaboard, limited access. Public institutions in New York, the most populous state in the Union, for example, enrolled only a handful of new students each year. Justin Turner, a professor at the University of Illinois, had pushed during the early 1850s for the creation of federally funded agricultural and industrial colleges. These schools would benefit the children of farmers and workers, to the betterment of the American economy. The call came to national attention when picked up by JUSTIN MORRILL, a Vermont senator. Morrill introduced a bill before Congress in 1857, calling for the distribution of public lands to the states. The profits gained from the sale of these lands would go to fund agricultural schools. President James Buchanan vetoed the bill after it cleared Congress in early 1859, arguing that giving public land to the states for sale violated the Constitution. Morrill reintroduced the bill two years later, although worried that the pressing demands of the Civil War might pull away any opportunity for debate. The proposal enjoyed widespread public support, however, helping it to clear Congress in the summer of 1862. The Morrill Act granted to each state 30,000 acres of federal land for each senator and representative it sent to Congress. Those states without enough public land within their own borders received acreage along the western frontier.

KEEP IN MIND AS YOU READ

1. Many western politicians initially opposed the Morrill Act, correctly fearing that the government would carve acres from their states to give to those in the more densely populated East.
2. The Morrill Act also called for land-grant colleges to teach military tactics. The program became the foundation for the later establishment of the Reserve Officers' Training Corps (ROTC).

3. The Confederate States were excluded from participating in the Morrill Act. "No State while in a condition of rebellion or insurrection against the government of the United States shall be entitled to the benefit of this act."
4. Congress had established precedent for the federal support of education in the Northwest Ordinance of 1787. The Northwest Ordinance directed that money from land sales in each township go to support public school construction and programs.

Document: The Morrill Act (July 2, 1862)

AN ACT Donating Public Lands to the several States and Territories which may provide Colleges for the Benefit of Agriculture and Mechanic Arts.

Be it enacted by the Senate and House of Representatives of the United States of America in Congress assembled, That there be granted to the several States, for the purposes here-inafter mentioned, an amount of public land, to be apportioned to each State a quantity equal to thirty thousand acres for each senator and representative in Congress to which the States are respectively entitled by the apportionment under the census of eighteen hundred and sixty: Provided, That no mineral lands shall be selected or purchased under the provisions of this Act.

SEC. 2. And be it further enacted, That the land aforesaid, after being surveyed, shall be apportioned to the several States in sections or subdivisions of sections, not less than one quarter of a section; and whenever there are public lands in a State subject to sale at private entry at one dollar and twenty-five cents per acre, the quantity to which said State shall be entitled shall be selected from such lands within the limits of such State, and the Secretary of the Interior is hereby directed to issue to each of the States in which there is not the quantity of public lands subject to sale at private entry at one dollar and twenty-five cents per acre, to which said State may be entitled under the provisions of this act, land scrip to the amount in acres for the deficiency of its distributive share: said scrip to be sold by said States and the proceeds thereof applied to the uses and purposes prescribed in this act, and for no other use or purpose whatsoever . . .

Source: Act of July 2, 1862 (Morrill Act), Public Law 37–108, which established land grant colleges, 07/02/1862; Enrolled Acts and Resolutions of Congress, 1789–1996; Record Group 11; General Records of the United States Government; National Archives, Washington, DC: http://www.ourdocuments.gov.

AFTERMATH

The Morrill Act ultimately gave more than 17 million acres of federal land to the states, from which they received about $7 million. More than 70 land-grant colleges opened their doors, including Washington State, Nebraska, Cornell, and Clemson. The generosity of the federal government helped to surge the number of colleges and universities in the United States to 356 by 1876, a three-fold increase from 25 years earlier. The number of students attending college began to rise, hitting 50,000 by the early 1870s. The figure represented only a small fraction of the college-age population. Still, under the Morrill Act, an affordable college education now was within reach of many Americans. The percentage of Americans attending college would continue to increase throughout the 20th century. Women especially benefited from the new educational opportunities and by the late 1800s comprised about one-third of all college students. A second Morrill Act, passed in 1890, extended land-grant provisions to the former Confederate States.

ASK YOURSELF

1. In passing the Northwest Ordinance, Congress declared that knowledge is "necessary to good government and the happiness of mankind." Do you agree, and why?
2. Few African Americans initially benefited from the Morrill Act. Should Congress have been more deliberate in securing access to land-grant schools for African Americans?

TOPICS AND ACTIVITIES TO CONSIDER

- How does the Morrill Act compare to the Northwest Ordinance? Explore the background and text to the Northwest Ordinance at Our Documents, National Archives: http://www.ourdocuments.gov.
- How does the Morrill Act compare to the GI Bill, which financed the education of large numbers of World War II veterans? Read the history of the GI Bill at "GI Bill Home," U.S. Department of Veterans Affairs: http://www.gibill.va.gov.

Further Reading

Cross, Coy F. *Justin Smith Morrill: Father of the Land-Grant Colleges.* East Lansing: Michigan State University Press, 1999.

Rainsford, George N. *Congress and Higher Education in the Nineteenth Century.* Knoxville: University of Tennessee Press, 1972.

Williams, Roger L. *The Origins of Federal Support for Higher Education: George W. Atherton and the Land-Grant College Movement.* University Park: Pennsylvania State University Press, 1991.

Web Sites

Learn more about Senator Justin Morrill at "Justin Smith Morrill Homestead," Vermont Division of Historic Preservation: http://www.historicvermont.org/morrill/.

Watch videos and see pictures from a 2009 Morrill Act Conference sponsored by the Abraham Lincoln Bicentennial Commission and held at the University of Illinois Champaign–Urbana at "Lincoln's Unfinished Work: the Morrill Act and the Future of Higher Education": http://www.abrahamlincoln200.org/morrill-act.aspx.

38. "A Physician's Story": *Continental Monthly* (December 1862)

INTRODUCTION

College graduates increasingly pursued professional career paths in the late 19th century, especially as physicians. By 1870 physicians outnumbered clergymen, lawyers, and bankers. That physicians dominated the professional world is perhaps not surprising, because few barriers stood between calling oneself "mister" and "doctor." Entrance requirements to the nation's 100 or so medical schools were slim, sometimes only the ability to write and speak English. Newly admitted students might complete the medical curriculum in one year, with few, if any, clinical requirements. Other aspiring physicians opted instead for apprenticeships with already established doctors. Here they learned through experience, before striking out on their own approximately three years later. The knowledge gained by medical students and apprentices was, by modern-day standards, shockingly little. Doctors had only vague knowledge about what caused diseases and how they spread. Understanding of the science of bacteriology was only beginning in the late 1860s, and doctors performed complex operations without much worry over the cleanliness of their medical tools and surroundings. Still, many doctors labored long hours and did their best to alleviate suffering. Few doctors made a profit, instead practicing their craft as a passion. The tongue-in-cheek excerpt from "A Physician's Story" details the disappointment experienced by a young and eager doctor in an unusually healthy and resilient small town. Like many rural physicians, the hero of the story saw himself as ready to treat any and all injuries and maladies.

KEEP IN MIND AS YOU READ

1. Americans generally imported medicines from Europe through the late 19th century or relied on home remedies. Doctors relied on juice from a green persimmon as a styptic (an agent used to stem bleeding from a cut or injury) and red poppy opium as an anesthetic. Many physicians made as much or more money from a drug store that they opened and operated as from the practice of their craft.

2. Dr. Nathan Smith Davis founded the American Medical Association in 1847. A young doctor practicing in western New York, Davis called for improving both

consumption: Recognized today as tuberculosis. A dreaded disease throughout much of world history, consumption seemed to consume people from the inside through fever, paleness, bloody coughing, and wasting away. The infection is spread through the air, when people who have the disease cough and sneeze. A vaccine became widely used by the mid-20th century, but cases of tuberculosis continue to appear around much of the world.

Hall's 'Journal of Health': Listed are several popular medical advice books. Books and medicines promising fantastic treatments were commonplace through the late 19th century, given little government or professional oversight.

locality: With little understanding of how disease spread, many Americans believed that the climate fostered many illnesses. Thus, malaria was attributed to swamp gases, especially prevalent in the South, rather than to mosquitoes.

whooped: A reference to whooping cough. The infection of the respiratory system causes severe coughing, ending in a whooping sound when the person inhales. Before a vaccine became available, whooping cough killed several thousand people, mainly infants and young children, each year.

Yellow Jack: A viral disease that gains its name from the jaundice symptoms that some patients acquired. Yellow fever became epidemic in several American cities, including Philadelphia in the late 1790s, New Orleans in the 1850s, and Memphis in the 1870s. The disease claimed thousands of victims in each city. A vaccine became available in the 1930s.

the standards of medical education and the health of the American public. Today, the AMA is the largest medical association in the United States.

Document: "A Physician's Story"

And here I may remark, literally *en passant*, that the town in which I had chosen to locate was salubrious to a painful and unnatural degree, the very last place in the world for a young physician in ordinary circumstances to seek his fortune, . . . The inhabitants all took **Hall's 'Journal of Health;'** they cherished Buchan's 'Domestic Medicine,' they studied the 'Handbook of Hygiene;' they were learned in the works of Fowler. Cold water was cheap and plentiful, they used it externally and internally—exercise was fashionable and inevitable, where every lady was her own help, and every gentleman his own woodsawyer; food was just dear enough to make surfeits undesirable, and medicine was so unpopular that nobody before me ever ventured to open a drug store; the old ladies dispensed a few herbs privately, and that was the end of it. People did not seem to die; if anything was the matter with they, they perseveringly 'kept on,' till it stopped, the disease retiring in despair from their determination to be well. . . . [M]umps and measles, chills and chicken pox, prevailed and disappeared without medical assistance, and though all the children in the village **whooped** like wild Indians, no anxious parent ever thought it necessary to call in a physician. . . . The **locality** was too far south for bronchitis and **consumption**, too far north for poisonous malaria fevers; and being inland, just inside the line of the coast scourges of cholera and **Yellow Jack**. In short, to quote the only epitaph in the village churchyard, 'Physicians was in vain.'

Source: "A Physician's Story," *Continental Monthly: Devoted to Literature and National Policy* 2, no. 6 (December 1862): 667–78. Listed at "The Nineteenth Century in Print: Periodicals," American Memory Collection, Library of Congress: http://memory.loc.gov/ammem/ndlpcoop/moahtml/snchome.html.

AFTERMATH

A significant push to overhaul American medical education occurred in the late 19th and early 20th centuries. Reformers hoped to standardize the training of physicians and to control entry into the profession through licensure. They were partially successful. Medical education became far more rigorous and included laboratory science and clinical training. However, upon taking their degree, many physicians resisted attempts to limit their freedom to determine treatment

ELIZABETH BLACKWELL

Elizabeth Blackwell was the first woman to graduate from an American medical school, taking her degree from Geneva Medical College in New York in 1849. Born in England, Blackwell immigrated to the United States with her family as a child. The Blackwell family was actively involved in the abolitionist movement and other reform efforts. The youngest of three Blackwell daughters became interested in becoming a physician after recognizing that many women would rather discuss their health with another woman. Blackwell won admission to Geneva Medical School only because the students reportedly believed her application a practical joke. Her hard work and perseverance eventually won over most of her fellow classmates. After graduating from Geneva, Blackwell founded the New York Infirmary for Women and Children in the 1850s. During the Civil War, Blackwell helped to select and train nurses to assist the Union army. Blackwell founded a medical college for women at the infirmary, before dying at 89 years of age in 1910. A stamp commemorating Blackwell as the first woman physician was issued by the Post Office in 1974.

and procedure. Doctors often continued to work from private offices and to make house calls. As for the physician in the CONTINENTAL MONTHLY, business soon picked up. "The spell is broken that held us in supernatural health." Various maladies afflicted young and old. Additionally, a planned railroad route "will bring foreign diseases and habits among us, and turn our peaceful Arcadia into a miniature New York." With disease, illness, and accident present and yet coming, the young physician predicted a "busy and prosperous future in store for me."

ASK YOURSELF

1. Should physicians continue to make rounds through the community, even if this means leaving behind much of their sophisticated medical equipment in the hospital?
2. Should physicians become specialized, or do general practitioners best serve the community?

TOPICS AND ACTIVITIES TO CONSIDER

- Find out more regarding the history and treatment of diseases at "Epidemic! The Natural History of Disease," San Diego Natural History Museum: http://www.sdnhm.org/exhibits/epidemic/index.html.
- How has the depiction of medicine changed over time? Find out at "Images from the History of Medicine," National Library Museum, United States National Institutes of Health: http://www.nlm.nih.gov/hmd/ihm/.

Further Reading

Cassedy, James H. *Medicine and American Growth, 1800–1860*. Madison: University of Wisconsin Press, 1986.
Haller, John S., Jr. *American Medicine in Transition, 1840–1910*. Urbana: University of Illinois Press, 1981.

Rosenberg, Charles E. *The Care of Strangers: The Rise of America's Hospital System.* New York: Basic Books, 1987.

Weissmann, Gerald. *Democracy and DNA: American Dreams and Medical Progress.* New York: Hill and Wang, 1995.

Web Sites

The Web site for the American Medical Association is: http://www.ama-assn.org.

The National Museum of Civil War Medicine in Frederick, Maryland, is listed at: http://www.civilwarmed.org.

39. "Knowledge Is Power," Lesson XXII, *McGuffey's New Fourth Eclectic Reader: Instructive Lessons for the Young* (1866)

INTRODUCTION

Americans had placed a high value on the educational basics of reading, writing, and arithmetic since the late colonial era, at least for white children. But formal education for young people only became the norm during the late 1870s, with the establishment of common schools (today's public schools) in all states. Leading educational reformers believed that publicly supported schools would both foster social equality among students from diverse economic backgrounds and produce future workers and managers capable of sustaining economic growth. The push to extend educational opportunities to all white children caused common school enrolment to boom. By 1870, 60 percent of white Americans between the ages of 5 and 19 attended publicly supported schools. This was nearly double the percentage of white children who had attended school in 1830. School children often read from a series of readers authored by WILLIAM MCGUFFEY. A college professor and Presbyterian minister, McGuffey taught reading skills and moral precepts to an equal degree. His readers were the most widely used schoolbooks in the mid- and late-19th century, selling more than 60 million copies. "Knowledge Is Power" is one of 79 stories published in an 1866 reader, including "Waste Not, Want Not"; "The Idle School-Boy"; "Story about Washington"; and "The Golden Rule."

KEEP IN MIND AS YOU READ

1. Other elementary textbook authors followed McGuffey's lead, although never achieving the same level of distribution and sales. Salem Town, also the author of a reader, declared that his goal was "to improve the literary taste of the learner, to impress correct moral principles, and augment his fund of knowledge." S. Augustus Mitchell expressed a similar sentiment in a geography text. Mitchell hoped that his lessons would "illustrate the excellence of Christian religion, the advantages of correct moral principles, and the superiority of enlightened institutions."

2. African Americans in the aftermath of the Civil War expressed an eagerness to learn, all-too-well aware that the denial of education had been a hallmark of the slave system. Southern black people worked with the federal government and various

northern-backed benevolent societies to establish schools of their own. About one-quarter of former slaves attended public schools by the 1870s, while others received educational instruction at their church. Students often used a series of five books, published by the American Tract Society during 1864 and 1865. The *Freedmen's* books highlighted basic educational skills, American and African American history, and religious instruction.

Document: "Knowledge Is Power"

"What an excellent thing is knowledge," said a sharp-looking, bustling little man, to one who was much older than himself. "Knowledge is an excellent thing," repeated he. "My boys know more at six and seven years old than I did at twelve. They can read all sorts of books, and talk on all sorts of subjects. The world is a great deal wiser than it used to be. Every body knows something of every thing now. Do you not think, sir, that knowledge is an excellent thing?"

"Why, sir," replied the old man, looking gravely, "that depends entirely upon the use to which it is applied. It may be a blessing or a curse. Knowledge is only an increase of power, and power may be a bad as well as a good thing." "That is what I can not understand," said the bustling little man. "How can power be a bad thing?"

"I will tell you," meekly replied the old man; and thus he went on: "When the power of a horse is under restraint, the animal is useful in bearing burdens, drawing loads, and carrying his master; but when that power is unrestrained, the horse breaks his bridle, dashes to pieces the carriage that he draws, or throws his rider." "I see!" said the little man.

"When the water of a large pond is properly conducted by trenches, it renders the fields around fertile; but when it bursts through its banks, it sweeps every thing before it, and destroys the produce of the fields." "I see!" said the little man, "I see!"

"When the ship is steered aright, the sail that she hoists enables her sooner to get into port; but if steered wrong, the more sail she carries, the further will she go out of her course." "I see!" said the little man, "I see clearly!"

"Well, then," continued the old man, "if you see these things so clearly, I hope you can see, too, that knowledge, to be a good thing, must be rightly applied. God's grace in the heart will render the knowledge of the head a blessing; but without this, it may prove to us no better than a curse." "I see! I see!" said the little man. "I see!"

EXERCISES—What is the subject of this lesson? When is knowledge useful? When is it injurious? May it always be useful? What marks are those used in the last sentence? In the last sentence, which are the adjectives? What is an adjective? What does the word *adjective* mean?

Source: William Holmes McGuffey, *McGuffey's New Fourth Eclectic Reader: Instructive Lessons for the Young*. New York: Clark & Maynard, 1866, pp. 78–80. Listed at "19th Century Schoolbooks," Digital Research Library, University of Pittsburgh: http://digital.library.pitt.edu/nietz/.

AFTERMATH

Students in the late 19th century had a different educational experience from their parents. Women now were more common as teachers. Educators believed classroom discipline and learning better based upon moral suasion rather than corporal punishment. Women supposedly possessed the innate skills as nurturers to maintain order and inspire students to learn. The fact that women had fewer professional paths open to them than men did, and thus worked for lower pay, also contributed to their growing numbers in the schools. School officials also grouped students together by age, the second noticeable difference in the classroom experience from before the Civil War. Educators otherwise had made little distinction between the learning needs among students of different ages. The result was that teachers instructed pupils who ranged in age and physical development from toddlers to young adults. With increasing numbers of children entering common schools by the mid- and late 1860s, school officials concentrated students by *age grading*. Under the practice, educators grouped children between 8 years of age and 13 years of age into intermediate schools, and teenagers between 14 years of age and 19 years of age into high schools. The age range of high school students in rural towns and villages often was younger (between 11 and 17 years of age), to enable students to sooner begin full-time work on family farms. Age grading in intermediate schools and high schools also influenced the ages of students attending college. By the end of the 19th century, most college students ranged between 18 years of age and 22 years of age.

ASK YOURSELF

1. Some critics argue that the attempt to instill national and moral values is no longer part of public education, thus taking the "common" out from common schools. Is this a fair assessment? And, if true, is the trend good or bad?

2. The *Fourth Eclectic Reader* would generally be used today between the third grade and the fifth grade. Do the questions in the Exercise section at the end of "Knowledge Is Power" seem at an appropriate level for children between the ages of eight and eleven? If not, are they too easy or too difficult?

TOPICS AND ACTIVITIES TO CONSIDER

- Some educators and parents worry today that the trend toward female teachers has gone too far, and that there are too few male teachers. Consider the topic at "Missing Male Teachers," at "Talk of the Nation," a program by National Public Radio, at: http://www.npr.org/blogs/talk/2008/09/missing_male_teachers.html.

- How did the daily experience of grade-school-age students in the mid- and late 19th century compare to your own? Find out at "Not For Ourselves Alone: A Day in the Life," PBS Kids: http://pbskids.org/stantonanthony/day_in_life.html.

TEXTBOOKS IN THE CONFEDERACY

Confederate educators churned out new textbooks, fearing a northern bias in prewar editions. Authors attempted to both teach children why the war was being fought and inspire them with stories of patriotism and bravery. An active defense of slavery was common, as well as extolling supposed Confederate martial prowess. One text claimed that slaves in the Confederacy were well clothed and fed, and "better instructed than in their native country." A math primer asked, "If one Confederate soldier can whip 7 yankees, how many soldiers can whip 49 yankees?" By the end of the Civil War, schoolbooks constituted nearly three-quarters of the youth literature published in the Confederacy.

Further Reading

Cremin, Lawrence A. *American Education: The National Experience, 1783–1876*. New York: Harper and Row, 1980.

Pulliam, John D. *History of Education in America*. 6th ed. Englewood Cliffs, NJ: Merrill, 1995.

Solomon, Barbara Miller. *In the Company of Educated Women: A History of Women and Higher Education in America*. New Haven, CT: Yale University Press, 1985.

Spring, Joel H. *The American School: From Puritans to No Child Left Behind*. Boston: McGraw-Hill, 2008.

Web Sites

Learn the history of American public schools at "School: The Story of American Public Education," a PBS documentary: http://www.pbs.org/kcet/publicschool/index.html.

Find out the educational requirement for elementary school at Brian R., Ben B., Zach S., "One Room School Houses, Boone County, Indiana": http://www.bccn.boone.in.us/schoolhouse/home.htm.

40. *Ragged Dick: Or, Street Life in New York with the Boot-Blacks* by Horatio Alger Jr. (1868)

INTRODUCTION

When not reading their schoolbooks, many children read dime novels. Briskly written, short in length, heavy on action, and, sometimes, lurid in detail, dime novels were sold at newsstands and through magazines. The paperbacks often sold for their name price, although, depending on the title, they might cost a nickel less or a nickel more. Some of the more popular titles received a printing of between 60,000 and 70,000 copies, a large run by period standards, and went through numerous reprintings. The American West was a popular subject, as were detective stories and romances. *Ragged Dick*, by Horatio Alger, first appeared in a monthly newspaper for children in 1867. The story received publication as a novel the next year, beginning the widely popular "Ragged Dick Series." Five more titles rounded out the series. Dick, a cheerful shoeshine boy with an Irish brogue, is introduced in this excerpt. Sleeping in a straw-filled wooden box, Dick is dirty and unkempt. Still, might one have taken soap and water and a new outfit to Dick, "he would have been decidedly good-looking. Some of his companions were sly, and their faces inspired distrust; Dick had a frank, straight-forward manner that made him a favorite." From such humble beginnings, Dick, by the end of the series, has risen to middle-class status and respectability. Hard work and willingness to learn are keys to Dick's upward climb, a larger message to the novel.

KEEP IN MIND AS YOU READ

1. Erasmus and Irwin Beadle became among the most successful publishers of dime novels. The Beadles paid authors anywhere from $50 to $250, based on sales expectations, to write novels that ran up to 100 pages. Initially binding the books in salmon-colored paper, the Beadles later switched to covers in other colors.
2. *Maleaska, the Indian Wife of the White Hunter*, written by Ann S. Stephens and published in 1860, was one of the best selling early dime novels. The book reportedly sold 65,000 copies in only a few months.
3. Dime novels also were popular in England. In Europe, however, the paperbacks were known as *penny dreadfuls*.

Document: Excerpt from Ragged Dick

Our ragged hero wasn't a model boy in all respects. I'm afraid he swore sometimes, and now and then he played tricks upon unsophisticated boys from the country, or gave a wrong direction to honest old gentlemen unused to the city. . . .

Another of Dick's faults was his extravagance. Being always wide-awake and ready for business, he earned enough to have supported him comfortably and respectably. There were not a few young clerks who employed Dick from time to time in his professional capacity, who scarcely earned as much as he, greatly as their style and dress exceeded his. But Dick was careless of his earning. Where they went he could hardly have told himself. However much he managed to earn during the day, all was generally spent before the morning. He was fond of going to the Old Bowery Theatre, and to Tony Pastor's, and if he had any money left afterwards, he would invite some of his Mends in somewhere to have an oyster stew; so it seldom happened that he commenced the day with a penny.

> **cigars:** Tobacco consumption was high in the United States in the 19th century, primarily through chew, snuff, pipes, and cigars. Tobacco consumption only soared higher with the machine production of cigarettes late in the century.

Then I am sorry to add that Dick had formed the habit of smoking. This cost him considerable, for Dick was rather fastidious about his **cigars**, and wouldn't smoke the cheapest. Besides, having a liberal nature, he was generally ready to treat his companions. But of course the expense was the smallest objection. No boy of fourteen can smoke without being affected injuriously. Men are frequently injured by smoking, and boys always. But large numbers of newsboys and boot-blacks form the habit. Exposed to the cold and wet they find that it warms them up, and the self-indulgence grows upon them. It is not uncommon to see a little boy, too young to be out of his mother's sight, smoking with all the apparent satisfaction of a veteran smoker.

There was another way in which Dick sometimes lost money. There was a noted gambling-house on Baxter Street, which in the evening was sometimes crowded with these juvenile gamesters, who staked their hard earnings, generally losing of course, and refreshing themselves with from time to time a vile mixture of liquor at two cents a glass. Sometimes Dick strayed in here, and played with the rest.

I have mentioned Dick's faults and defects, because I want it understood, to begin with, that I don't consider him a model boy. But there were some good points about him nevertheless. He was above doing anything mean or dishonorable. He would not steal, or cheat, or impose upon younger boys, but was frank and straight-forward, manly and self-reliant. His nature was a noble one, and had saved him from all mean faults. I hope my young readers will like him as much as I do, without being blind to his faults. Perhaps, although he was only a boot-black, they may find something in him to imitate.

Source: Horatio Alger Jr., *Ragged Dick: Or, Street Life in New York with the Boot-Blacks.* Boston: A. K. Loring, 1868, pp. 16–18. Listed at Internet Archive: http://www.archive.org/ stream/raggeddickorstre00alge/raggeddickorstre00alge_djvu.txt.

AFTERMATH

Children and young adults were not the only ones with their eyes glued to the printed page; women also became voracious readers of novels. By the start of the Civil War in 1861,

Harper's Magazine estimated that women made up four-fifths of the reading public. Profits were to be made, and many publishers sought after female authors to better turn wives and mothers into customers. The subsequent outpouring of books starred heroines who overcame adversity, often created by less than ideal men. Writers of domestic novels shied away from politics, believing it was too controversial for their audience. Instead, according to Sarah Hale, a nationally known writer and advocate, female authors emphasized "domestic scenes and deep emotions." Even with limited boundaries, writes of domestic novels sometimes ran into trouble. Nathaniel Hawthorne, one of the preeminent authors in American history, scoffed at his countrymen's interest in a "damned mob of scribbling women." Mark Twain viewed domestic novels as too light on plot and too heavy on sentiment. Domestic novels declined in popularity in the aftermath of the Civil War, as ladies magazines and journals gained in circulation. But the genre did not die out completely; it was the forerunner of today's mass-market romance novel.

ASK YOURSELF

1. Many contemporary novelists argue that a book needs to hook its audience within the first several pages, to keep it reading the remainder. Does the excerpt from *Ragged Dick* hold your interest? Would you read the rest of the novel, if given the opportunity?

2. One modern-day critic claims that dime novels declined in popularity by the late 1800s because they were "out of step" with the values and attitudes of American society. Would stories emphasizing morality, hard work, and individualism fare well in bookstores today?

TOPICS AND ACTIVITIES TO CONSIDER

- How did cover art help dime novels to gain in popularity? See some of the novel covers at "Dime Novels," Rare Book & Special Collections Division, Library of Congress: http://www.loc.gov/exhibits/treasures/tri015.html.

- Are dime novels and domestic novels similar to today's romance novels? Find out more at "Romance Scholarship," RomanceWiki: http://www.romancewiki.com/Romance_Scholarship.

Further Reading

Arac, Jonathan. *The Emergence of American Literary Narrative, 1820–1860.* Cambridge, MA: Harvard University Press, 2005.

Johannsen, Albert. *The House of Beadle and Adams and Its Dime and Nickel Novels: The Story of a Vanished Literature.* 3 vols. Norman: University of Oklahoma Press, 1950–62.

Margolis, Stacey. *The Public Life of Privacy in Nineteenth-Century American Literature.* Durham, NC: Duke University Press, 2005.

Sasa, Ghada Suleiman. *The Femme Fatale in American Literature.* Amherst, NY: Cambria Press, 2008.

Sullivan, Larry E. and Lydia Cushman Schurman, eds. *Pioneers, Passionate Ladies, and Private Eyes: Dime Novels, Series Books, and Paperbacks.* New York: Haworth Press, 1996.

Web Sites

See more examples of dime novels at "Dime Novels and Penny Dreadfuls," Academic Text Service, Stanford University Libraries: http://www-sul.stanford.edu/depts/dp/pennies/home.html.

Search for dime novels and tens of thousands of other popular fiction titles at the Rare Book and Special Collections Reading Room, Library of Congress: http://www.loc.gov/rr/rarebook/.

41. "Harvest of Death": Photograph by Timothy O'Sullivan (1863)

INTRODUCTION

Dime novels and domestic novels served as distractions from the horrors of the Civil War, brought home all too vividly to the American public through photographs. Although a relatively new visual medium by 1861, photography was widely practiced during the Civil War. The process of picture-taking was daunting. Photographers had to wait upwards of 30 seconds, sometimes more, for the intended image to burn onto the wet plate. The variable exposure time made possible only pictures of landscapes, still objects, and unmoving people and animals. If there was any motion, the picture would blur and the image would be lost. Despite the technological difficulties, wartime photographers shot perhaps as many as one million photographs. Most were group and individual portraits, but some photographs showed the aftermath of battle. "Harvest of Death," by Timothy O'Sullivan, shows corpses the day after the fighting at Gettysburg during the summer of 1863. The picture shocked a nation that until that time had rarely, if ever, seen any depiction of wartime dead. Alexander Gardner, who operated the studio where "Harvest of Death" was displayed, defended the image. The picture served a "useful moral" by showing all too visibly the "blank horror and reality of war." In 1866 Gardner published "Harvest of Death" in his *Photographic Sketch Book of the War*. Gardner introduced the picture with these words:

> Slowly, over the misty fields of Gettysburg—as all reluctant to expose their ghastly horrors to the light—came the sunless morn, after the retreat by [Confederate General Robert. E.] Lee's broken army. Through the shadowy vapors, it was, indeed, a "harvest of death" that was presented; hundreds and thousands of torn Union and rebel soldiers—although many of the former were already interred—strewed the now quiet fighting ground, soaked by the rain, which for two days had drenched the country with its fitful showers.

KEEP IN MIND AS YOU READ

1. Mathew Brady, a contemporary of O'Sullivan, was among the most famous Civil War photographers. Born in upstate New York in 1823, Brady won permission from the federal government soon after the start of the Civil War to chronicle

the operations of the Union army. Brady eventually amassed 5,700 negatives of war subjects, primarily in the eastern theater. Financially strained by his wartime efforts, Brady died in near poverty in 1896.

2. Photographers were less common in the Confederacy, due to a scarcity of supplies. Photographic equipment received little emphasis as the Confederacy attempted to smuggle military supplies through the ever-tightening Union naval blockade. Confederate photographers did take several widely circulated pictures of Fort Sumter, South Carolina. The Union controlled fort surrendered on April 14, 1861, after enduring a two-day Confederate bombardment. The Confederate attack upon Fort Sumter marked the opening battle of the Civil War.

Document: "Harvest of Death"

Harvest of Death.

Source: Alexander Gardner (Timothy H. O'Sullivan), *Gardner's Photographic Sketch Book of the War*, vol. 1—Prints and Photographs Division, Library of Congress, Washington, DC, LC-B8184–7964-A: http://www.loc.gov/pictures/item/2006685384/.

AFTERMATH

Sketch artists also followed Union and Confederate armies, drawing the war with pencil and paper. Illustrators had an advantage over photographers, because they recorded battles, marches, and other action scenes on the spot. However, war artists had to confront a range of professional obstacles. Illustrators often had their fine lines and details lost, as engravers carved the drawing onto thick blocks of wood for imprinting on newspapers. Sketch artists also had to endure daily life in the field, with all its attending physical discomforts and hardships. If wood blocks and bad food and hard marches were not enough to deter anyone from putting pencil to drawing paper, illustrators also had to endure jibes from soldiers that their drawings and maps provided valuable information to the enemy. Still, despite obstacles in the home office and on the front lines, sketch artists illustrated for the American public—then and now—what military life during the four years of fighting was like. Lieutenant General Ulysses S. Grant, the general-in-chief of the Union armies during 1864–65, reportedly recognized the long-term influence of illustrator-journalists. "We are the men who make history," Grant is said to have told one artist, "but you are the men who perpetuate it."

ASK YOURSELF

1. Does seeing a photograph of men killed in battle, such as O'Sullivan's picture, have more influence on a viewer than seeing a pencil drawing of a similar scene? Why or why not?
2. What are some public photographs that have made an impression on you? Why?

TOPICS AND ACTIVITIES TO CONSIDER

    ∾ Do pictures of American war dead lower national morale? The issue is in the news recently, with the federal government reversing a long-standing ban on the news media taking pictures of the coffins of American war dead. Find out more at Elisabeth Bumiller, "Pentagon to Allow Photos of Soldiers' Coffins," February 26, 2009, *New York Times*: http://www.nytimes.com/2009/02/26/us/26web-coffins.html.

THE BOHEMIAN BRIGADE

The Civil War was the most widely reported war in American history, although depth and reliability often were spotty. Reporters followed after the armies and often pooled resources and information. Far more journalists recorded the ongoings of the Union army, freed from the manpower and financial constraints faced by the Confederacy. Often hard-drinking and beyond the reach of army regulations, members of the so-called Bohemian Brigade detailed the war for the home front. Like soldiers writing home, reporters faced no government censorship in their dispatches. The result sometimes led to tension, with high-ranking officers believing too much information regarding their plans divulged for public consumption. Newspaper correspondents also occasionally fell victim to the practice of writing first and verifying second, in the rush to beat deadlines. Still, well before the days of e-mail and the Internet, reporters kept the public informed of the war effort.

﹌ "Harvest of Death" is arguably the most famous of the 100 photographs printed in *Gardner's Photographic Sketch Book*. What impression do the other photographs give of military life during the Civil War? Does the accompanying text sensationalize each image? See the images at "Gardner's Photographic Sketch Book of the War," Division of Rare and Manuscript Collections, Cornell University: http://rmc.library.cornell.edu/7milVol/.

Further Reading

Davis, William C., ed. *The End of an Era*. Garden City, NY: Doubleday, 1984.

Davis, William C., ed. *Touched by Fire: A Photographic Portrait of the Civil War*. William A. Frassanito, photographic consultant. 2 vols. Boston: Little Brown, 1985–1986.

Frassanito, William A. *Early Photography at Gettysburg*. Gettysburg, PA: Thomas Publications, 1995.

Lee, Anthony W. and Elizabeth Young. *On Alexander Gardner's Photographic Sketch Book of the Civil War*. Berkeley: University of California Press, 2007.

Savas, Theodore P. *Brady's Civil War Journal: Photographing the War 1861–65*. New York: Skyhorse Publishing, 2008.

Zeller, Bob. *The Blue and Gray in Black and White: A History of Civil War Photography*. Westport, CT: Praeger, 2005.

Web Sites

The Library of Congress has compiled a searchable index of over 1,000 photographs at "Selected Civil War Photographs": http://memory.loc.gov/ammem/cwphtml/cwphome.html. Visit the American Museum of Photography, a virtual museum, at: http://www.photographymuseum.com.

Theodore Davis, a former sketch artist accompanying the Union army, remembers some of his experiences in "How a Battle Is Sketched," in *St. Nicholas*, a children's magazine. Read the article at History Matters, American Social History Productions: http://www.historymatters.gmu.edu/d/6833.

42. "THE BLUE AND THE GRAY" BY FRANCIS MILES FINCH (1867)

INTRODUCTION

Finding reconciliation in the aftermath of the death and destruction so vividly captured in "Harvest of Death" loomed ominously before the nation in 1865. It must have felt as though the wounds inflicted by the war might never fully heal, leaving the nation deeply scarred. Initially, little national discussion regarding the war occurred. Northerners and southerners were too busy mourning their dead and making up for lost time. *The Blue and the Gray*, written by Francis Finch and published two years after the end of the Civil War, helped to prod the nation into finding a shared memory. Finch—a lawyer in New York at the time—reportedly received inspiration to write the poem after hearing that a women's memorial association in Columbus, Mississippi, had tended to the graves of both Union and Confederate dead in a local cemetery.

KEEP IN MIND AS YOU READ

1. The Grand Army of the Republic (GAR) was established in 1867 for Union veterans. Initially the group was hierarchical, with ranks and titles. Faced with small enrollment, the GAR became more fraternal in the late 1860s. Members participated in national and local encampments and memorial days. Enrollment in the GAR peaked in 1890, with nearly 500,000 members. The GAR also had a political agenda. The organization successfully pushed for veterans' pensions and the establishment of retirement homes for former Union soldiers and sailors. Members generally voted for the party of Abraham Lincoln, leading some wags to quip that GAR stood for "Generally All Republican." (The Democratic Party suffered in the postwar North due to its association with the secession movement in the Old South.) The last member of the GAR died in 1956, and the organization was formally dissolved.

2. The United Confederate Veterans (UCV) was the southern counterpart to the GAR. Founded in 1889, the UCV served as a benevolent, social, and historical association. Members especially attempted to provide for disabled veterans and widows of former Confederate soldiers, since the federal government provided no financial assistance. At the height of its popularity, the UCV listed about 160,000

members. The last national reunion of the UCV met in Norfolk, Virginia, in 1951.

Document: "The Blue and the Gray"

By the flow of the inland river, / Whence the fleets of iron have fled,
   Where the blades of the grave-grass quiver, / Asleep are the ranks of the dead:
   Under the sod and the dew, / Waiting the Judgment Day:
   Under one, the Blue; / Under the other, the Gray.

These in the robings of glory, / Those in the gloom of defeat,
   All with the battle-blood gory, / In the dusk of eternity meet:
   Under the sod and the dew, / Waiting the Judgment Day
   Under the laurel, the Blue; / Under the willow, the Gray.

From the silence of sorrowful hours, / The desolate mourners go,
   Lovingly laden with flowers, / Alike for the friend and the foe:
   Under the sod and the dew, / Waiting the Judgment Day:
   Under the roses, the Blue; / Under the lilies, the Gray.

So, with an equal splendor / The morning sunrays fall,
   With a touch impartially tender, / On the blossoms blooming for all:
   Under the sod and the dew, / Waiting the Judgment Day:
   Broidered with gold, the Blue; / Mellowed with gold, the Gray.

So, when the summer calleth, / On forest and field of grain,
   With an equal murmur falleth / The cooling drip of the rain:
   Under the sod and the dew, / Waiting the Judgment Day:
   Wet with the rain, the Blue; / Wet with the rain, the Gray.

Sadly, but not with upbraiding, / The generous deed was done.
   In the storms of the years that are fading / No braver battle was won:
   Under the sod and the dew, / Waiting the Judgment Day:
   Under the blossoms, the Blue; / Under the garlands, the Gray.

No more shall the war-cry sever, / Or the winding rivers be red;
   They banish our anger forever / When they laurel the graves of our dead!
   Under the sod and the dew, / Waiting the Judgment Day:
   Love and tears for the Blue; / Tears and love for the Gray.

Source: Francis M. Finch, *The Blue and the Gray, and Other Verses.* New York: H. Holt, 1909. Listed at Internet Archive: http://www.archive.org/details/blueand grey00fincrich.

AFTERMATH

Reunion came with surprising speed, given the ferocity with which the Union and the Confederacy had fought. Veterans often led the way. By the late 19th century, a trickle of former soldiers returning to the battlefields that had marked their youth turned into a flood. Veterans emphasized the valor and heroism of the men who had worn blue and gray, rather than the reasons behind the start of the war. Highlighting a shared American bravery helped to quiet past sectional arguments. Additionally, the focus on battlefields kept the war within the domain of white Americans. Black soldiers had not fought at Gettysburg and Antietam, two of the more widely commemorated battles because of their perception as military and political turning points. Survivors of the fighting in Pennsylvania and Maryland rarely mentioned the wartime sacrifices of black soldiers, because that was beyond their immediate focus. The public soon followed, and the Civil War became remembered primarily as a contest between whites. Confederate veterans also increasingly came to agree that the end of slavery had been a good thing. The institution had stymied long-term economic growth in the region, by discouraging agricultural innovation. Amid the goodwill, the plight of former slaves in the South simply was not the concern of white veterans. Reconciliation happened, but the integration of African Americans into the fabric of American society remained a question for future generations to grapple with.

ASK YOURSELF

1. Positive memories often crowded out inconvenient memories in the commemoration of the Civil War. Do individuals tend to do the same in remembering the events of their life? Does distance make the past seem more pleasant?
2. How does *The Blue and the Gray* match up to letters written by soldiers listed in the section on military life? Did soldiers seem to regard their service in the war as a "generous deed," and their adversaries with "love and tears"?

TOPICS AND ACTIVITIES TO CONSIDER

- How might veterans design a monument to commemorate the role of their unit in the Civil War? See pictures and read description of the Union and Confederate monuments at Gettysburg at Stephen Becker, "Virtual Gettysburg": http://www.virtualgettysburg.com/exhibits/monuments/.

CONFEDERADOS

Some former Confederates immigrated with their families to Brazil during the postwar era, where they became known as "Confederados." Estimates vary as to how many white southerners moved to Latin America, but some scholars place the number in the low thousands. Motives for the move varied, from unwillingness to accept ultimate Union victory to desire to make a new economic start. Brazilian Emperor Dom Pedro II encouraged Americans to move to his country to cultivate cotton. Brazil also continued to practice slavery, although the institution was abolished in 1888. Americana, in southern Brazil, was one of the communities established by Confederados. About 10 percent of the city's 200,000 residents today claim Confederate ancestry. In other parts of Brazil, the American Descendants Association meets to preserve their mid-19th-century heritage. Still, it is important not to overexaggerate the wanderlust of Confederate veterans. The vast majority of former gray-clad soldiers remained in the South, working to rebuild their lives and their home region.

       👋 How did commemoration of the Civil War compare to that of the Vietnam War in the late 20th century? Find out at a Web site that asks, "How should we remember a war that we 'lost'?" at Edward J. Gallagher, "The Vietnam Wall Controversy," Department of English, Lehigh University, Bethlehem, Pennsylvania: http://www.lehigh.edu/~ejg1/vietnam/.

Further Reading

Blair, William Alan. *Cities of the Dead: Contesting the Memory of the Civil War in the South, 1865–1914.* Chapel Hill: University of North Carolina Press, 2004.

Blight, David W. *Beyond the Battlefield: Race, Memory, and the American Civil War.* Amherst: University of Massachusetts Press, 2002.

Fahs, Alice and Joan Waugh, eds. *The Memory of the Civil War in American Culture.* Chapel Hill: University of North Carolina Press, 2004.

Foster, Gaines M. *Ghosts of the Confederacy: Defeat, the Lost Cause, and the Emergence of the New South, 1865–1913.* New York: Oxford University Press, 1987.

Logue, Larry M. and Michael Barton, eds. *The Civil War Veteran: A Historical Reader.* New York: New York University Press, 2007.

McConnell, Stuart C. *Glorious Contentment: The Grand Army of the Republic, 1865–1900.* Chapel Hill: University of North Carolina Press, 1992.

Web Sites

More information on Union veterans is found at Grand Army of the Republic Museum and Library, Philadelphia, Pennsylvania: http://garmuslib.org.

The Sons of Confederate Veterans labels itself as the "direct heir of the United Confederate Veterans, and the oldest hereditary organization for male descendents of Confederate soldiers." The site is listed at: http://www.scv.org.

RECREATION AND LEISURE

43. "Clubs and Club Life": *The Galaxy* (1876)

INTRODUCTION

American men spent much of their leisure time at clubs, lodges, and fraternal organizations during the late 19th century. According to Robert Walker, a social historian writing during the 1970s, one out of every five adult males participated in a nonchurch-affiliated group by 1890. The high numbers occurred because members gained a sense of order and stability amid the change that characterized the postwar era. The Freemasons, Independent Order of Odd Fellows, Grand Army of the Republic, and other fraternities and clubs provided a constant against a seemingly fast-paced and ever-more-complex world. Additionally, male-only organizations provided an opportunity for fun. Parades, dinners, and picnics provided members and their guests a sense of belonging. In an article penned for *THE GALAXY*, an unidentified author, writing under the pen name "An Old New Yorker," encouraged unmarried men especially to join one of the many clubs that existed in the city. For a relatively small annual due, a bachelor was provided with almost all the benefits of home. This included rooms for reading, eating, and socializing. The author described several clubs in detail, including the Union Club. Organized in the 1830s, the Union Club quickly became an elite group. Membership was capped at 1,000 men, almost exclusively from upper-crust backgrounds. For most readers of *The Galaxy*, knowledge of the Union Club came through the word-tour provided by "An Old New Yorker." That the Union Club received almost as much space as the other New York clubs combined indicates that many Americans, then as now, find interesting the lifestyle of the rich and the famous.

KEEP IN MIND AS YOU READ

1. The Union Club was staunchly conservative. Members reportedly did not expel individuals who fought for the Confederacy, despite considerable public backlash.
2. Membership in the Union Club was expensive, as a way to keep its elite status. In addition to contributing a one-time $300 initiation fee, members had to pay $75 in annual dues.
3. Perhaps as a way to repair some of the damage for failing to renounce its Confederate members, the Union Club during the postwar era admitted many military officers

to its ranks. Army and navy officers did not count against the 1,000 member total, and were exempt from membership dues.

4. "An Old New Yorker" deflected arguments that if young bachelors joined a club, they might never marry. "Man is drawn toward woman by a mysterious power far greater than that which causes the magnetic needle to point steadfastly toward the North Pole," he assured. "In cultivated communities the social ease and freedom from restraint of club life will never militate against the refined charm of female society."

Document: "Clubs and Club Life"

A few words descriptive of the interior economy of the Union Club . . . may prove of interest to the general reader. The house is opened at 7 A.M. from May 1 to November 1, and at 8 A.M. from November 1 to May 1. A servant is at all times stationed at the door. . . . It is his province to see that none but those who are entitled to admission penetrate within the walls of the sacred edifice. . . . To the left of the hall immediately on entering is the office. Here meals are ordered, letters sought, and information of all kinds given by the clerk. We speak advisedly when we say information of all kinds. The questions which the clerk is called upon to answer during the twenty-four hours embrace all subjects and range over every branch of human knowledge. . . .

The chief reading and lounging room runs the whole length of the building on Fifth Avenue. Four large windows form admirable lookouts. Here are kept the daily and weekly papers, both foreign and domestic, a small collection of books of reference, some maps, and two tables furnished with all the materials necessary for writing. . . . The usual dining hour is six or half past. At about eight the diners straggle in for coffee and cigars, and disperse soon after for the theater, the opera, the card room, or outside social engagements. Twelve years ago it was a rare thing to see a man lounging about the club in evening dress without he had been bidden there to dine. Now almost every other man you meet after dinner is in full dress. The large front reading room is a sort of *foyer* where news is gathered and spread.

Each group has its *specialité*. In one corner may be seen the solid men, who have passed the age of frivolities, calmly discussing stocks, bonds, railroads, real estate, and business, failures, and **defalcations**. Further on, politics, elections, and municipal affairs are treated of from a taxpayer's standpoint. Another group are deep in horse racing, yacht racing, pigeon shooting, mail stage coaching, and of late fox hunting. These younger gentlemen . . . are many of them men of large fortune, cosmopolitan in tastes and habits. They pass a great deal of their time abroad, and are as much at home on the *asphalts* of the **Boulevard or Pall Mall** as here in New York.

On the second floor are the card rooms, billiard rooms, and a small apartment devoted to non-smokers . . . The card rooms come in play about nine o'clock in the evening. The only games permitted are whist, all fours, euchre, and cribbage, and the stakes cannot exceed twenty dollars. . . . Euchre [recently] came in and took forcible possession of the card rooms. The older members still cling to whist. Two or three tables accommodate now all the

Atlantic cables: The first successful transatlantic cable was laid in 1866. Americans might now have almost instant access to European economic and political news.

Boulevard or Pall Mall: Trendy streets and neighborhoods in Paris and London.

defalcations: Embezzlements.

whist players; the balance are given over to the invaders, who look upon whist as too slow a game in this age of steam, electricity, and **Atlantic cables**. Perhaps they are right.

Source: "Club and Club Life," *The Galaxy* 22, no. 2 (August 1876): 227–38. Listed at American Memory Collection, Library of Congress: http://memory.loc.gov/ammem/ndlpcoop/moahtml/snchome.html.

AFTERMATH

Outside the city, the National Grange of the Patrons of Husbandry, popularly known among Americans as the Granger movement, was among the largest of the postwar fraternal orders. Established by farmers during the late 1860s, the Granger movement protested the perceived victimization of agriculture by railroads, banks, and other moneyed interests. Hard economic times suffered by farmers during the 1870s caused the Grangers to gain rapidly, with 850,000 members. The widespread backing allowed the Grangers to establish both cooperatives to pool otherwise expensive agricultural equipment and banks that catered to farmers and their families. Numbers also allowed the Grangers to push through national and state legislation restricting rates charged by the railroads for a public utility, such as agriculture. The Grange also took time to have fun. Local groups sponsored a range of membership activities, including picnics and dances. The food, games, and singing that accompanied these gatherings provided a sense of community while helping to maintain membership.

ASK YOURSELF

1. Given the popularity today of electronic social networking sites like Facebook and Twitter, do social clubs and organizations that meet in person seem out of date? Is there value to paying to meet in person with local friends, when one might meet online with friends from across the nation for free?
2. If invited to join an exclusive social organization like the Union Club, would you? Why or why not?

THE YMCA AND YWCA

The Young Men's Christian Association and the Young Women's Christian Association provided a religious alternative to secular clubs and organizations. The YMCA came to the United States from England during the mid-1850s, and the YWCA about 10 years later. By the mid-1870s, the YMCA counted nearly 1,000 branches in the United States and Canada, with 100,000 members. The two organizations emphasized Christian faith and devotion, especially Bible readings and lectures. The YWCA was especially active in attempting to provide a safe alternative to young women from the perceived ills of city life. The YMCA and YWCA also attempted to expand the mind beyond the religious, with study classes, music concerts, and athletic games. Although perhaps most widely known today for the former hit song by the group the Village People, the YMCA and the YWCA remain active across the United States.

TOPICS AND ACTIVITIES TO CONSIDER

- ❧ Do college fraternities and sororities need letters, pins, and other paraphernalia to mark membership? Should nonmembers be allowed to collect such items? See Katherine Rosman, "O Brother (and Sister), Where Art Thy Pins?" *New York Times,* August 11, 2002: http://www.nytimes.com/2002/08/11/style/o-brother-and-sister-where-art-thy-pins.html?src=pm.

- ❧ How have fraternal organizations been depicted in print? Was George Washington a Mason? Find out these answers and many more at the Exhibitions page for the National Heritage Museum in Lexington, Massachusetts: http://www.nationalheritagemuseum.org/Default.aspx?tabid=155. According to its Web site, the National Heritage Museum is an "American history museum founded and supported by the 32nd Scottish Rite Freemasons in the Northern Masonic Jurisdiction of the United States of America."

Further Reading

Clawson, Mary Ann. *Constructing Brotherhood: Class, Gender, and Fraternalism.* Princeton, NJ: Princeton University Press, 1989.

Ferguson, Charles W. *Fifty Million Brothers: A Panorama of American Lodges and Clubs.* New York: Farrar and Rinehart, 1937.

Nordin, D. Sven. *Rich Harvest: A History of the Grange, 1867–1900.* Jackson: University Press of Mississippi, 1974.

Schmidt, Alvin J. *Fraternal Organizations.* Westport, CT: Greenwood Press, 1980.

Web Sites

Read descriptions of the various buildings occupied by the Union Club during the 20th century at Christopher Gray, "Inside the Union Club, Jaws Drop," *New York Times,* February 11, 2007: http://www.nytimes.com/2007/02/11/realestate/11scap.html.

The official Web site of the Grange movement, headquartered in Washington, DC, is: http://www.nationalgrange.org.

44. PUBLICITY PHOTO FOR P. T. BARNUM'S AMERICAN MUSEUM (C. MID-1850S–MID-1860S)

INTRODUCTION

After strolling past the Union Club, New Yorkers and visitors to the city might head to P. T. BARNUM's American Museum. One of the more flamboyant entertainers and raconteurs in the nation's history, Barnum opened the American Museum on the corner of Broadway in 1842. The five-story building featured a lecture hall, where theatrical productions, magic shows, and other cultural and entertainment events occurred. Curiosities of all sorts abounded throughout the rest of the museum, including a flea circus, the Feejee Mermaid (in reality, the torso of a monkey grafted onto the tail of a fish), and several supposedly sacred relics. Barnum courted sensationalism—well aware that controversy often generated profit—and he also exhibited human curiosities. Lavinia Warren was among the most well known. Born in Massachusetts in 1841, Warren stood 32 inches high and weighed about 30 pounds. Although noted for her "singular intelligence," Warren most captivated the American nation for her 1863 marriage to General Tom Thumb, a dwarf who also starred at Barnum's American Museum. Attendance soared as gawkers, perhaps needing a diversion from the bloodshed of the ongoing Civil War, formed long lines. *Harper's Weekly,* the popular illustrated magazine, perhaps best caught the prevailing mood by quoting one of the enthusiasts who, after seeing Warren and her new husband, asked, "'What more could we desire?'"

KEEP IN MIND AS YOU READ

1. On some days, as many as 15,000 people visited the American Museum, paying a 25-cent admission fee. Between 1842 and 1865, 38 million people toured the museum. The numbers made the site one of the more popular tourist attractions of the mid- and late 19th century.
2. Barnum's American Museum was destroyed by fire during the mid-summer of 1865. The origins of the fire are still unknown, and speculation ranges from accident to arson. Barnum soon after opened another museum, only to see it too destroyed by flames in 1868.
3. Barnum sometimes rubbed the upper crust of New York society the wrong way for supposedly pandering to the masses. The Lecture Room came in for especial criticism. In a letter to *The Nation,* published soon after the destruction of the original

museum, an anonymous writer took Barnum to task for providing "vulgar" theatrical productions. The writer sniffed that, "It has been many years since a citizen could take his wife or his daughter to see a play on that stage." Barnum quickly defended himself and his museum. True, he did sometimes display rather outlandish curiosities, but visitors might see these exhibits alongside educational displays (Barnum labeled these displays as "whales, giants, dwarfs, Albinoes, dog shows, et cetera"). As for the lecture room, no whiff of disrespectability occurred. "No vulgar word or gesture, no profane expression, was *ever* allowed on my stage! Even in Shakespeare's plays, I unflinchingly and invariable cut out vulgarity and profanity." After all, Barnum pointed out, his ability to draw large numbers of visitors depended on "my keeping a good reputation for my Museum."

Document: Photo of Lavinia Warren, Managed by P. T. Barnum

AFTERMATH

Undaunted by the loss of the American Museum, Barnum went on to become involved in the circus business. He established a traveling circus in 1871 that, by the next year, billed itself as "The Greatest Show on Earth." The claim was true, if judged against other traveling circuses. Barnum provided far more entertainment than other shows, with acrobats, clowns, dwarfs, giants, and exotic animals (including several elephants, a hippopotamus, and a giraffe—all rarely viewed beasts in the United States at the time). He also introduced a second circus ring to his shows, allowing the entertainment to continue nearly nonstop. Barnum also beat his circus competitors through his mastery of logistics. The Greatest Show on Earth traveled by rail, rather than wagon. Riding in 61 specially designed cars, Barnum's circus covered up to 100 miles in a single night. The mobility allowed Barnum to skip small towns where the gate receipts might have been too low. In the 1880s Barnum joined forces with James Bailey. The resulting Barnum & Bailey Circus introduced a three-ring performance, and toured Europe and the United States. The show continues through today as Ringling Bros. and Barnum & Bailey Circus.

ASK YOURSELF

1. Barnum claimed that he showed "human curiosities" like Lavinia Warren and Tom Thumb for their educational and scientific value. Might this be offensive to modern-day American sensibilities, as taking advantage of people who are physically different from the majority of the population? Or, in business and entertainment, is anything fair game?
2. Have you gone to the circus? To a curiosity museum? Would you go back? Why or why not?

Lavinia Warren.

Source: "Miss Lavinia Warren," LC-DIG-cwpbh-02976, Library of Congress, Prints and Photographs Division, Washington, D.C.: http://www.loc.gov/pictures/item/brh 2003004240/PP/.

TO THE THEATER!

Going to the theater was one of the more popular forms of public entertainment in the United States during the Civil War and Reconstruction era. *Our American Cousin* and *The Black Crook* are perhaps the most well-known plays from the 1860s and 1870s. *Our American Cousin* was a comedy that premiered in 1858. Asa Trenchard, the main character, is an American who goes to England to meet his aristocratic relatives. Laughs abound as the unsophisticated Trenchard interacts with his boorish but wealthy extended family. Although panned by modern-day critics for its "creaky" humor, the play ran for five consecutive months—a very successful showing for the time. Whether genuinely funny or formalistic, *Our American Cousin* has gained notoriety as the play Abraham Lincoln was watching at Ford's Theater, in Washington, D.C., when he was assassinated. *The Black Crook* was a musical that premiered the year after Lincoln's death. The audience was perhaps less interested in the lavish sets that accompanied the play than in staring at the 100 scantily dressed ballerinas who danced to the music. "The scenery and the legs are everything," Mark Twain reportedly gushed after seeing the production. With music, dancing, and a unified theme, *The Black Crook* is considered by many scholars as the starting point for popular 20th-century musicals, such as *South Pacific, The Sound of Music,* and *West Side Story.*

TOPICS AND ACTIVITIES TO CONSIDER

- What attracted women to the American Museum and other 19th-century entertainments? Find out at Ann Fabian, "Women in P. T. Barnum's New York City," The Lost Museum, American Social History Productions: http://chnm.gmu.edu/the-lost-museum/.
- Who burned Barnum's American Museum in 1865? Try to solve the mystery at The Lost Museum: http://www.lostmuseum.cuny.edu/office.php.

Further Reading

Adams, Bluford. *E Pluribus Barnum: The Great Showman and the Making of U.S. Popular Culture.* Minneapolis: University of Minnesota Press, 1997.

Barnum, Phineas T. *The Life of P. T. Barnum, Written by Himself.* Introduction by Terence Whalen. (Reprint: Urbana: University of Illinois Press, 2000.)

Cook, James W. *The Arts of Deception: Playing with Fraud in the Age of Barnum.* Cambridge, MA: Harvard University Press, 2001.

Davis, Janet M. *The Circus Age: Culture and Society under the American Big Top.* Chapel Hill: University of North Carolina Press, 2002.

Dennett, Andrea Stulman. *Weird and Wonderful: The Dime Museum in America.* New York: New York University Press, 1997.

Saxon, A. H. *P. T. Barnum: The Legend and the Man.* New York: Columbia University Press, 1989.

Web Sites

The Lost Museum offers background essays on Barnum and his times as well as an interactive, virtual tour of the American Museum. The site is maintained by American Social History Productions, housed at the Graduate Center, City University of New York, in collaboration with the Center for History and New Media, George Mason University. The address is: http://www.lostmuseum.cuny.edu/home.html.

For ways to use the Lost Museum Web site in the classroom, see Michael O'Malley, "Barnum's World," Center for History and New Media, George Mason University: http://chnm.gmu.edu/exploring/19thcentury/barnumsworld/index.php. O'Malley is an associate professor of history and art history at George Mason University.

45. "The Baseball Glove Comes to Baseball": Albert Spalding (1875)

INTRODUCTION

Today, with every pitch and swing from Major League Baseball games analyzed online, and almost every off-field move by the players discussed in magazine and, sometimes, posted on Twitter, it is hard to imagine baseball in simpler times. Union and Confederate soldiers had enjoyed the game in camp, because it was easy to play. A ball and a bat and an open field were the only requirement to start a game (and even here, a walnut wrapped in string and a sturdy branch might substitute as the playing equipment). Soldiers brought home their passion for playing baseball, and the sport boomed in popularity. The National Association of Base Ball Players, founded in 1858, was the game's first national organization. An amateur league in which players received no money for their participation, the National Association expanded rapidly. Between 1860 and 1867, the number of teams joining the league jumped from 50 to 202. The rapid increase in the number of teams convinced many Americans that baseball was the nation's sport of choice. A writer for *Sports and Games,* one of the first national magazines devoted exclusively to the title topic, agreed. The author gave the opinion in the late 1860s that baseball was the "national game of the United States." Albert Spalding, who threw as a pitcher for the Boston Red Stockings and, later, for the Chicago White Stockings remembered that the game was almost too basic. A bat and a ball remained the only standard equipment, as they had during the Civil War. Players who wore gloves to protect their hand were treated with some derision, because of their supposed lack of toughness.

KEEP IN MIND AS YOU READ

1. Scores generally ran high in baseball games that were played during the Civil War. The pitcher had to hit each base runner with the otherwise bouncy and oversized ball to record an out, a feat that required nearly as much luck as skill. In one contest, a team from the 13th Massachusetts defeated a team from the 104th New York, by a score of 66 to 20. In another nail-biter, teams from two New York regiments battled to a 58 to 19 final score.

2. The National Association of Base Ball Players barred African Americans from membership in 1867. The Babylon (New York) Black Panthers, the first professional black baseball team, took the field in 1885. The team later was named the Cuban Giants, to appeal to a wider audience. The thought was the name change would garner greater publicity, by sounding more exotic and disguising the fact that the team was black.

3. The Cincinnati Red Stockings was the nation's first professional team. Players received salaries ranging from $800 to $1,400 and toured the country in 1869, taking on amateur teams.

4. Spaulding fared well professionally, founding a sporting goods company named after him during the late 1870s. Spaulding sporting goods still is in operation today.

Document: "The Baseball Glove Comes to Baseball"

The first glove I ever saw on the hand of a ball player in a game was worn by Charles C. Waite, in Boston, in 1875. He had come from New Haven and was playing at first base. The glove worn by him was of flesh color, with a large, round opening in the back. Now, I had for a good while felt the need of some sort of hand protection for myself. In those days clubs did not carry an **extra carload** of pitchers, as now. For several years I had pitched in every game played by the Boston team, and had developed severe bruises on the inside of my left hand. When it is recalled that every ball had to be returned, and that every swift one coming my way, from infielders, outfielders or hot from the bat, must be caught or stopped, some idea may be gained of the punishment received.

Therefore, I asked Waite about his glove. He confessed that he was a bit ashamed to wear it, but had it on to save his hand. He also admitted that he had chosen a color as inconspicuous as possible, because he didn't care to attract attention. He added that the opening on the back was for purpose of ventilation.

Meanwhile my own hand continued to take its medicine with utmost regularity, occasionally being bored with a **warm twister** that hurt excruciatingly. Still, it was not until 1877 that I overcame my scruples against joining the "kid-glove aristocracy" by donning a glove. When I did at last decide to do so, I did not select a flesh-colored glove, but got a black one, and cut out as much of the back as possible to let the air in.

Happily, in my case, the presence of a glove did not call out the ridicule that had greeted Waite. I had been playing so long and had become so well known that the innovation seemed rather to evoke sympathy than hilarity. I found that the **glove**, thin as it was, helped considerably, and inserted one pad after another until a good deal of relief was afforded. If anyone wore a padded glove before this date I do not know it. The "pillow mitt" was a later innovation.

Source: "The Baseball Glove Comes to Baseball, 1875," Eye-Witness to History: http://www.eyewitnesstohistory.com.

extra carload: Pitchers in the late 19th century threw far more often than they do today. Spalding recorded 253 wins and 65 losses during his seven-year career with Boston and Chicago. In the modern-era, pitchers throw only once every four or five games.

glove: Early baseball gloves lacked any padding, other than the leather exterior.

warm twister: In this case, a sharply hit ball back to the pitcher.

AFTERMATH

Perhaps there never was a simpler time in baseball. The very popularity of the game allowed corruption to creep in to the National Association. Some communities offered talented players high-paying jobs to live in their towns, civic pride overcoming their sense of sportsmanship. Chicago was one of the worst offenders in this regard. The Excelsior Club paid Spalding (prior to his playing for Boston) $40 a week to work as a grocery clerk in the city. Spaulding may have made a fine clerk, but he made a better pitcher, the true reason for his receiving the otherwise generous job offer. Gambling also was an issue in the amateur league. Some observers accused individual players of accepting bribes to influence their play on the field. Worse, some observers accused entire teams of taking money to throw the outcome of a game. Members of the National Association vigorously protested the illicit payment of both players and teams. By the early 1870s, however, fans and players alike recognized that the league was amateur in name only.

The creation of the National League of Professional Baseball Clubs in 1876 helped to stem the tide of corruption. Professional teams from New York, Philadelphia, Hartford, Boston, Chicago, Cincinnati, Louisville, and St. Louis initially constituted the league. The organization of the National League gave rise to many of the characteristics of modern-day baseball. Teams competed at the major league and minor league levels, and players received contracts. Professional baseball also introduced new types of equipment, to minimize the risk of player injury. Infielders and outfielders fielded with padded mitts, and catchers wore gloves and masks. Some old-time players scoffed at the equipment changes, as Spalding's reminiscence suggests. "We used no mattress on our hands, No cage upon our face" ran one chant popular among former players. "We stood right up and caught the ball with courage and with grace." Yet for better or for worse, the days of bruised faces and swollen hands as commonplace among baseball players were forever gone.

ASK YOURSELF

1. Given the rash of negative publicity regarding professional baseball today—from players accused of taking steroids to players behaving poorly off the field—is baseball still the "nation's pastime"?
2. Spalding's initial worries over wearing a glove reflect a larger societal issue in the United States, still in effect today, between toughness (not wearing a glove) and safety (wearing a glove). What are some other examples, and where do you side in the debate?

COLLEGE FOOTBALL

College football, like amateur and professional baseball, gained in popularity during the late 19th century. American college students had long played various forms of football, but the first recorded intercollegiate game occurred between Rutgers and Princeton in 1869. Princeton, Harvard, and Yale soon dominated the sport, earning them "The Big Three" as a nickname. The games played by the three schools became highlights of the fall social season. When any of The Big Three played one of the others, the number of spectators soared even higher. The contest between Princeton and Yale on Thanksgiving Day in 1878 drew 4,000 fans. Although these numbers are small in an age when some college football stadiums boast 100,000 seats, they were extremely large for the time. Within the next several years, the Princeton-Yale game would draw 40,000 spectators.

TOPICS AND ACTIVITIES TO CONSIDER

☙ Want to know the career won–lost record for Albert Spalding? Want to know the history and statistics for now defunct professional teams, such as the Buffalo Bisons and Chicago Whales? Find out the answers to these questions and many more at "Baseball-Reference.Com," Sports Reference LLC: http://www.baseball-reference.com/teams/.

☙ How do academics use baseball as a teaching tool, from the "Social History of Baseball" to "Baseball and Statistics"? Find out more at "Baseball Course Syllabi," Society for American Baseball Research, Cleveland, Ohio: http://sabr.org/.

Further Reading

Kirsch, George B. *Baseball in Blue and Gray: The National Pastime during the Civil War.* Princeton, NJ: Princeton University Press, 2003.

Lomax, Michael E. *Black Baseball Entrepreneurs, 1860–1901: Operating by Any Means Necessary.* Syracuse, NY: Syracuse University Press, 2003.

Morris, Peter. *But Didn't We Have Fun? An Informal History of Baseball's Pioneer Era, 1843–1870.* Chicago: Ivan R. Dee, 2008.

Nemec, David. *The Great Encyclopedia of Nineteenth Century Major League Baseball.* Tuscaloosa: University of Alabama Press, 2006.

Ryczek, William J. *When Johnny Came Sliding Home: The Post-Civil War Baseball Boom, 1865–1870.* Jefferson, NC: McFarland, 1998.

Spalding, Albert G. *America's National Game: Historic Facts Concerning the Beginning, Evolution, Development, and Popularity of Base Ball, with Personal Reminiscences of Its Vicissitudes, Its Victories, and Its Votaries.* Introduction by Benjamin G. Rader. Reprint; Lincoln: University of Nebraska Press, 1992.

Sullivan, Dean A., ed. *Early Innings: A Documentary History of Baseball, 1825–1908.* Lincoln: University of Nebraska Press, 1995.

Web Sites

The Web site for Negro Leagues Baseball Museum, located in Kansas City, Missouri, is: http://www.nlbm.com.

An excellent history of baseball and its influence on American culture is "Baseball: A Film by Ken Burns," Public Broadcasting System: http://www.pbs.org/kenburns/baseball.

46. "Christmas, 1871": *Manufacturer and Builder* (1871)

INTRODUCTION

The observance of Christmas, marking the birth of Jesus in Bethlehem, was spotty in the United States through the early 19th century. The Puritans in New England disapproved of the holiday as a vestige of the Roman Catholic Church. Observance of the day was banned in parts of the Massachusetts colony for two decades during the late 1600s. Following the Revolutionary War, many Americans believed that the celebration of Christmas was too British for their tastes. Attitudes changed dramatically beginning in the 1820s. The publication of several short stories by the popular author Washington Irving in 1820 explored the meaning of Christmas. These titles included "Christmas," "Christmas Eve," and "Christmas Dinner." Two years later, the American-born Clement Clarke Moore published "A Visit from St. Nicholas." Beginning with the now famous line "Twas the Night before Christmas," the poem helped to establish images of Santa Claus that continue through today. The publication of the Charles Dickens's *A Christmas Carol* in 1843 only further drew attention to Christmas. Although Dickens was a British author, his story of Scrooge and the Cratchit family emphasized goodwill and compassion. All government employees had an opportunity to observe Christmas at home with their families beginning in 1870, when President Ulysses S. Grant signed a bill declaring the day a federal holiday. The next year, the editors at *Manufacturer and Builder,* a nationally circulated magazine, acknowledged the excitement and cheerfulness generally exhibited across the land prior to the dawning of Christmas morning. Parents delighted in spending time with relatives, while children suddenly became "remarkably well-behaved." Even the local policeman, otherwise "wrapped up" in the power of his trappings, "is seen to unbend and exchange a pleasant nod and smile with the passersby." Given the joy of the season, the editors hoped that Americans would remember the less fortunate.

KEEP IN MIND AS YOU READ

1. Christmas trees, mistletoe, and Christmas cards all had become part of the season by the start of the Civil War. School break, stretching several days on either side of Christmas, also had become customary.

2. Some Americans worried that the religious significance of Christmas was becoming lost amid the commercialization. HARRIET BEECHER STOWE included a character in *The First New England Christmas,* published in 1850, who sees Christmas as a burden because of the effort to find appropriate presents. "Dear me, it's so tedious!" the overwhelmed shopper bemoans. "Everybody had got everything that can be thought of."

Document: "Christmas, 1871"

Now we don't propose to conclude these few lines with a moral lecture. We don't believe in any dry sermonizing, having a tendency to make one morally wretched, at this time of year, nor do we think that we need entertain any skeleton at our feast by allowing ourselves to be constantly reminded that, although we may be enjoying ourselves for the moment, an entire colony of little Hottentots in Bollawallah Jee is without adequate protection from predatory gorillas, ... But this we do say—if your own home is cheerful and bright, so you can render it even more radiant by throwing a gleam of sunshine into the doors of those that are dark and cheerless.

Remember the sorrowing as well as the joyous. Homeless ones wander in the streets of our cities. Do what you can to console them. Remember those that are suffering, and have been driven from homes as pleasant as yours by the merciless flames. Remember those exposed to the dangers and perils of the deep. Do what you can to alleviate their sufferings, add your mite in their behalf, and then when you kneel at the altar, in prayer and thanksgiving for His wondrous birth, you can do so with the consciousness that you have afforded to others besides yourself a merrier, happier, and holier Christmas.

Source: *Manufacturer and Builder* 3, no. 12 (December 1871): 267. Listed at Making of America, Library of Congress: http://memory.loc.gov/ammem/ndlpcoop/moahtml/snchome.html.

AFTERMATH

Running a close second to the celebration of Christmas was the Philadelphia Centennial Exposition, opened during May 1876 for a six-month run. Although other patriotic celebrations occurred to mark the nation's 100th birthday, the Centennial Exposition was the most spectacular. The 30,000 exhibits were designed to demonstrate that the American people, in the words of one official, "whilst engaged in their daily and necessary pursuits, enjoy a larger measure of personal comfort and dignity than those of any other nation." After paying a 50-cent admission fee, visitors walked through exhibitions on manufacturing and science, agriculture, machinery, and horticulture. Those individuals with energy still remaining strolled through exhibits that included the U.S. Government Building, the Woman's Building, the Nevada Quartz Mine, the Bible Pavilion, the Butter and Cheese Factory, and many others. Refreshment might be found at a variety of ethnic restaurants, popcorn stands, cigar booths, and, after some controversy, beer gardens. Exposition goers who had recovered their energy after partaking in food and drink might make their way to see the Torch of Liberty from the as-yet unfinished Statue of Liberty. The exhibition drew record crowds. The first day alone drew 200,000 visitors, including President Ulysses S. Grant. By the close of the exposition during the late fall, 10 million people had toured the grounds. A similar rate of attendance today would draw in 75 million people, or about one out of every four Americans.

ASK YOURSELF

1. Is the message delivered in "Christmas, 1871" similar to messages given today? Why or why not?
2. Would you attend an exposition commemorating the 250th birthday of the United States in 2026? Would you if you had to travel to do so?

TOPICS AND ACTIVITIES TO CONSIDER

- What are the origins of the Christmas tree? Is Santa Claus based on a historical figure? Find out the answers to these and many other popular Christmas customs and practices at "Christmas," A&E Television Networks: http://www.history.com/content/christmas.
- Does Christmas overshadow all other holidays? Read a tongue-in-cheek editorial at Guy Trebay, "Excuse Me, Where's Thanksgiving?" *New York Times,* November 14, 2008: http://www.nytimes.com/2008/11/16/fashion/16store.html?scp=11&sq=%22merry%20christmas%22&st=cse.

Further Reading

Giberti, Bruno. *Designing the Centennial: A History of the 1876 International Exhibition in Philadelphia.* Lexington: University Press of Kentucky, 2002.

Marling, Karal Ann. *Merry Christmas! Celebrating America's Greatest Holiday.* Cambridge, MA: Harvard University Press, 2000.

Nissenbaum, Stephen. *The Battle for Christmas.* New York: Alfred A. Knopf, 1996.

Restad, Penne L. *Christmas in America: A History.* New York: Oxford University Press, 1995.

Rydell, Robert W. *All the World's a Fair: Visions of Empire at American International Expositions, 1876–1916.* Chicago: University of Chicago Press, 1984.

Web Sites

"The History of the Holidays," A&E Television Networks: http://www.history.com/topics/holidays.

Read more about the Centennial Exposition at "The Centennial Exposition of 1876," American Experience, Public Broadcasting Service: http://www.pbs.org/wgbh/amex/grant/peopleevents/e_expo.html.

47. "The Checkered Game of Life": An Advertisement in *The Nursery: A Monthly Magazine For Youngest Readers* (1877)

INTRODUCTION

One of the more popular board games in American history came about through Abraham Lincoln's decision to grow a beard after winning the presidential election of 1860. Milton Bradley, a young lithographer working in Massachusetts that fall, had been busily selling an image of a clean-shaven candidate Lincoln. The market for a picture of a beardless president-elect plummeted almost overnight. Undaunted, Bradley put his drawing skills to work on a board game. The resulting "Checkered Game of Life" was a nearly instant success. Bradley quickly sold out his first run of several hundred copies. By the end of 1861, 45,000 copies of the game had sold. Distraction from the Civil War and ease of play contributed to the success of the game. More important, "The Checkered Game of Life" emphasized moral uplift. Players moved their marker around a checkered game board, marked every other square by virtues and vices. Landing on a virtue square generally scored a player five points. Some of these squares included "Happiness," "College," and "Success." Landing on a helping hand square moved a player ahead to a virtue. For example, landing on the "Bravery" square advanced a player eight spaces to the five-point "Honor" square. "Wealth" and "Happy Old Age" were the exception to the five-point virtue squares, scoring 10 points and 50 points, respectively. Vices—such as intemperance and gambling—sent a player back by so many squares. Landing on the "Prison" square lost a player a turn, while moving onto the "Suicide" square took a player out from the game. This advertisement in *The Nursery*, which began publication in Boston in 1867, offers to sell Milton Bradley's game for $1.00.

KEEP IN MIND AS YOU READ

1. To order "The Checkered Game of Life," the editors asked for a check drawing on a bank in Boston, New York, or Philadelphia. "All other checks subject us to expense in collecting: to cover this, add fifteen cents." Money also was acceptable, if "in a letter carefully sealed and directed, and prepaid by stamps." If the buyer had trouble making correct change, the magazine accepted postage stamps as currency. In all of this, the editors warned, "remittances are at the risk of the sender."

2. Chess and checkers also were popular board games. During the Civil War, many soldiers whiled away the hours in camp, maneuvering for either a "check mate" or a triple jump.

3. In 1960 Bradley's game was updated and rereleased as "The Game of Life." The game has since gone through several new editions, including a computerized version.

Document: *"The Checkered Game of Life"* (1877)

This game is so simple that any child who can read may learn to play it. It is not simply a game of chance, but in every move there is an opportunity for the exercise of the judgment. . . . Two, three, or four can play, and each player is represented by one counter, or man, which is entered at infancy, and by various means regulated by the throw of a tetotum, or die, passes through school, college, industry, success, perseverance, etc., to wealth or happy old age; or through idleness, intemperance, gambling, crime, etc., to disgrace, poverty, ruin, suicide, or prison.

Source: "Checkered Game of Life," Premium-List, in *The Nursery: A Monthly Magazine for Youngest Readers* 21, no. 1 (January 1877): 9. Listed at Project Gutenberg: http://www.gutenberg.org/files/28129/28129-h/28129-h.htm.

AFTERMATH

Adults who found "The Checkered Game of Life" too tame for their tastes might move outside to try their hand at croquet. Introduced from England at the end of the Civil War, croquet boomed in popularity across the United States because it allowed men and women to play together. Young men and women took quick advantage to flirt and socialize with one another while trying to knock their brightly colored balls through the wickets. The writers of an early croquet rule book feared that some women played two games at once. They warned prospective players that "Young ladies are proverbially fond of cheating at this game; but they only do so because they think the men like it." Croquet sets sold exceptionally well during the 1870s. Some sets even included wickers equipped with candle sockets, so that players could continue their game well into the night (similar to present-day glow-in–the-dark sporting equipment).

In addition to croquet, bicycle riding and lawn tennis were popular outdoor activities. Early bicycles were, in retrospect, poorly constructed. The seat was perched above a high front wheel that, when combined with a small back wheel, made for an unsteady ride. Women kept pace on tricycles with the pedals fitted to one side, so as not to separate their knees. The bicycle design more familiar to modern-day readers, with standard-size wheels and a drop frame for women, began to appear during the late 1870s, to widespread popularity.

Lawn tennis also attracted a crowd. Players softly patted the ball back and forth with their racquet over a net stretched across any level piece of ground. Players who appeared on either side of the net were well-groomed and dressed, because they were not expected to run for the ball. Instead, players allowed balls to pass by them if hit too far to either side. The emphasis on fashion as much as physical skill held appeal, because lawn tennis, like croquet, proved an opportunity for young men and women to play together.

ASK YOURSELF

1. Do board games still teach values today? Does "Monopoly" impart skill in managing money, or "Risk" and "Connect Four" impart skill in strategic thinking?
2. Does playing sports continue to provide an opportunity for social interaction? Have you made friends while bike riding, playing tennis, or any other outdoor sport?

TOPICS AND ACTIVITIES TO CONSIDER

- What do the board games played during the late 19th and early 20th centuries say about American culture and values? Research the question at "The Games We Played: American Board and Table Games from the Liman Collection," Henry Morrison Flagler Museum, Palm Beach Florida: http://www.flaglermuseum.us/exhibits/past-exhibits/the-games-we-played.
- How has the game of croquet been depicted in film? What are the still unresolved mysteries about the origins of croquet? Find the answers to these questions and others in the article database at "Croquet in America: From Backyard Game to Worldclass Sport," United States Croquet Association: http://www.croquetamerica.com/croquet/history.

Further Reading

Crego, Robert. *Sports and Games of the 18th and 19th Centuries.* Westport, CT: Greenwood Publishing, 2003.

Cross, Gary, ed. *Encyclopedia of Recreation and Leisure in America.* Farmington Hills, MI: Charles Scribner's Sons, 2004.

Dawson, Melanie. *Laboring to Play: Home Entertainment and the Spectacle of Middle-Class Cultural Life, 1850–1920.* Tuscaloosa: University of Alabama Press, 2005.

Dulles, Foster Rhea. *America Learns to Play: A History of Popular Recreation, 1607–1940.* 2nd ed. New York: D. Appleton-Century, 1965.

Web Sites

Strategies for using "The Checkered Game of Life" in the classroom are found at Paula Petrik, "Checkered Game of Life," Exploring U.S. History, Center for History and New Media, George Mason University: http://chnm.gmu.edu/exploring/19thcentury/checkeredgame/assignment.php. Petrik is a professor of history and art history at George Mason University.

A description of the larger meaning of "The Checkered Game of Life" is found at Jill Lepore, American Chronicles, "The Meaning of Life," *The New Yorker*, May 21, 2007: http://www.newyorker.com/reporting/2007/05/21/070521fa_fact_lepore.

APPENDIX 1: BIOGRAPHICAL SKETCHES OF IMPORTANT INDIVIDUALS MENTIONED IN TEXT

Alcott, Louisa May: Author, best known for writing *Little Women*. Alcott was born in Massachusetts in 1832, to a father (Bronson) who was a writer, educator, and idealist and to a mother (Abigail May) who was a reformer and abolitionist. While growing up, Alcott met Ralph Waldo Emerson, Henry David Thoreau, William Lloyd Garrison, and other writers and activists her parents associated with. These acquaintances, along with her parent's influences, led Alcott to support abolitionism, feminism, and other reform movements. During 1862–63, Alcott worked as a nurse at a Union hospital in Georgetown. Alcott fell ill and went home to recuperate. She published *Hospital Sketches* later that year. Alcott based the book on her letters to her family, and the humorous, sometimes sharp, tone won national attention. At the urging of her father, Alcott wrote *Little Women* in 1868. Alcott followed with other titles, but none ever reached the same level of critical acclaim and financial success. Alcott died in 1888. Mercury poisoning may have contributed to the relatively early death. After she had fallen ill during the Civil War, Alcott was given calomel, a mercury-laced medicine, to help recover. Calomel was widely given in the United States through the late 19th century as both an emetic (to induce vomiting) and a laxative.

Alger, Horatio, Jr.: Well-known author of children's and young-adult literature. Born in Massachusetts in 1832, Alger graduated from Harvard Divinity School (1860) and began work as a Unitarian minister. Alger soon left the First Unitarian Church and Society of Brewster, Massachusetts, under suspicion of having molested two young boys. The charges later proved most likely true, but were little publicized. After leaving Brewster, Alger worked with various organizations in New York City to help and offer aid to impoverished children. Alger's novels were widely read during the 19th century. He often emphasized a rags-to-riches theme, emphasizing social and economic uplift through hard work and morality. Alger died in Massachusetts from heart disease in 1899. Today, the Horatio Alger Association of Distinguished Americans, named after the author and established in 1947, offers scholarship opportunities to young people who have demonstrated, among other qualities, "determination in overcoming adversity."

Allen, Elizabeth Akers: A poet and journalist; born Elizabeth Chase, in Strong, Maine, in 1832. Allen began to write poetry while a teenager, under the pen name Florence Percy. The verses sold well enough that she traveled to Europe on the proceeds. While abroad, she served as a reporter for the *Portland* (Maine) *Transcript* and the *Boston Evening Gazette*. In 1860, she married Benjamin Paul Akers, a sculptor, who died the next year. She worked as a clerk in Washington, DC, during the Civil War. In 1865 she married Elijah Allen. The next year, she published *Poems*. The collection included "Rock Me to Sleep," which soon was set to music. The song immediately gained national popularity, although Alexander Ball, another poet, for many years attempted to claim authorship. Allen served as literary editor of the *Daily Advertiser* in Portland, Maine, before dying in 1911.

Anthony, Susan B.: A founding figure in the 19th-century women's rights movement. Anthony was born in 1820 in Massachusetts. She became a teacher in the late 1830s, the only profession open to middle-class women at the time. Anthony later quit teaching but recognized the link for women between economic independence and gaining greater rights. During the Civil War, Anthony, along with Elizabeth Cady Stanton, organized the Women's National Loyal League. The organization called for the constitutional abolition of slavery. In the immediate postwar era, Anthony was greatly disappointed when women were not granted the right to vote by the 15th Amendment (granting suffrage to black men). With single-minded determination, Anthony spent her remaining years pushing for women to have access to the ballot. Anthony pushed for the right to vote at the national level, worried that gains in individual states might later be reversed. Never married and without a family, Anthony treated suffrage leaders as her own. In turn, she earned the almost unwavering loyalty of younger generations. Anthony died in 1906, but the subsequent granting of the right to vote to women was as much her triumph as any other women's rights leader.

Barnum, P. T. (Phineas Taylor): Owner and operator of the American Museum, one of the most popular tourist sites in 19th-century America. Although primarily known as an entertainer and showman, and justifiably so, Barnum had interest in politics. He won election to the Connecticut legislature, his native state, as a Republican in 1865. He later ran twice for Congress but failed to carry either election. In 1875, after establishing his traveling circus, Barnum served as mayor of Bridgeport, Connecticut. He worked conscientiously in the office, establishing gas lighting along the streets and improving the water supply. Barnum died in 1891, just shy of his 81st birthday. He is buried in Bridgeport. Barnum's story is available today through *The Life of P. T. Barnum: Written by Himself* (1855).

Beecher, Catharine: Born in 1800 in New York, the oldest child of the Congregational minister and moral reformer Lyman Beecher. Catharine Beecher became an early advocate for greater educational opportunities for women. Toward that end, Beecher founded the Hartford Female Seminary in Connecticut in 1823. Her success as an educator (Beecher taught at the Hartford Female Seminary until 1831) added weight to Beecher's call for women to serve as teachers, a profession dominated almost exclusively by men to that time. Beecher argued that women possessed a greater moral suasion to keep order in the classroom, rather than having to rely upon physical force. The argument became increasingly popular across much of the nation, leading to the rapid feminization of the teaching profession by the late 19th century (a shift added by the fact that women teachers worked for less pay than their male counterparts). Beecher expanded her view from the classroom to the parlor by the 1840s. Beecher turned to the pen to push for the increased power of women within the home through the publication of titles such as *Letters to Persons Who Are Engaged in Domestic Service* (1842) and *Treatise on Domestic Economy* (1843). She was not, however, calling for greater public activism by women.

Beecher opposed a high-profile role for women in the abolitionist movement, a sore point for many other female reformers. Beecher died in Elmira, New York, in 1878.

Beers, Ethel Lynn: American poet, born in 1827 in New York. Contemporaries described Beers as "of medium stature, with dark hair and eyes." Beers is most famously known for "The Picket Guard," published in *Harper's Magazine* in 1861. The poem quickly was put to music and became widely known across the Union and the Confederacy as "All Quiet Along the Potomac Tonight." A contemporary literary critic said of Beers, "She carries her conscience into all of her work, her chief desire, as she once expressed it, being to write no word or line that should mislead an earnest soul." Beers died in 1879, the day after her collected poems were published.

Bennett, James Gordon, Jr.: Publisher of the *New York Herald,* a widely circulated newspaper that ran between 1835 and 1924. Bennett was born in 1841, and when he was 25-years old he took over the *Herald*, established by his father. Bennett helped to boost circulation of the *Herald* through flamboyant stunts, such as financing the Henry Stanley expedition in Africa. When asked if this was a proper use of money, Bennett reportedly replied that the true objective of a newspaper "is not to instruct but to startle." Bennett moved to Europe in 1877, after a series of controversial public episodes. Ten years later, he established a Continental edition of the *Herald*. Overseeing both editions of the newspaper proved difficult. Soon after Bennett died in 1918, the *New York Tribune* bought the *Herald*. The resulting *New York Herald Tribune* was published into the mid-1960s.

Bonner, Robert: Newspaper publisher, born in Northern Ireland in 1824. Bonner immigrated to the United States with his family and as a teenager worked as an apprentice for the *Hartford* (Connecticut) *Courant*. He later worked as a correspondent for the New York *Evening Mirror*. Bonner saved enough money as a reporter to purchase the *Merchant Ledger,* a financial weekly paper, in 1851. Bonner soon after changed the name of the paper to the *New York Ledger*. Bonner soared subscriptions to the *Ledger* by hiring popular writers to pen multipart stories and essays. Writings by the poet William Cullen Bryant and the popular author Fanny Fern received a circulation of 400,000 copies. When Bonner retired, he handed the reigns to his three sons. The *Ledger* came into hard times without Bonner's direct oversight, and published its last issue in 1898. Bonner died the following year.

Currier, Nathaniel: Founder of the popular lithograph firm, Currier and Ives. Currier was born in Massachusetts in 1813. Currier learned the art of lithography while an apprentice to a print shop in Boston. In 1835, Currier started his own lithographic business. He created a picture during the same year, illustrating a fire that had recently swept through the business district in New York City. The print sold quickly, and Currier recognized the business opportunity available in depicting current events. Currier followed soon after with scenes from a hotel fire in New Orleans and a steamboat explosion in Long Island Sound. The success of these prints helped Currier to gain a weekly insert in the *New York Sun* in 1840. Currier retired from his firm in 1880, turning the business over to his son. He died at home in Massachusetts eight years later.

Davis, Jefferson Finis: Confederate president. Davis was born in Kentucky in 1808, one year before Abraham Lincoln. He graduated from West Point in 1828, and served in the army for the next seven years. Davis took up farming in Mississippi, where he met Sarah Knox Taylor. The daughter of future president Zachary Taylor, Sarah Taylor died of malaria only three months after marrying Davis in 1835. Ten years later, Davis married Varina Howell. The Davis's eventually had six children, one of whom died accidentally while young. Davis won election to Congress as a Democrat in 1845. Except for a brief period of military service during the Mexican War, where he suffered a wound, Davis remained in the public eye almost continuously until his death in 1889. Davis served as Secretary of War under President Franklin Pierce during the 1850s, performing well. When Mississippi seceded from the Union in early 1861, Davis resigned his Senate seat. The appointment to president by the Confederate Congress caught Davis by some surprise, as he was expecting a military commission. As president, Davis often proved prickly and overbearing. Yet Davis was a true believer, and his strength of conviction helped to hold the Confederacy together. Davis was captured by Union forces after the fall of Richmond, the Confederate capital, in the spring of 1865. He served two years in prison before the federal government released him, without initiating a treason trial. Davis remained unapologetic, and in 1881 published his memoirs. *The Rise and Fall of the Confederate Government* maintained that the South had exercised a legally defensible course of action in attempting to form its own nation.

Douglas, Stephen: Author of the Kansas-Nebraska Act. Born in Vermont in 1813, Douglas studied law before moving to Illinois. Douglas helped to organize the Democratic Party in his new home state, before winning election to the House of Representatives in 1843. Two terms and four years later, Douglas was elected to the Senate. A passionate advocate of American expansion, Douglas supported the annexation of Texas and the ensuing war with Mexico. The question over the westward expansion of slavery plagued Douglas during the 1850s. Despite winning reelection to the Senate in 1858 (after holding a series of now famous debates with Abraham Lincoln), Douglas found his popularity on the wane. He strove unsuccessfully to find a middle ground on the slavery issue. Although privately opposing slavery, Douglas publicly espoused the idea of popular sovereignty. In 1860, Douglas ran for president at the head of a Democratic Party now hopelessly split into a northern and a southern faction. Douglas worked hard to avoid the sectional split that occurred after the election of Lincoln to the White House. Failing that, he loudly supported the Union after the start of the Civil War. Douglas died soon after, in the summer of 1861, as much perhaps from a broken spirit as from physical exhaustion. A fiery speaker and seemingly tireless individual, Douglas, who stood only five feet four inches tall, won national acclaim during his Congressional career as the Little Giant.

Everett, Edward: Known most widely as "other" speaker at the dedication of the Gettysburg Cemetery, behind Abraham Lincoln. The tag is unfair, because Everett had a distinguished public career. Born in 1794, Everett won election to both houses of Congress as a Whig. He also served as president of Harvard University and governor of Massachusetts. From 1852 to 1853 Everett served as Secretary of State in the administration of Millard Fillmore. Hoping to avoid the looming threat of civil war, Everett unsuccessfully ran as the vice presidential candidate on the Constitutional Union ticket during the 1860 presidential election. Everett died in 1865, and is buried in Cambridge, Massachusetts.

Gardner, Alexander: Born in Scotland in 1821, Gardner is regarded as one of the premier photographers of the Civil War. Gardner worked as assistant for Mathew Brady, another well-known photographer, during the 1850s. With the start of the Civil War, Gardner often traveled with the Union Army of the Potomac. He may have taken the majority of the pictures of the famous Union army that were ever publicly displayed. Gardner established his own studio in 1862, giving individual photographers credit for their work. Prior to this time, most studio owners listed photographs taken by their assistants under their own name. After the war, Gardner published *Gardner's Photographic Sketch Book* *of the War.* The volume listed images taken by Gardner and his assistants, and was the first published collection of Civil War photographs. The volume sold poorly, perhaps because many of the images portrayed battlefield dead (such as "Harvest of Death"). Gardner continued to work during the postwar era, taking many photographs of people and places in the American West. Gardner died in 1882.

Grant, Ulysses S.: General-in-chief of the Union army, and the first three-star general in American history since George Washington. Born in Ohio in 1822, Grant graduated from West Point in 1843 and served in the Mexican-American War. Grant fought well, and won promotion for his battlefield bravery. He later served in a variety of far-flung posts, and resigned his commission in 1854. Grant fared poorly as a civilian, undertaking a variety jobs and doing well in none of them. Based on his previous military experience, Grant received commission as a colonel at the start of the Civil War. Seizing the opportunity, Grant fought aggressively. He scored a major battlefield victory in leading the Union forces that captured Fort Henry and Fort Donelson on the Tennessee and Cumberland Rivers during early 1862. Grant saw his star somewhat dim that April, when his army suffered a surprise attack at Shiloh, Tennessee. The Union army eventually won the ferocious two-day battle, but whispers started that Grant had been drunk and unfit to command. The rumors never were confirmed, although Grant reportedly sometimes lapsed into heavy drinking when his men were safely encamped in winter quarters. Grant continued to win battlefield victories, forcing the surrender of Vicksburg, Mississippi, during the summer of 1863, and breaking a Confederate siege of the Union-held Chattanooga, Tennessee, that fall. The hard-fighting and military successes of Grant earned him promotion to general-in-chief of the Union army in early 1864. Grant took the field with the Army of the Potomac that spring, where he battled Confederate General Robert E. Lee and the Army of Northern Virginia. After ferocious and sustained fighting and maneuvering, Grant effectively ended the war in Union triumph by forcing the surrender of Lee at Appomattox Court House. After the war, Grant served as president of the United States for two terms (1868–76). Although personally honest, Grant saw his administration marred by financial and political scandal. Grant died in 1885 from throat cancer, soon after finishing his *Personal Memoirs.*

Hale, Sarah Josepha: Editor of *Ladies' Magazine* and *Godey's Lady's Book* throughout much of the mid-19th century. She was born as Sarah Buell in New Hampshire in 1788, to a Revolutionary War Veteran. In 1813, she married David Hale. Widowed seven years later, Hale turned to writing to help support her five children. Hale published *Northwood* in 1827, to much popular acclaim. The same year, Hale assumed the editorship of *Ladies' Magazine.* She penned "Mary Had a Little Lamb," in 1830, one of the more popular children's rhymes in American history. Hale became editor (although Hale preferred the title "editress") of *Godey's Lady's Book* in 1837, a position she held for the next 40 years. The magazine had a wide readership, and influenced women's fashion and home decoration. Hale kept stayed active outside her work in editing *Godey's.* A strong proponent of higher education for women, Hale helped to found Vassar College in New York. Perhaps most famously, in 1863, after a nearly two-decade-long campaign, Hale helped to make Thanksgiving a national holiday. Previously, Thanksgiving had been celebrated only in New England. Hale died at home in Philadelphia in 1879.

Hawthorne, Nathaniel: Born in Massachusetts in 1804, Hawthorne spent much of his early career as a struggling writer. With money tight, Hawthorne supplemented his income as a novelist and short-story writer by working as a customs official in Boston and, later, Salem. Hawthorne achieved his greatest literary prominence in the 1850s, with the publication of *The Scarlet Letter* and *The House of the Seven Gables*. The novels are considered masterpieces of American literature because of their use of the past to interact with characters' present. In 1852, Hawthorne received the consulship of Liverpool, England, from his long-time friend, then-President Franklin Pierce. The consulship was lucrative but, after a few years, Hawthorne resigned. Hawthorne became increasingly wary of the continued industrialization that marked the United States prior to his death in 1864. Hawthorne is today considered one of the great literary figures in the nation's history.

Hayes, Rutherford: Nineteenth president of the United States. Born in Ohio in 1822, Hayes graduated from Harvard Law School and practiced law in Cincinnati. Hayes married Lucy Ware Webb, an abolitionist and fellow Ohioan, in 1852. The couple had eight children, only five of whom survived into adulthood. Hayes joined the Republican Party in the 1850s, and offered legal defense to captured runaway slaves. He served in the Union army during the Civil War, winning promotion to major general for battlefield gallantry. In the postwar era, Hayes served as governor of Ohio. While in office, he helped to found the Ohio State University. Hayes narrowly won the presidential election of 1876, defeating Democratic Samuel Tilden. Hayes brought a reputation of honesty to the White House, a welcome relief in the wake of the business scandals that had plagued the administration of Ulysses S. Grant (1868–76). In addition to ending Reconstruction, Hayes confronted a railroad strike in 1877. Hayes deployed federal troops when the labor disputes turned violent in several cities, eventually restoring the peace. Hayes refused to run for reelection in 1880, believing that presidents should serve for only one term (although Hayes argued that the term length should be increased to six years). Hayes died from complications of a heart attack in 1893.

Ives, James: Partner in the popular lithographic company, Currier and Ives. Born in New York in 1824, Ives married Caroline Clark, who was related by marriage to the Currier family. Ives gained the attention of Nathaniel Currier for his business acumen and artistic knowledge. Ives went to work for Currier in the early 1850s, and won promotion to full partner in 1857. Ives continued to work at the business until he died in 1895.

Johnson, Andrew: Wartime governor of Tennessee and 17th president of the United States. Johnson was born to humble beginnings in North Carolina in 1808. As a teenager, Johnson moved with his family to Tennessee. Self-educated, Johnson possessed a no-frills personality that helped him to connect with the small farmers of Tennessee. With their support, Johnson won election as governor of Tennessee in 1853 and as a U.S. Senator three years later. Johnson retained his seat in Congress after the outbreak of the Civil War, the only senator from a Confederate state to do so. After Union forces had occupied much of Tennessee by early 1862, Johnson received appointment as governor from Abraham Lincoln. The task was difficult, because much of western and central Tennessee, where the Union army had its strongest presence, was openly pro-Confederate. Johnson managed to reinstate civil authority throughout much of the state by late the following year. The strong performance helped Johnson to win a spot on the Republican ticket in 1864, as vice president. Johnson assumed the presidency the next year, following the assassination of Abraham Lincoln. As president, Johnson was too lenient for many Republicans on the defeated Confederate States. He made little effort to oversee the social and political restructuring of the South from the antebellum era. With former Confederate officials winning election to Congress and blacks returned to slavery in everything but name, Republicans seized control of dictating Reconstruction policies. Johnson was nearly removed from office, after suffering impeachment in 1868. Johnson served out the remainder of his presidential term and returned to Tennessee, where he died in 1875. Johnson usually ranks mid to low on listings of the "best and worst" American presidents.

Johnston, Joseph E: Confederate general. An outstanding organizer and consummate military professional, Johnston also was sensitive over issues of rank and, arguably, too cautious. Born in Farmville, Virginia, in 1807, Johnston earned appointment to West Point in 1825. He graduated four years later, in the top one-third of his class. Johnston served as an engineer, and earned distinction during the war with Mexico. Johnson received commission to brigadier general in the Confederate army with the start of the Civil War. The Virginian fought well at Bull Run during the summer of 1861, helping to throw back a Union assault and win a major Confederate victory. The following spring, Johnson commanded the Confederate army defending Richmond from the Union offensive on the Virginia Peninsula. Johnston was wounded on May 31 at the Battle of Seven Pines, and needed several months to recuperate. Johnston's replacement outside Richmond was the now legendary Robert E. Lee. Johnston directed the Confederate defense of Atlanta in the summer of 1864, before being relieved for acting too cautiously. Whether Johnston was overly timid is a matter of debate through today, as the Confederate army in the West was outnumbered. The husbanding of military resources by Johnston might have doomed the Confederate defense of Atlanta to inexorable defeat anyway, but the aggressive battlefield action displayed by his successor certainly contributed to the loss of the city that fall. Johnston received command of the Confederate forces in the Carolinas in early 1865, where he could do little against Union numbers and logistics. Johnston defended his wartime leadership in his memoirs, published in 1874. Johnston died in Columbia, South Carolina, in 1891.

Lee, Robert Edward: Although ultimately defeated at Appomattox Court House, Virginia, in the spring of 1865, Lee ranks as one of the most formidable generals of the Civil War. Lee was born in Virginia in 1807, the fourth child of "Light Horse" Harry Lee, a Revolutionary War hero. Appointed to West Point in 1825, Lee graduated second in his class without having received a demerit, a remarkable record. He received a commission in the Corps of Engineers, where he worked on several different projects. In 1831 Lee married Mary Custis, the great granddaughter of Martha Washington. The Lees eventually had seven children, three of whom served as Confederate officers. Lee served with distinction during the Mexican War, where he won promotion for his battlefield bravery. Lee continued to serve prominently during the 1850s, holding a three-year term as superintendent of West Point and leading the marines who recaptured Harpers Ferry, Virginia, from John Brown and his followers. With the outbreak of the Civil War, Lee received an offer to hold a senior command in the U.S. forces. Lee refused, under the argument that he could not fight against Virginia. Quickly commissioned a Confederate general, Lee early in the war served largely behind the scenes as a special military advisor to President Jefferson Davis. Lee rose to national prominence when he assumed command of the military force outside Richmond that he later named the Army of Northern Virginia. From early June 1862 through the end of the war, Lee turned the Army of Northern Virginia into one of the most formidable armies in world history. Often fighting outnumbered, Lee displayed aggressive and skilled leadership. The cost in casualties was high, with the Army of Northern Virginia only a shadow of its former self by the Appomattox Campaign. After the war, Lee served as president of Washington College (now Washington and Lee) in Lexington, Virginia. Lee died in 1870, and is buried in a mausoleum on the Washington and Lee campus that is open to the public. Lee urged reconciliation in the postwar era, although some modern-day scholars argue that he harbored more bitterness toward the North than is commonly acknowledged. Even if so, Lee, by the time of his death, was a widely admired figure in the North for his battlefield skill and, in defeat, his magnanimity. In the South, Lee was a beloved figure who came to personify the best of the former Confederacy.

Lincoln, Abraham: Modern-day historians rank Lincoln as one of the nation's greatest presidents. Some contemporaries thought differently and savaged Lincoln for everything from his gangly appearance to his lack of formal education. Those who doubted Lincoln's intelligence and focus often found differently. Lincoln quickly grew into his role as commander and chief. He learned from his mistakes, and maintained an unshakable will to win. Despite the high number of casualties suffered by the Union, Lincoln never became jaded. He remained intensely interested in the common soldier and, in turn, won their affection. Lincoln also endured personal tragedy, when Willie, his twelve-year-old son, died from illness in early 1862. Lincoln had a turbulent relationship with his often-mercurial wife, Mary Todd. Although sometimes shrill and stubborn, Mary Todd worked hard to create a homelike atmosphere in the White House. Scholars today generally agree that while often stormy, the Lincolns' relationship was fairly strong. Lincoln was assassinated by John Wilkes Booth while attending a play at Ford's Theatre. An actor and southern sympathizer, Booth slipped into the box where Lincoln was watching *My American Cousin*, a popular play at the time, and shot him in the head. Lincoln died the next morning, on April 15.

McClellan, George Brinton: Commander of the Union Army of the Potomac before his removal during late 1862, and Democratic presidential candidate during 1864. By almost all measurable standards, McClellan seemed a man destined to greatness. Born in Pennsylvania in 1826, McClellan graduated second in his class from West Point 20 years later. Commissioned a second lieutenant in the Corps of Engineers, McClellan won promotion to captain for his distinguished service during the Mexican War. McClellan continued to serve in the army through the mid-1850s, most notably teaching at West Point and serving as an American observer of the Crimean War. He resigned his commission in 1857, going on to serve as vice president of the Illinois Central Railroad and, later, president of the Ohio and Mississippi Railroad. Commissioned a major general at the start of the Civil War, McClellan won national fame for winning two relatively small battles—by late war standards—in western Virginia. Lincoln tapped McClellan during the mid-summer of 1861 to command the Army of the Potomac, the main Union army in the eastern theater. Although a masterful organizer and administrator, McClellan revealed several leadership weaknesses. He never seemed willing to take the field unless every detail down to the last ration was accounted for. He also readily believed faulty intelligence reports that vastly overinflated Confederate numbers. Frustrated by the lack of energy in prosecuting the war, Lincoln removed McClellan from command in late 1862. After the war, McClellan recaptured some of his old success. Before his death in 1885, he worked at several business ventures and served as governor of New Jersey. McClellan also wrote his self-serving *McClellan's Own Story*, published in 1887.

McGuffey, William: Author of textbooks read by millions of grade-school students in the late 19th century. McGuffey was born in Pennsylvania in 1800, and moved with his family as a young child to Ohio. McGuffey graduated from Washington College in Pennsylvania and, in 1826, became a professor at Miami University, Ohio. He married Harriet Spinning the next year, eventually having five children. McGuffey also was ordained a Presbyterian minister while teaching at Miami. In 1836, he became president of Cincinnati College. McGuffey moved several more times over his career, including serving as president of Ohio University and teaching at the University of Virginia. McGuffey died in Charlottesville in 1873.

Morrill, Justin: A representative and senator from Vermont, who won fame for authoring the land-grant bill to colleges and universities that bears his name. Morrill was born in 1810 and worked as a merchant for many years. He spent his early years in Congress as a Whig but, by the mid-1850s joined the newly established Republican Party. Morrill also authored the Tariff Act of 1861, which favored American industry. During his time in Congress, Morrill served as the chairman on the Committee on Public Buildings and Grounds and as regent of the Smithsonian Institution. Morrill died in Washington in 1898.

O'Sullivan, Timothy: Nationally known Civil War photographer. Records indicating the exact date of O'Sullivan's birth are lost, but most scholars place it in 1840 in Ireland. Immigrating to the United States with his parents as a young boy, O'Sullivan grew up in New York City. O'Sullivan worked as a photographer for Mathew Brady early in the Civil War. He left in 1863 to work for Alexander Gardner, who gave credit to his operatives for the pictures they had taken (unlike Brady and many other studio owners and photographers). O'Sullivan continued to work as a photographer in the postwar era, accompanying several expeditions to the Far West. O'Sullivan died of tuberculosis in 1882.

Sherman, William T: One of the most famous generals to emerge from the Civil War, Sherman had a quick temper that, when not directed against them, his soldiers enjoyed. Born in Lancaster, Ohio, in 1820, Sherman had as a brother John, a later United States senator. William Sherman earned an appointment to West Point, where he graduated sixth in his class (from 42 graduates) in 1840. Sherman served in the Mexican War, but saw little action. He resigned his commission in 1853, to work in business and, later, law. Sherman accepted the superintendency at a military school in Louisiana six years later (the school was the forerunner for Louisiana State University, in Baton Rouge). At the start of the Civil War, the Ohio native received a commission as a brigadier general in the Union army. Sherman fought well at Shiloh in the spring of 1862 and played a significant role in the Union capture of Vicksburg the next year. In the fall of 1864, Sherman, now a major general, led the Union army that captured the major Confederate transportation and manufacturing hub at Atlanta. Later that same year, Sherman led a Union army that marched east through Georgia and captured Savannah. The March to the Sea is ranked by many military historians as one of the most brilliant campaigns of the war, by demonstrating the vulnerability of the Confederate interior. After the war, Sherman served for several years as general-in-chief of the army and published his memoirs. The former Union general died in New York City in 1891.

Stanton, Edwin McMasters: Secretary of War during the Lincoln administration and the Johnson administration. Brilliant, often sharp-tongued, and seemingly indefatigable, Stanton played a major role in helping the Union to triumph during the Civil War. Born in Ohio in 1814, Stanton became a noted lawyer during the antebellum era. He won appointment as attorney general under President James Buchanan in late 1860, where he served until Lincoln was inaugurated a little over two months later. Lincoln called Stanton back from private life during early 1862, to join his cabinet. The two men worked well together, despite political differences (Stanton was a Democrat). Stanton worked strenuously to make the Union army one of the best supplied and equipped in the world. Stanton died in 1869, after he had received confirmation to the Supreme Court but before he had assumed his seat.

Stanton, Elizabeth Cady: A major figure in the women's rights movement. Born in 1815 in Jonestown, New York, Elizabeth Cady enjoyed an early life of prosperity. The only blemish to the upbringing, from her perspective, was receiving an education at Emma Willard's Academy. Although considered one of the best schools for young women in the country, the Academy was not a college. She met Henry Stanton, an abolitionist, at the home of her cousin, also an abolitionist. Elizabeth and Henry married in 1840 and, as a honeymoon, attended the World's Antislavery Convention in London. Stanton met and befriended Lucretia Mott, a leading abolitionist, at the meeting. Stanton and Mott organized the women's right convention in Seneca Falls (where the Stanton family had recently moved) in 1848. Stanton met Susan B. Anthony three years later, and the two friends pushed for an end to slavery and the granting of women's suffrage. Stanton took a wider view than Anthony, and also called for women to leave unhappy marriages. Compounding the controversy—because other women's rights leaders argued that divorce for all but the most dire reasons weakened the family—Stanton advocated the right to self-sovereignty. Self-sovereignty meant that women, if they wanted, should take steps to avoid pregnancy. Perceived by many Americans as a call for greater sexual freedom, and an interference with God's plans for married couples, Stanton increasingly moved to the edges of the women's movement. Stanton only fed into the idea that she was becoming too radical by associating Victoria Woodhull, who openly, and notoriously, advocated free love. Stanton also became vocally distrustful of organized religion, leading to conflict with many fellow suffrage leaders. Although largely outside the mainstream by her death in 1902, Stanton had played a major role in advancing the women's movement.

Stowe, Harriet Beecher: Born in Litchfield, Connecticut, the younger sister of Catharine Beecher. She moved to Cincinnati in 1832 when her father became president of Lane Theological Seminary. The sight of slaves in northern Kentucky, and escaping slaves in Ohio, opened her to the horrors of the institution. She married Calvin Ellis Stowe, a professor at Lane, in 1836. The Stowes moved to Maine, where Harriet penned *Uncle Tom's Cabin*. Published in 1852, the novel far outdistanced other works in sales. *Uncle Tom's Cabin* followed the travails of one slave family. Although often taking a paternalistic attitude toward African Americans, Stowe was one of the first authors to treat blacks as individuals. Well received in the North but despised in the South, *Uncle Tom's Cabin* contributed to growing sectional tensions. Abraham Lincoln, when he later met Stowe, only half jokingly accused her as bearing some blame for the start of the Civil War. Stowe died in 1896 in Hartford, Connecticut. The Stowe house today is a public museum and research library.

Twain, Mark: One of the great American writers. Twain was beginning to rise to national prominence by the end of the Reconstruction era, and exercised enormous influence through his words and writings for the remainder of the century. Born Samuel Clemens in 1835, Twain grew up in Hannibal, Missouri. His boyhood experiences while living in the port town on the Mississippi River, as well as working aboard steamboats during the 1850s, provided the backdrop for *The Adventures of Tom Sawyer* (1876) and *Adventures of Huckleberry Finn* (1884). The two books, although sometimes appearing dated to modern-day sensibilities, are classics of American literature. Twain reportedly served for two weeks in a Confederate militia company in 1861, before deciding that military life did not suit his tastes. Twain later published a humorous account of his short-lived military experience. After traveling much of the West and working as a reporter, Twain toured the Mediterranean in the late 1860s. His description of his overseas travels in

Innocents Abroad (1869) earned a wide audience. Twain married Olivia Langdon in 1870, and the couple ultimately had four children (Langdon, the only son, died from disease as a toddler). Twain continued to write from his home in Connecticut, his satire and wit maintaining a national audience. Twain's criticism of the seeming superficiality of American life in *The Gilded Age*, published in 1873, gave name to the last two and one-half decades of the nineteenth century. Twain died in 1910.

Willard, Frances: Social reformer and antialcohol crusader. Willard was born in upstate New York in 1839, although the family moved to Wisconsin six years later. Willard dedicated her life to temperance and women's rights. After serving briefly as president of Evanston College for Ladies (that later became part of Northwestern University), Willard became actively involved with the Woman's Christian Temperance Union. Willard moved to England in 1892, discouraged over her inability to push the WCTU to campaign more vigorously for women's suffrage. Willard died six years later of influenza.

APPENDIX 2: GLOSSARY OF TERMS MENTIONED IN TEXT

Abolition of Slavery: The abolitionist movement first gained momentum in the Second Great Awakening during the early 1830s. The Second Great Awakening was a religious revival that swept across much of America, prompting many reformers to attack perceived earthly evils. The abolitionists believed that slavery was a sin against God and needed to be ended immediately. Plans for what to do with the slaves once freed remained rather hazy. The abolitionist movement was more vocal than earlier attempt to end slavery, which called for either the colonization of freed slaves outside the United States or the freeing slaves over an extended period of time through gradual emancipation.

Antebellum: Before the Civil War, generally referring to the time period between 1815 and 1861.

Antietam, Maryland: General Robert E. Lee, the commander of the Confederate Army of Northern Virginia, invaded Maryland during the autumn of 1862. Lee hoped to score a major battlefield victory on northern soil, and thereby gain European recognition of the Confederacy. This likely would have ended the war with an independent Confederate States, because England and France would have stepped in to negotiate a settlement. The fighting around Antietam Creek resulted in an almost unimaginable level of carnage. By the end of the one-day battle, 23,000 Union and Confederate soldiers were killed, wounded, and missing. September 17, 1862 remains the bloodiest single-day battle in American history.

The Atlantic Monthly: Founded in Boston in the late 1850s. The magazine circulated nationally after the Civil War, and focused primarily on literary and cultural topics.

Book of Genesis: The first book of the Old Testament in the Bible. The book is perhaps most famous for describing the creation of Earth and all living things upon it.

Border States: In 1861, Missouri, Kentucky, and Maryland existed between the twenty states of the Union and the eleven states of the Confederacy. All three states remained in the Union throughout the Civil War, and all three states provided more volunteers to the Union army than the Confederate army.

Captain: A captain commanded a company of, at least on paper, 100 men. Ten companies formed a regiment, under the command of a colonel. (In ascending order, company and regimental officers are lieutenant, captain, major, lieutenant colonel, colonel.)

Carpetbaggers: Northerners who moved south during the Reconstruction era often became the subject of caricature, as unscrupulous Yankees bent on deepening their own pockets. In reality, many carpetbaggers hoped to improve educational and economic opportunities in the South.

Cash Crop: Agricultural produce sold for profit rather than grown for consumption.

Census: The Constitution mandates that the federal government conduct a census every 10 years, to record population totals. The results determine representation in the House of Representatives as well as federal funding for various state programs.

Chancellorsville, Virginia: The fighting at Chancellorsville in early May 1863 is considered one of Confederate General Robert E. Lee's greatest triumphs. Lee outmaneuvered and outfought a larger and better supplied Federal army, under the leadership of Major General Joseph Hooker. The Confederate victory at Chancellorsville prompted Lee to undertake a second invasion of the North in late June.

Continental Monthly: A journal that began publication in early 1862 and circulated across the North. The last issue was published only a little over two years later.

Corporal: The lowest noncommissioned rank, below a sergeant.

Deep South: The seceded states by the time of Lincoln's inauguration, in order of their secession, were South Carolina, Mississippi, Florida, Alabama, Georgia, Louisiana, and Texas.

Electoral College: During the presidential election of 1864, the Union states and the border states (Missouri, Kentucky, and Maryland) voted. No Confederate States participated.

Ethnic Soldiers: Soldiers who were born overseas or born to immigrant parents.

54th Massachusetts: Recruited around Boston and mustered into federal service in March 1863, the 54th Massachusetts was one of the first African American regiments to serve in the Union army. Free blacks supplied much of the regiment's manpower. The unit quickly became a showcase black regiment, with its colonel and lieutenant colonel coming from prominent abolitionist families. The 54th Massachusetts continued to serve after the failed Union attack on Battery Wagner, fighting in Florida and South Carolina. The unit is among the better known Union regiments today, if not perhaps the best known, due to the box office popularity of the film *Glory*, directed by Edward Zwick and released in 1989.

Fredericksburg: The Union army crossed the Rapidan River and seized Fredericksburg, Virginia, on December 11, 1863. Two days later, the Union army assaulted strong Confederate defensive lines on a series of low hills behind the town. The attacks ended in bloody failure, seriously dampening Union morale.

Freedmen's Bureau: Officially designated the Bureau of Refugees, Freedmen, and Abandoned Lands; created by Congress in 1865. The Freedmen's Bureau carried a wide range of responsibilities, including providing temporary food, shelter, and medical aid for the destitute. The Freedmen's Bureau also oversaw the opening of schools for former slaves, its most long-lasting accomplishment. Nearly 3,000 schools were in operation four years after the end of the Civil War, as well as a number of colleges. Major General Oliver O. Howard, who was noted for his religiosity and integrity, oversaw the Freedmen's Bureau. Howard's personal qualities were in stark contrast to those displayed by the inefficient and corrupt officials who often saddled the organization. Congress ended the work of the Freedmen's Bureau in 1869 in all areas but education, which ended a few years later. Although supported by most former slaves during its career, the Freedmen's Bureau was despised by even more southern whites.

The Galaxy: Founded by the Church brothers, William and Francis, in 1866, the magazine featured the early writings of both Henry James and Mark Twain. *The Galaxy* merged in 1878 with the *Atlantic Monthly*.

Gospel of Matthew: One of four accounts in the New Testament recounting the life of Jesus.

Internal improvements: Transportation networks that helped to link together the American economy, such as roads, canals, and railroads.

Legislation: The Pacific Railroad Act of 1862 authorized the Union Pacific and the Central Pacific to begin construction of the transcontinental railroad. Each railroad company received federal funds and land for each mile of track laid, after the first 40 miles were completed. An 1864 act increased the amount of money and land offered.

Lithographs: First invented in the late 1700s by Alois Senefelder in Bavaria. In essence, lithography involved etching an image into smoothed limestone. A chemical reaction induced by the lithographer caused printing ink to cling to one part of the etched image and not the other. The stone then served as the printing block, with the image transferred to paper. The flat printing surface allowed for a longer printing run and a more detailed print image.

Manassas, Virginia: Union Brigadier General Irvin McDowell maneuvered his 35,000 men during the mid-summer of 1861 to capture the strategic railroad junction at Manassas, located between Washington and Richmond. The Union army attempted to outflank the 22,000 Confederate defenders, under the command of General Pierre G. T. Beauregard. After confused fighting that lasted throughout most of the afternoon, the Confederates threw back a last Union attack. Tired and dirty, the retreating Union soldiers soon gave way to panic and fled back to Washington over the next several days. The Union lost 2,896 men, nearly one-half of whom were missing or captured. The Confederates suffered 1,982 casualties.

March 4, 1861: The date of Abraham Lincoln's first inauguration. Until the ratification of the 20th Amendment in the early 1930s, inauguration day occurred in early March. This meant that the president-elect had to wait nearly four months before taking office. Today, the president-elect takes the oath of office at 12 noon on January 20.

The Missouri Compromise of 1820: Admitted Missouri into the Union as a slave state, and Maine into the Union as a free state, thereby maintaining equal representation in the Senate. Recognizing that the expansion of slavery into the western territories needed addressing, Congress drew an imaginary line through the Louisiana Purchase at 36°30'. Any territory coming in north of the latitude came in free (excluding Missouri), while any territory coming in south of the line came in slave.

Noah: One of the most well-known figures from the Old Testament. Noah builds an ark upon the command of God, to shelter his family and two of every type of animal from the flood that engulfs Earth.

Port Hudson: Port Hudson, Louisiana, fell to Union forces in the mid-summer of 1863, after a lengthy siege. The surrender of the city came on the heels of another Confederate capitulation at Vicksburg, Mississippi, and opened control of the Mississippi River to the Union.

Promontory Summit, Utah: Some confusion occurred as to where the ceremony marking the completion of the Transcontinental Railroad actually occurred. Many reports had Leland Stanford and Thomas Durant driving the gold spike at Promontory Point, about 35 miles from Promontory Summit. Today, the National Park Service maintains a National Historic Site at Promontory Summit.

Property: Slave owners defined slaves as property rather than people. Such a dubious distinction worked to the benefit of the Union during the spring of 1861. Union army officers began to argue that, since slaves were property, any liberated slaves and runaway slaves might stay within the Federal lines as "contraband of war." That summer, under the Confiscation Act of 1861, Congress declared that any fugitive slave used to aid the Confederate war effort was a legitimate prize of war and to be set free. For the remainder of the war, Union soldiers referred to slaves who came within their lines as "contraband."

Protestants: Any Christian who belongs to a church whose origins date to the break with the Roman Catholic Church in the early 1500s. Protestants believe that Scripture is the ultimate authority in the church, rather than the pope in Rome.

Ratify: Three-quarters of state legislatures, or 28 of 37 states, had to approve the 14th Amendment and 15th Amendment after they received passage in Congress.

Republican Ticket: To reflect its broader political support across the North, the Republican Party ran as the Union Party during the 1864 election. Many Democrats who supported Lincoln's war aims, known across the Union as "war Democrats," supported the Union Party. Still, the basis of support came from Republicans, and many northerners continued to refer to the Lincoln ticket as the Republican Party.

Reservations: Under the Indian Appropriations Act of 1851, the federal government began to set aside land specifically for use by various Native American tribes. Today, about 310 Indian reservations exist. Taken all together, Indian reservations total about 55.7 million acres of land (or slightly more than 2% of the territory of the United States). The Bureau of Indian Affairs, an agency of the United States Department of the Interior, oversees each reservation. Because each Native American tribe exercises limited national sovereignty, laws vary by reservation.

Romanize: Many late-19th-century American Protestants believed that Catholic immigrants gave their allegiance to the pope in Rome, rather than to the Constitution. The pope is the head of the Catholic Church and viewed as God's representative on Earth. To allow Catholics to continue to enter the country risked allowing in individuals who would unthinkingly follow the pope's commands, and thus Romanize the United States.

Scalawags: Some white southerners supported the Republican Party during the Reconstruction era because they came from regions that had remained strongly pro-Union during the Civil War, such as eastern Tennessee, northern Alabama, and western North Carolina. Other scalawags were members of the old Whig Party that shared the Republican emphasis on government support for economic development.

Slave Power Conspiracy: An idea, increasingly held in the free states during the 1850s, that slave owners were determined to spread slavery across the United States or, failing this, to break apart the American Union.

Spirituals: A religious song, created by enslaved blacks. The term *spiritual* became widely used beginning in the 1860s. Religious songs of African American origin later became known as black spirituals, to distinguish them from other spiritual music.

Transportation and Market Revolutions: The American infrastructure improved dramatically in the wake of the War of 1812. Roads, canals, and railroads opened up the country like never before. Taken together, the surge in routes and methods to move goods and people is known as the *transportation revolution*. American industry took advantage. Producers shipped goods to customers across the country, rather than for a local market. The boom in national sales is known as the *market revolution*.

Vicksburg, Mississippi: The city of Vicksburg represented one of the last Confederate strongholds on the Mississippi River by the summer of 1863. Union forces placed the city under siege in late May, after an unsuccessful attempt to do so in late 1862. The Confederate defenders increasingly battled disease and lack of supplies, as did the civilian population. The city surrendered to Union forces on July 4, the day after the Union victory at Gettysburg. The fall of Vicksburg helped to secure the Mississippi River for the Union. The capture of Vicksburg soared morale in the Union as much as it deflated it in the Confederacy, because many observers believed the city all but impregnable.

Westward expansion: A frontier, or a thinly populated edge of settlement, existed in American history through the close of the 19th century. In the mid-1850s, the western frontier included most of the West today. By 1854, only six states existed west of the Mississippi River: Louisiana (1812), Missouri (1821), Arkansas (1836), Texas (1845), Iowa (1846), and California (1850). Today, in the continental United States, twenty-two states are west of the Mississippi River.

Wilson's Creek, Missouri: The first major battle of the Civil War fought west of the Mississippi River. The fighting went back and forth throughout most of the morning of August 10, 1861, before the Union forces, running low on ammunition, retreated toward Springfield. Although casualties were roughly equal—a combined 2,500 men killed, wounded, and missing—the Confederates claimed victory because they maintained possession of the battlefield. The triumph buoyed Confederate spirits and contributed to the divided loyalties that wracked Missouri over the next four years.

BIBLIOGRAPHY

SELECTED PRINTED SOURCES

Boatner, Mark Mayo III. *The Civil War Dictionary*. Rev. ed. New York: David M. McKay, 1988.

Bowman, John S., ed. *The Civil War Almanac*. New York: Facts on File, 1983.

Copeland, David A., ed. *The Antebellum Era: Primary Documents on Events from 1820 to 1860*. Westport, CT: Greenwood Press, 2003.

Current, Richard N., et al., eds. *Encyclopedia of the Confederacy*. 4 vols. New York: Simon and Schuster, 1993.

Davis, David Brion and Steven Mintz, eds. *The Boisterous Sea of Liberty: A Documentary History of America from Discovery through the Civil War*. New York: Oxford University Press, 1998.

Faust, Patricia L., ed. *Historical Times Illustrated Encyclopedia of the Civil War*. New York: Harper and Row, 1986.

Gienapp, William E., ed. *The Civil War and Reconstruction: A Documentary Collection*. New York: W. W. Norton, 2001.

Greene, A. Wilson and Gary W. Gallagher. *National Geographic Guide to the Civil War National Battlefield Parks*. Washington, DC: National Geographic Society, 1992.

Linden, Glenn M., ed. *Voices from the Reconstruction Years, 1865–1877*. Fort Worth, TX: Harcourt Brace, 1999.

Long, E. B. and Barbara Long. *The Civil War Day by Day: An Almanac, 1861–1865*. Garden City, NY: Doubleday, 1971.

McPherson, James M., ed. *The Atlas of the Civil War*. New York: Macmillan, 1994.

Nevins, Allan. *The Emergence of Modern America*. New York: Macmillan, 1927.

Perman, Michael, ed. *Major Problems in the Civil War and Reconstruction: Documents and Essays*. 2nd ed. Boston: Houghton Mifflin Co., 1998.

Richter, William L. *Historical Dictionary of the Civil War and Reconstruction*. Lanham, MD: Scarecrow Press, 2004.

Risley, Ford, ed. *The Civil War: Primary Documents on Events from 1860 to 1865*. Westport, CT: Greenwood Press, 2004.

Roller, David C. and Robert W. Twyman, eds. *Encyclopedia of Southern History*. Baton Rouge: Louisiana State University Press, 1979.

Sizer, Lyde Cullen and Jim Cullen, eds. *The Civil War Era: An Anthology of Sources*. Malden, MA: Blackwell, 2005.

Smith, John David, ed. *Black Voices from Reconstruction, 1865–1877*. Gainesville: University Press of Florida, 1997.

Sutherland, Daniel E. *The Expansion of Everyday Life, 1860–1876*. New York: Harper and Row, 1989.

Wilson, Charles Reagan and William Ferris, eds. *Encyclopedia of Southern Culture*. Chapel Hill: University of North Carolina Press, 1989.

Woodworth, Steven E. *The American Civil War: A Handbook of Literature and Research*. Westport, CT: Greenwood Press, 1996.

SELECTED NONPRINT SOURCES

Films and Television

Civil War Journal: The Commanders. 2 DVDs. History Channel, 2001.

Civil War Journal: The Conflict Begins. 2 DVDs. A&E Home Video, 2001.

Cold Mountain. DVD and Blu-Ray. Miramax, 2003.

Gettysburg. DVD and Blu-Ray. Turner Home Entertainment, 1993.

Gods and Generals. DVD and Blu-Ray. Warner Home Video, 2003.

Great Battles of the Civil War. 2 DVDs. Smithsonian Institution, 1992.

The American Civil War. 14 DVDs. A&E Television Networks, 2000.

The Civil War. A Film by Ken Burns. 5 DVDs. PBS, 1990.

Music

Gettysburg: Music from the Original Motion Picture Soundtrack–Deluxe Commemorative Edition. Music by Randy Edelman. 2 Compact discs. Milan Records, 1998.

Glory: Original Motion Picture Soundtrack. Music by James Horner. Compact disc. Virgin Records, 1990.

Music of the Civil War, Original Instruments. Americus Brass Band. Compact disc. Summit Records, 1991.

The Civil War. Traditional American songs and instrumental music featured in the film by Ken Burns. Original soundtrack recording. Compact disc. Elektra Nonesuch, 1990.

The Civil War: Its Music and Its Sounds. 2 compact discs. Mercury, 1990.

The Civil War Music Collector's Edition. 3 compact discs. Time-Life Music, 1991.

Songs of the Civil War. Compact disc. Sony, 1991.

Web Sites

CivilWar.com is divided into 10 sections, covering, among other topics battles, weapons, travel, and information for teachers. The site is sponsored by Premier Internet, Inc. The site hopes to "present the history of the Civil War accurately and in a compelling way which honors all Americans." The link is: http://www.civilwar.com/.

The Civil War Preservation Trust is the largest nonprofit organization in the United States "devoted to the preservation of our nation's endangered Civil War battlefields." For more about the Civil War Preservation Trust's accomplishments, as well as a wealth of other information on the Civil War, see: http://www.civilwar.org.

To research if one of your ancestors fought in the Civil War, visit the "Civil War Soldiers and Sailors System," sponsored by the National Park Service. The site is searchable by last name, regiment, and state. The address is: http://www.itd.nps.gov/cwss/.

The National Park Service oversees many of the battlegrounds of the Civil War, including Shiloh, Antietam, and Gettysburg. For information on each site, see: http://www.nps.gov.

INDEX

About the Editors

Lawrence A. Kreiser, Jr., is an associate professor of history at Stillman College in Tuscaloosa, Alabama.

Ray B. Browne, prior to his death in 2009, was a professor emeritus in the Department of Popular Culture at Bowling Green State University.

Professors Kreiser and Browne coauthored *The Civil War and Reconstruction*, a volume in Greenwood Press's American Popular Culture through History series, in 2003.